Library of
Davidson College

The Development of
State-Chartered Banking in Texas

from Predecessor Systems until 1970

The Development of State-Chartered Banking in Texas

from Predecessor Systems until 1970

Joseph M. Grant
Lawrence L. Crum

Bureau of Business Research
The University of Texas at Austin

International Standard Book Number 87755-219-3
Library of Congress Catalog Card Number 76-24778
Copyright 1978, Board of Regents,
The University of Texas System

Contents

	Page
List of Illustrations	ix
List of Tables	xi
Preface	xiii

Chapter

1. BANKING IN TEXAS BEFORE STATEHOOD 3
    Banco Nacional de Texas 3
    The First Chartered Commercial Bank in Texas 6
    Early Banking Legislation 7
    Attempts to Establish a National Bank for the
        Republic of Texas 10
    Opposition to Banking in Texas 11

2. BANKING IN THE STATE OF TEXAS
        BEFORE 1865 15
    Constitutional Prohibition of Banking 15
    The Banking Operation of R. & D. G. Mills 16
    The Commercial and Agricultural Bank 17
    Litigation against the Commercial and
        Agricultural Bank and R. & D. G. Mills 18
    Other Private Firms Engaged in Banking 20

3. BANKING IN TEXAS FROM 1865 TO 1905 23
    Development of Private Banking during
        Reconstruction, 1865-1876 23
    National Banks in Texas during Reconstruction 25
    Bank Chartering under the State Constitution of 1869 .. 26
    Era of Private and National Banks, 1876-1900 30

v

4. THE TEXAS STATE BANK LAW OF 1905 37
   Growing Support for State-Chartered Banking 37
   Provisions of the New Banking Law 42

5. THE FIRST FIVE YEARS UNDER THE BANKING
      LAW OF 1905 47
   Demand for Charters 48
   The First Five Years of the State Banking System 48
   The Panic of 1907 53
   Impact of the Panic of 1907 57
   Economic Impact of the State Banking System 57
   The "Free-Banking Period," 1905-1913 61
   Review and Reform of the Texas State Bank Law 63

6. INSURANCE OF BANK DEPOSITS IN TEXAS 71
   History of Deposit Insurance in the United States 71
   Agitation for Deposit Insurance in Texas 74
   Influence of Thomas B. Love and William
      Jennings Bryan 75
   Influence of the Panic of 1907 76
   Division of Opinion between State
      and National Bankers 77
   Deposit-Guaranty Legislation 80
   Provisions of the Texas Guaranty Law 82
   Preference for the Guaranty Fund 85
   Summary 87

7. BANKING UNDER THE GUARANTY FUND 91
   Growth of the State Banking System 91
   Effect of Economic Conditions, 1910-1920 92
   Revision of the State Bank Chartering Procedure 97
   Federal Reserve Act 99
   State Bank Failures 103
   Modifications of the Texas State Bank Law 107
   Governor Colquitt's Bank Bill 108
   Indictment of Commissioner Charles O. Austin and
      Impeachment of Governor James E. Ferguson 109

    Some Concluding Observations on the 1910-1920 Era .. 113

8. **THE TROUBLED TWENTIES** 117
    Decline of the State Banking System 118
    The Economic Climate of the Twenties 118
    State Bank Liquidations in the Twenties 126
    Bank Failures 129
    Voluntary Liquidations 154
    Efforts of the Department of Banking to
        Avert Bank Failures 156
    New State Banking Laws Enacted during the Twenties ... 163

9. **REPEAL OF THE DEPOSITORS GUARANTY LAW** .. 171
    Favorable Experience before the 1920-1921
        Recession 171
    The Beginning of the End of the Guaranty Fund Law .. 173
    Agitation for Repeal of the Guaranty Fund Law 174
    Arguments against the Guaranty Fund 176
    Response of the Thirty-ninth Legislature 181
    Shifts to the Bond Security Plan and the National
        Banking System 181
    Failure of the Thirty-ninth Legislature to Repeal
        the Guaranty Fund 183
    Repeal of the Depositors Guaranty Law 184
    Review of the Depositors Guaranty Law 186

10. **THE DEPRESSION AND ITS AFTERMATH,**
        1930-1939 193
    Continued Decline of the State Banking System 193
    The Economic Setting 194
    State Bank Liquidations in the Thirties 217
    Bank Failures 218
    Voluntary Liquidations 229
    Role of the R.F.C. and the F.D.I.C. in
        Rehabilitation 230
    State Bank Legislation Enacted during the Thirties 235

11. **UNPRECEDENTED GROWTH OF THE STATE**
        BANKING SYSTEM, 1940-1970 243

The State Banking System during World II 243
The Texas Banking Code of 1943 252
Postwar Development of the State Banking System ... 253

Appendix 273

List of Illustrations

Commissioner	Page
W.J. Clay	275
Thos. B. Love	275
William E. Hawkins	275
Frederick Von Rosenberg	276
B.L. Gill	276
W.W. Collier	276
Jno. S. Patterson	276
Chas. O. Austin	277
Geo. Waverly Briggs	277
J.C. Chidsey	277
J.T. McMillin	277
Ed Hall	278
J.L. Chapman	278
Chas. O. Austin	278
James Shaw	278
E.C. Brand	279
Irvin McCreary	279
Zeta Gossett	279
Fred C. Branson	279
Lee Brady	280
John Q. McAdams	280
H.A. Jamison	280
L.S. Johnson	280
J.M. Falkner	281

List of Tables

Table		Page
1.	Private Banks in Texas, 1877-1905	31
2.	Texas Private Banks Reporting to the Comptroller of the Currency, Selected Years, 1880-1904	33
3.	National Banks in Texas, 1865-1905	34
4.	State Banks Chartered and in Operation in Texas, 1907-1969	49
5.	Growth of State and National Banks in Texas, 1914-1919	93
6.	State Bank Liquidations in Texas, 1907-1939	94
7.	Approximate Farm Cash Income in Texas from Specified Products, Selected Years in the 1920s	122
8.	Average Prices Received by Texas Farmers, 1919-1939	124
9.	Commercial Bank Failures in the United States and Texas, 1920-1939	128
10.	Texas Cotton Acreage, Production, and Value, 1920-1940	135
11.	Causes of State Bank Failures in Texas, 1920-1925	140
12.	Oil Production in Eastland and Stephens Counties, 1917-1926	145
13.	Price of Crude Oil, 1919-1924	146
14.	Causes of State Bank Failures in Texas, 1921-1930	153
15.	Special Assessments, Withdrawals, and Losses of the Texas Depositors Guaranty Fund, 1910-1927	172
16.	Texas National and State Bank Deposits on Selected Call Dates, 1920-1928	178
17.	Banks Participating in the Guaranty Fund and Bond Security System in Texas, January 1, 1925, through February 2, 1927	185

18. Selected U.S. Economic Indicators, 1929-1942 199
19. Commercial Bank Failures in the United States,
    1929-1939 200
20. Texas Oil Production and Value, Selected Years,
    1910-1940 215
21. State Bank Voluntary Liquidations in Texas,
    1930-1939 229
22. Texas Banks and Bank Resources and Deposits,
    1905-1969 246

Preface

The absence of a comprehensive, well-documented history of state-chartered commercial banking in Texas provided the motivation for writing this book. Through its sponsorship of the study, the Association of State Chartered Banks in Texas has contributed in a significant way to the further development of the resources of historical literature of Texas. We feel, though, that the utility of the study extends beyond the realm of academic worth alone. It should enable bankers and bank users alike to better understand the current banking structure in Texas and the nature and full scope of the commercial banking business as it has developed to the present time. The chronicle and analysis of the evolution of deposit banking and deposit insurance should be particularly informative and instructive.

In banking, as in most fields, much can be learned from the experiences, including the mistakes, of past performance. Both the management of banking institutions and the governmental surveillance of banking in the public interest have improved measurably during the twentieth century, and to an appreciable extent the improvement has entailed remedial action and policies that emanated from adverse, often near-disaster, experiences. These experiences, especially the difficulties of the two decades prior to World War II, and the improvements in banking that they gave rise to are brought to light and examined in this study. Other features of banking operations, structure, and supervision, which provide opportunities for further improvement in performance, are also analyzed. In general, though, specific recommendations for change by either bank managers or supervisors are not considered to be within the purview of this historical study.

The system of state-chartered banks in Texas was born with the enactment of the legislation of the State Bank Law of 1905. The myriad facets of the development of the system through 1969 are the mainstream of the subject matter of this volume. Naturally, though, to provide a complete history, we have begun with the earliest semblance of bank operations in Texas, in the era antedating the Republic. The most extensive coverage in this work is logically accorded to the most turbulent decade in the life of the state banking system—the 1920s.

Banking is intensely person-oriented, and the human element is borne out in many ways in our writing. Not least among these are the anecdotes and the brief dramatizations with which we have approached and reviewed some of the most important issues in the history of the state banking system.

The strengthening of this system is to a notable extent a reflection of the development of the state Banking Department. Every effort has been made to point out the most important contributions of specific banking commissioners. To complement the writing we have, with the cooperation of the state Banking Department, included in the volume photographs of all the banking commissioners for whom reproducible photographs were available.

The authors wish to express their sincere appreciation to the Association of State Chartered Banks for sponsoring this study. In particular we wish to thank A. J. Lewis, chairman of the board of the Jefferson State Bank in San Antonio and chairman of the History Committee of the Association of State Chartered Banks, for his invaluable counsel and unerring enthusiasm for the history. The other members of the History Committee also provided substantial assistance and encouragement. They include William Z. Gossett, L. B. Manry, Jr., Fred T. Brooks, Maurice Burns, D. E. Blackburn (deceased), J. O. Gillham (deceased), and P. R. Hamill. A very prominent acknowledgment is also due Berl E. Godfrey, current president of the Association of State Chartered Banks, and P. B. Garrett, chairman of the Education Committee of the Association, for the attention they accorded the history project from 1968 to 1970.

It would have been impossible to accomplish our purposes without the wholehearted support the state Banking Department afforded by furnishing virtually unrestricted access to the records of the department. Banking commissioner John M. Falkner and his successor, Robert E. Stewart, provided more cooperation than could reasonably have been asked for and exhibited continuous interest in our research and writing. Perhaps no single person deserves more recognition for assistance to us in pursuing research details than Mabel Boles of the state Banking Department.

Finally, we wish to express our gratitude to Sam O. Kimberlin, Jr., executive vice-president of the Texas Bankers Association, and Milton Boswell, editor of the *Texas Bankers Record*, for providing access to records and facilities, and to C. B. Sullivan and W. A. Sandlin (both deceased), former state bank examiners, for recapturing some of their experiences in Texas banking in the 1920s and 1930s and otherwise providing us with data to authenticate our exposition of developments during that time span.

Though we benefited from assistance in many forms and from many sources in writing this history, we alone are responsible, of course, for whatever errors and deficiencies the work may contain.

Joseph M. Grant
Lawrence L. Crum

Austin, Texas
Spring 1977

The Development of
State-Chartered Banking in Texas

from Predecessor Systems until 1970

I

Banking in Texas before Statehood

Before 1822 there were no formal banking institutions in Texas. The only money in circulation consisted of a limited amount of Mexican silver coin, some gold, and a few bank notes brought to Texas by immigrants. Ninety percent of all transactions were effected through barter or on credit.

In 1821 Texas became a province of Mexico, which had won its independence from Spain in that year. Agustin de Iturbide, who had led the movement for independence, had set up an empire and proclaimed himself emperor. One of Emperor Iturbide's first official acts was to appoint José Felix Trespalacios as colonel of the army and political chief of the province of Texas. This event ultimately led to the establishment of the Banco Nacional de Texas, the first bank in Texas and the first chartered bank west of the Mississippi River.

Banco Nacional de Texas

During the years after the execution of Father Miguel Hidalgo, who first proclaimed the independence of Mexico on September 16, 1810, José Felix Trespalacios fought relentlessly with the forces of the revolution. For ten years he was hunted and pursued throughout Mexico, and he was finally forced to flee the country for Havana and then New Orleans. During this period of exile, Trespalacios was first introduced to the rudiments of paper money and banking.

After Agustin de Iturbide won Mexico's independence, Trespalacios returned to Mexico and was appointed governor of

Texas. Upon arriving in San Antonio, the provincial capital, Governor Trespalacios discovered that one of the basic problems of the province was the irregularity with which gold and silver specie, used to pay troops and public officials, was sent from the subtreasury in San Luis Potosí to San Antonio. Long periods usually elapsed between paydays, and in the meantime the troops and their families had to live on credit extended by local merchants. Even when the specie did arrive, the troops were so elated that they spent a considerable amount of their pay at the local saloon. The result was that little was left to pay the merchants, who were thus forced to wait for another shipment of specie, uncertain whether they would be paid even then.

In order to expedite the payment process and alleviate the miseries induced by the existing system, Governor Trespalacios proposed the establishment of a national bank with the authority to issue notes fully redeemable in specie—the amount of notes issued being regulated by the amount of silver and gold expected to meet the payroll of the province.

Because of the urgency of the situation, Trespalacios set about to establish the bank prior to receiving the emperor's approval, which he was confident would be forthcoming. The plan was presented to the city council of San Antonio and unanimously approved. It was decided that the note issue of the bank should be legal tender for all transactions, including the payment of taxes, and that it would be guaranteed by the specie expected from the government and could not exceed that amount. In order to enhance its accessibility and prestige, three members of the council were made officers of the bank and were required to countersign all notes. On October 21, 1822, Governor Trespalacios promulgated a decree establishing the first bank in Texas.

The first notes were issued on November 1, 1822, and were transmitted to the commander of the garrison at La Bahia (Goliad) to meet the monthly payroll. On November 9, 1822, the commander replied that everyone was pleased with the new arrangement and that the paper money was well received and generally accepted. By December the notes of the Banco Nacional de Texas were apparently being circulated without difficulty.

In the meantime, however, a report from Governor Trespalacios detailing the establishment of the bank and requesting official approval had reached Emperor Iturbide. What happened upon its receipt is not recorded in the annals of history. However, it is likely that the idea of a paper currency as set forth in the report, received at a time when Mexico faced severe financial problems, appealed to the emperor, since shortly thereafter he authorized the national issuance of paper money. By the national decree issued December 29, 1822, treasury notes were declared legal tender and after January 1 all payments made either to or by the Mexican treasury were to be one-third paper money and two-thirds specie.

The national decree was a serious blow to the Banco Nacional de Texas, for if full specie payment for the troops were to cease, the notes of the bank could not be redeemed at face value as promised. Moreover, the Texas notes would have a rival currency. On February 5, 1823, the provincial government reluctantly published the national decree acquainting the citizens with the new currency. Naturally, public confidence was severely shaken.

Although the national decree probably meant the functional end of the Banco Nacional de Texas, its actual demise resulted from a treasury circular released by order of the emperor on February 5, 1823, specifying that the notes of the bank would be replaced by the national issue. This decision further undermined the confidence of the Texans, who felt as though they had been defrauded. They had initially been promised redemption in specie, and now they were being offered notes issued by the national treasury for their Banco Nacional de Texas notes. The question in their minds was: would the government stand behind the new notes? With the seeds of doubt planted, they refused all offers of exchange, and only after seven years of petitioning and bargaining was the issue finally settled by President Vicente Guerrero, who ordered the national treasury to pay the amount due the Texans for their Banco Nacional de Texas notes.

The Banco Nacional de Texas was important in the banking history of Texas, not only because it was the first bank in the state, albeit in a very limited sense, but also because of the general distrust of bank note issues that it helped to engender. This distrust was manifest in the failure of the lawmakers of Texas to provide for a state banking system until the enactment of the Texas State Bank Law in 1905.[1]

The First Chartered Commercial Bank in Texas

Although the Banco Nacional de Texas was designated as a bank, it performed only one banking function—that of note issue. Other banking services during the first half of the nineteenth century were provided by mercantile firms that conducted a limited banking business as an adjunct to their ordinary activities. It was frequently necessary for these firms to extend credit to their customers, discount promissory notes, and accept drafts. In addition, they were called upon to receive specie for safekeeping and to make small loans. One such firm was R. & D. G. Mills, which is reported to have been engaged in banking activities at Brazoria and Columbia as early as 1832.

The firm of Thomas F. McKinney and Samuel May Williams had also assumed banking functions in the early 1830s. Williams began his business career in Baltimore and later was secretary to General Andrew Jackson in New Orleans. In 1821 he came to Texas to serve as secretary to Stephen F. Austin, a position he held until 1835. In his capacity as secretary to Austin, Williams had frequent business dealings with McKinney and eventually formed a partnership with him to conduct a mercantile business at Quintana, Texas. The firm grew rapidly and soon had business extending to New Orleans and Philadelphia. As it prospered, it assumed numerous banking functions, and in 1835 Williams obtained the first bank charter in Texas. On April 30, 1835, the congress of the state of Coahuila and Texas, by Decree Number 308, granted to Samuel May Williams a twenty-year charter for the "Banco de Commercia y Agricultura."

The charter of the bank provided for a minimum capital of $300,000, with $100,000 in specie paid in and held in the vault before business could begin.[2] Other provisions permitted the bank to issue bank notes, to lend money at a rate of 8 percent per annum for a period not exceeding six months and 10 percent when the loan was in excess of six months, and to establish branches throughout the state. The charter also required the governor of the state to appoint a commissioner who was to examine the "concerns of the association" each year.

Although the charter was granted in 1835, the Banco de Commercia y Agricultura did not open for business until 1847. From the records of the firm of McKinney and Williams, it is evident that the partnership had some difficulties in meeting obligations promptly. In addition, it had been actively engaged in raising funds for the Republic of Texas and, in fact, provided the main financial support for the Republic, including the financing of the Texas Revolution.[3] Because of this burden and the financial panic of 1837, numerous attempts to raise the necessary capital to open the "Banco de Commercia y Agricultura" were unsuccessful.

Early Banking Legislation

Three years before the Texas Declaration of Independence, the representatives of the people of Texas met in convention in March 1833 to prepare a constitution for the state. At this convention Branch T. Archer, a delegate to the convention, proposed that a clause providing for "a bank or banks" be included in the constitution. Although he was supported by most of the leaders of the convention, the opposition was successfully led by Sam Houston, the most influential individual at the convention. Houston was a long-time friend and supporter of Andrew Jackson, who had just been reelected president of the United States on a platform of opposition to the Bank of the United States. Houston, like Jackson, was bitterly opposed to banking. He argued that a sound banking system could not be hoped for, as "human cupidity and stringent times would prove stronger than constitutional provisions."[4] The constitution was written to include the following provision: "No bank nor banking institution nor office of discount and deposit nor any other moneyed corporation nor bank establishment shall ever exist during the continuance of the present constitution."[5] This constitution was never approved by the Mexican government.

The constitution of the Republic of Texas, adopted by the convention at Washington-on-the-Brazos on March 17, 1836, and ratified by the people on September 5, 1836, contained no reference to banks or banking. The journals of the convention only report that Asa Brigham, a delegate from Brazoria, introduced the following resolution: "Resolved by this convention, that a national bank be founded and that the provisional government, when formed, may grant a charter to that effect."[6] After its introduction the house took a recess and the subject was not considered subsequently by the convention.

On December 16, 1836, the congress of the Republic of Texas passed an act which authorized the establishment of the "Texas Railroad, Navigation, and Banking Company." The act provided that the company was authorized to engage in banking activities and also to construct a system of internal navigation and transportation. This system was to connect the waters of the Rio Grande and the Sabine by means of internal navigation and railroads.

The provisions of the act relating to banking privileges stipulated that the company was to have minimum capital of $5,000,000. However, it was provided that the bank could not commence business until $1,000,000 in specie had been paid in and a bonus of $25,000 in gold or silver had been paid to the treasury of the Republic of Texas. The bank was prohibited from charging interest of more than 10 percent per annum, for issuing any note with a denomination smaller than five dollars, or from establishing more than two branches without the consent of congress. The charter was to be valid for a period of forty-nine years.[7]

The act authorizing the Texas Railroad, Navigation, and Banking Company was approved by President Houston, but immediately thereafter a substantial amount of opposition to it arose. As a result President Houston reversed his position and under his influence Republic Treasurer Asa Brigham refused to accept the bonus because it was not tendered in gold or silver within eighteen months, as required by the act.

The principal opponent of the Texas Railroad, Navigation, and Banking Company was Dr. Anson Jones of Brazoria County, who was to become the last president of the Republic of Texas. The following passage from Dr. Jones's memoirs reveals his attitude toward the company:

In 1837, I successfully combated a mammoth banking institution (the Texas Railroad, Navigation and Banking Company), and destroyed it. Had this institution been permitted to take root and fasten itself upon the country, it could never have been gotten rid of, but by serious civil commotion or a revolution, and would have been most ruinous in its consequences to the best interest of Texas.[8]

The attitude of Dr. Jones toward banking was shared by many of his fellow Texans. Between 1835 and 1837 bank notes of wildcat banks in Mississippi, Louisiana, Tennessee, Alabama, and Georgia were brought to Texas by immigrants. The panic of 1837 resulted in the downfall of many of these banks and left the holders of their bank notes with worthless paper. As a result paper money was regarded with great distrust. On December 14, 1837, an act passed by the congress of the Republic of Texas made it unlawful to issue or circulate "any note, bill or paper of purported value."

In spite of the law prohibiting note issuance and their inability to raise the necessary capital to open the Commercial and Agricultural Bank, McKinney and Williams continued to serve as bankers for the Republic.

In consideration for the advances they had made to the Republic, congress, on February 3, 1841, passed an act authorizing McKinney and Williams to issue $30,000 of their promissory notes in small denominations to circulate as money. The act required that collateral be pledged against these notes in the form of mortgages on real estate and on Negroes and that the note issue could not be in excess of 50 percent of market value of the collateral. However, due to the opposition of the people to the issuance of notes by banks, congress revoked this power in 1844. This legislation, entitled "An Act to Suppress Private Banks," prohibited any persons, group of persons, or corporations from issuing bills or promissory notes to circulate as money, and it provided that all previous laws granting such authority were abrogated.[9] Thus all previous charters were repealed and the law prohibiting the issuance of bank notes, originally passed on December 14, 1837, was reaffirmed by this last banking act of the congress of the Republic of Texas. At the time of annexation to the union, Texas law prohibited note issuance, then an indispensable function of banking.

Attempts to Establish a
National Bank for the Republic of Texas

Many individuals, including politicians, attempted to establish banks and banking in the Republic of Texas. Efforts were made to amend the charter of the Texas Railroad, Navigation, and Banking Company and to establish other banking institutions. In 1839 a bill was introduced in congress seeking to establish the National Bank of the Republic of Texas.

On December 31, 1838, President Mirabeau B. Lamar, in his message to the third congress, had recommended that a national bank be established. The bank was to be the government's fiscal agent, a regulator of exchange, a bank of discount, loan, and deposit, and a bank of issue. Branches were to be established to provide convenient banking facilities to all parts of the Republic. The directors were to be elected jointly by both houses of congress, and the president and cashier were to be appointed by the president of the Republic.

At the time the National Bank of Texas was proposed, Texas was experiencing severe financial difficulties. The economy was still suffering from the effects of the Panic of 1837 and of the many worthless bank notes that remained in circulation. In addition, the Republic's own paper currency was in jeopardy because it had been over issued. President Lamar saw the national bank as a means for providing relief to the people during these troubled times. He believed that by a special pledge of the public domain and guarantee of full convertibility into specie a safe bank would be assured. Unfortunately, however, Texas had little specie, its credit was practically nonexistent, and its "boundless acreage of fertile land had no market value." Because of these conditions, the bill to incorporate the National Bank of the Republic of Texas, which was introduced in the house of representatives, was vigorously opposed and was rejected by a vote of sixteen to fourteen on January 21, 1839.

During this period of financial distress there was another effort to establish a national bank for Texas.[10] The bank was to be funded with the proceeds of a bond issue in the amount of $7 million to be floated in France. However, negotiations with the

French minister of finance were severed before the loan was secured and the bank never materialized.

An interesting incident is related about the French minister to Texas. Apparently the minister, M. de Saligney, had a horse that was being watched over by his servant in a stable in Austin, Texas. A "herd of swine" owned by an Austin innkeeper, named Bullock, wandered into the stable; in driving out the swine, the servant accidentally killed one. Bullock responded to this incident by giving the servant a severe thrashing. M. de Saligney, in turn, complained to the local government, and Bullock was summarily arrested but then released, with the secretary of the Texas treasury responsible for bond. Shortly thereafter, de Saligney ventured into the hotel and Bullock ejected him. Again de Saligney registered a complaint. Another arrest followed and a subsequent release. By this time the argument had developed into an international incident that was being discussed on the streets, in newspapers, and in congress. Public sentiment was with Mr. Bullock. As a result the recall of the French minister was requested and negotiations for the loan were abruptly halted. It seems that M. de Saligney had close family ties to the French minister of finance. One writer of the day, who was obviously opposed to the proposed bank, was quoted as saying, "as the geese saved Rome, so Mr. Bullock's pigs saved Texas."

Opposition to Banking in Texas

The prevailing attitude toward banking in Texas during the last days of the Republic was an outgrowth of the existing social and economic conditions. The Panic of 1837 had left the United States in the midst of its most severe depression, which lasted until 1843; the distressed economic conditions gave rise to widespread bank failures. The annual report of the comptroller of the currency for 1876 shows that the number of banks in the United States increased from 788 in 1837 to 901 in 1840 and then decreased sharply to 691 by 1843. During the latter period, total loans and discounts of all banks decreased from $463 million to $255 million, and capital decreased from $358 million to $229 million. The many bank failures and concomitant defaults on bank notes were severely felt by the Texans, and, generally speaking, they resulted in a revulsion of public feeling against banks and bankers. In addition, the leadership of the Republic from December 1841 until annexation on February 16, 1846, was in the hands of Sam Houston and Dr. Anson Jones, the Republic's two most prominent opponents of banking.

Notes

1. Much of the information in this section comes from Carlos E. Castañeda, *The First Chartered Bank West of the Mississippi: Banco Nacional de Texas* (reprinted from *Bulletin of the Business Historical Society*, December 1951), pp. 1-15.
2. Decree no. 308, "Laws and Decrees of Coahuila and Texas," *Gammel's Laws of Texas* (Austin: Gammel Book Company, 1898) 1:406.
3. Thomas B. Love, "Some East Texas Banking History," in T. C. Richardson, *East Texas—Its History and Its Makers*, ed. Dobney White (New York: Lewis Historical Publishing Company, 1940), p. 1342.
4. Thomas B. Love, "Banking Legislation in Texas—Past, Present and Future," address before the Texas Bankers Association, Fort Worth, June 5, 1908, p. 3.
5. Ibid., p. 5.
6. Ibid., p. 6.
7. "An Act to Incorporate the Texas Railroad, Navigation, and Banking Company," *Gammel's Laws of Texas* 1:1188.
8. Love, "Some East Texas Banking History," p. 1347.
9. Ibid., p. 1350.
10. John Jay Knox, *A History of Banking in the United States* (New York: Bradford Rhodes & Company, 1903), p. 618.

2

Banking in the State of Texas before 1865

Constitutional Prohibition of Banking

After annexation had been agreed upon, the first state constitutional convention met at Austin on July 4, 1845, to draft a constitution for the state of Texas. The convention resurrected the question of banking and settled it for years to come.

Sam Houston, the most influential Texan of his time, was elected a delegate to the convention but, instead, decided to travel to Tennessee in order to pay his respects at the bedside of his dying friend, General Andrew Jackson. Although Jackson died a few days before the convention, Houston did not return to Texas in time to take his seat. In spite of Houston's absence, his influence and that of the deceased Andrew Jackson determined the fate of banking in Texas for a considerable span of time. The convention adopted a resolution that each delegate should wear crepe on his arm in honor of General Jackson. In a letter dated January 12, 1845, Jackson had exhorted Houston and the people of Texas to repudiate banking in the new constitution.[1]

The constitutional convention responded accordingly and on August 6 passed the following clause by a vote of forty-seven to seven: "No corporate body shall hereafter be created, renewed, or extended, with banking or discounting privileges."[2] In the debate that followed, General Thomas Rusk, the president of the convention, said:

Thousands upon thousands [of individuals] have been ruined by [banks]. I consider it a bright page in the history of General Jackson, that he had the honor of giving the blow which will destroy them upon this continent. And I wish by no vote of mine, here or elsewhere, to authorize the institution of a bank, which may benefit a few individuals, but will carry, here as elsewhere, ruin, want, misery, and degradation in its train.³

After the debate on the prohibition of banking was over, the question of prohibiting note issue was considered, and a resolution prohibiting the issuing or circulating of notes was introduced. If adopted, this provision would have prohibited the Commercial and Agricultural Bank or the Texas Railroad, Navigation, and Banking Company, as well as individuals representing them, from issuing or circulating notes if their charters were held valid by the state government. As a compromise, the following was proposed: "The legislature shall prohibit by law individuals from issuing bills, checks, promissory notes, or other paper to circulate as money."⁴ This provision did not prohibit any valid corporation or firm from issuing notes or any individual from circulating notes. It was unanimously approved by the convention, without debate. Even so, opposition to the Commercial and Agricultural Bank and the Texas Railroad, Navigation, and Banking Company continued during the convention, although without success.

It is evident from the convention proceedings that leniency was shown toward the Commerical and Agricultural Bank and the Texas Railroad, Navigation, and Banking Company. However, it is not certain why these corporations were left alone. Was it the intent of the convention to give these institutions a banking monopoly in the state or merely to leave the decision to the courts? It is certain that the exercise of banking privileges by any other corporation was absolutely denied.

The Banking Operation of R. & D. G. Mills

On April 7, 1846, the state legislature passed a law, in compliance with the constitution, making it a criminal offense for any person or persons to issue notes to circulate as money. However, shortly after the passage of this bill and probably even before its passage, "Mills Money," issued by the firm of R. & D. G. Mills, was in wide circulation.

R. & D. G. Mills was a partnership formed by Robert Mills and his younger brother, David G. Mills, to conduct a mercantile business in Brazoria. In 1849 they moved the business to Galveston and admitted to the partnership John W. Jockusch, the Prussian consul in Galveston. This firm was stronger than that of McKinney and Williams, from the standpoint of both management and capital, and Robert Mills was purported to be the richest man in the state and the most influential merchant in Texas. Mills's trading enterprise included interests in firms in New Orleans, New York, Liverpool, and Havana, and he owned and operated many sailing vessels and several steamships. The Mills brothers also owned four large sugar and cotton plantations comprising some 3,300 acres under cultivation and 100,000 acres of raw land. In 1857 the trading company was reported to have been worth $5 million.

The firm of R. & D. G. Mills provided a valuable service to the people of Texas in furnishing them with a circulating medium. Although Texas law prohibited the issuance of any bill, promissory note, or other paper to circulate as money, it did not prohibit the circulation of the notes of foreign banks endorsed by a Texas firm. At that time the worthless notes of the Northern Bank of Mississippi at Holly Springs were in wide circulation in all denominations. In order to facilitate business transactions, R. & D. G. Mills endorsed these notes and placed them into circulation in an amount estimated to be between $30,000 and $300,000. With the name of R. & D. G. Mills on the paper the bills were considered to be "equivalent to gold" and were thus in wide demand. These notes came to be known as "Mills Money."

The Commercial and Agricultural Bank

During the years of the Republic, McKinney and Williams had continued their banking operations and also their negotiations to operate under the charter granted by the state of Coahuila and Texas. Finally, some twelve years after the charter had been granted, the Commercial and Agricultural Bank opened its doors on December 30, 1847, in spite of the constitutional prohibition of chartered banks. The bank, located in Galveston, was the *first incorporated bank in Texas*. Very little data concerning the finances or operations of the bank throughout its life are extant. Letters and other manuscripts indicate that the capital of the bank probably never exceeded $300,000, although the amount actually paid in cannot be determined. The financial condition of the bank in 1849 was apparently sound, as indicated by a letter written by former Cashier J. M. McMillan to President Williams congratulating him on "the good appearance of the bank's balance sheet" and suggesting that the bank's profits could be increased "when you have sufficient real capital."

Although the demand for loans from the new bank was active and a large number of loans were made, many of the borrowers were destitute and had difficulty meeting their obligations. Samuel May Williams was apparently a man of great compassion who responded freely to the needs of the pioneers of Texas. Numerous loans were made to new settlers, most of whom had exhausted their resources journeying to Texas. In addition, many loans were made to Texans who were experiencing extreme financial difficulties because of the economic conditions prevailing at the time. These people had very little collateral, and the loans were made merely upon faith in the borrower's promise to repay. Requests for loans ranging from $25 to $1,000 came from all parts of the state. Little information is available concerning the bank's total deposits; however, existing drafts and receipts reveal that deposits were received from all parts of Texas.

Shortly after the bank opened in Galveston, a branch was established in Brownsville to serve Mexican-American interests. It is reported that the bank carried on a rather large volume of business, although the Mexicans refused to accept the bank's notes. Unfortunately, the operations of the branch and the Galveston bank were severely curtailed because of litigation pending against the bank throughout most of its life.

Litigation against the Commercial and Agricultural Bank and R. & D. G. Mills

On March 20, 1848, less than three months after the opening of the Commercial and Agricultural Bank, the legislature passed an act to suppress banking. This act prohibited any corporation, company, or association from engaging in banking activities or issuing notes to circulate as money and carried a penalty consisting of a fine of not less than $2,000 or more than $5,000 for its violation.[5]

The report of the attorney general to the governor, dated October 27, 1849, reveals that four suits were filed against the organizers of the Commercial and Agricultural Bank for issuing notes. One of the suits was brought to court, but the state lost its case in district court. The question of the validity of the banking business was not considered.

In 1853 the attorney general filed suits for violation of the 1848 law against the partners of R. & D. G. Mills and against the proprietors of the Commercial and Agricultural Bank. The state obtained judgments in both cases; however, in 1859 the Supreme Court overruled the lower court's decision in the Mills case on the basis that the Act of 1848 did not refer to the issuing of paper money by an unincorporated firm. At the same time, the judge held that the charter of Commercial and Agricultural Bank was absolutely void. This decision, along with the death of Samual May Williams on September 13, 1858, resulted in the closing and liquidation of the bank and its branch in Brownsville. The goodwill of the bank was assumed by Ball, Hutchings & Company. It is interesting to note that the Commercial and Agricultural Bank had continued to operate until 1859, even though its twenty-year charter granted by the state of Coahuila and Texas in 1835 had expired.

Although the firm of R. & D. G. Mills withstood the legal assault of the state, the Civil War precipitated its demise. Robert Mills gambled and lost his mercantile fortune by engaging in blockade-running during the war. He returned to Galveston after the war, "broken in spirit and in finances." The firm of R. & D. G. Mills was bankrupt, and Robert Mills, in order to pay off his creditors, auctioned his homestead mansion, carriages, furniture, and personal belongings, though the laws of the time would have permitted him to shield much of this property from his creditors.

An indication of the strength of R. & D. G. Mills and the Commercial and Agricultural Bank during the 1850s was provided during the financial panic of 1857. At that time the banks had approximately $1 million in aggregate in bank notes outstanding, subject to redemption in specie on demand. When news of the financial panic reached the coastal area, runs on the two banks developed on October 19 and 20, 1857. R. & D. G. Mills met all demands for redemption, while the Commercial and Agricultural Bank only closed its doors for a few hours on October 20. Both banks opened their doors on the morning of October 21 and were again paying in specie.

Other Private Firms Engaged in Banking

In the late 1840s and 1850s other firms began businesses that included banking functions. H. Runge & Company of Cuero began mercantile operations in 1845 in Indianola. At the time of its failure on January 16, 1932, it claimed to be the oldest banking institution in Texas. D. Yturri, Brownsville, opened for business in Brownsville in 1848. In 1854 two new private banks began commercial operations in Texas. B. A. Sheperd opened an office in Houston to engage exclusively in banking—"B. A. Sheperd, Exchange and Collection Office"—and also in 1854 Ball, Hutchings & Company was established. The latter company, the same firm that assumed the goodwill of the Commercial and Agricultural Bank, was a partnership of John Sealy, John H. Hutchings, and George Ball. Ball, Hutchings & Company was later succeeded by the private bank, Hutchings, Sealy & Co., which merged with the South Texas National Bank in 1930 to become the Hutchings-Sealy National Bank. In 1958 the Hutchings-Sealy National Bank merged with the First National Bank of Galveston, the first chartered national bank in the state, to form the First Hutchings-Sealy National Bank of Galveston. The firm of D. & A. Oppenheimer was established in San Antonio in 1858 and is still in business. Undoubtedly, there were numerous other firms conducting a limited banking business, but they are unrecorded in the annals of history.

Notes

1. Love, "Banking Legislation in Texas," p. 13.
2. *Constitution of 1845*, Article 7, Section 30.
3. *Journals and Debates, Texas Convention*, 1845, p. 461.
4. Ibid.
5. *Gammel's Laws of Texas* 3:234.

3

Banking in Texas from 1865 to 1905

During the Civil War banking services continued to be provided by private banks, since there were no banks of issue in the state. Ball, Hutchings & Company, R. & D. G. Mills, B. A. Sheperd, and others operated throughout this period.

After the war, on February 7, 1866, a constitutional convention convened in Austin and subsequently readopted with only minor amendments the constitution that had been in effect on January 28, 1861, that is, the Constitution of 1845. The prohibition of the chartering of state banks remained in force. However, the National Bank Act of 1863, passed by the U.S. Congress, did permit banks with national charters to operate within the state of Texas, although the scarcity of capital in the post-Civil War days made it extremely difficult to raise $50,000, the minimum capital required. As a result the establishment of private banks was encouraged and the private banking system developed simultaneously with the growth of national banks.

Development of Private Banking
during Reconstruction, 1865-1876

According to the *Texas Almanac for 1867*, fifteen private banks were operating in Texas at the end of 1866.[1] Seven of these were located in Galveston, two in Houston, two in San Antonio, and one each in Austin, Belton, Brenham, and Waco.

The environment under which private banks operated was one of complete freedom, as they were responsible to no supervisory authority and were free to follow whatever policies they desired. There were no restrictions on entry; any individual or firm wishing to do so could operate a "banking" business regardless of the amount of net worth, or capital, that could be provided to support it. They could make loans for any purpose whatsoever, in any amount, for any duration, and for whatever rate of interest the market would bear as long as the usury laws were not violated.

Although complete freedom existed, the banking activities of the merchant-bankers were rather rudimentary by present standards. During the Reconstruction, banking services were conducted primarily in connection with the cotton export business. This undoubtedly accounted for the large concentration of banking firms in Galveston, which was the largest city in Texas and the principal port during this era. As the financial and commercial center of Texas, Galveston attracted numerous financial enterprises. For example, the firm of J. S. and J. B. Sydnor was willing to make "liberal advances on consignments of all kinds of merchandise," and Burns & Lee acted as "wholesale dealers in foreign and domestic exchange."[2] Other banking services offered by the private firms included the collection and remittance of drafts and advances to cotton growers.

In some other parts of the state the banking activities of merchants were less sophisticated than those of the Galveston financiers. For example, the Charles Schreiner business in Kerrville, which was founded in 1869, operated in a small building, sixteen by eighteen feet. There were no banks in this part of the state, and the cattlemen of the area turned their gold and silver over to the store for safekeeping. Upon order the store would pay the cattlemen's bills in the village. The firm had no safe and the coins were deposited in a box beneath the floor of the store, with a "barrel of salt" covering the loose boards. Although the business was robbed frequently, no funds "deposited" for safekeeping were ever lost, and Schreiner never failed to pay specie on demand.[3] This pioneer financial business survives to the present day.

Profits attainable by the private bankers were apparently attractive, since a relatively large number of private banking firms were established. By the end of 1868 there were twenty-five private banks operating in Texas, according to the *Texas Almanac for 1869*.[4]

Only eleven of the firms listed in the *Texas Almanac for 1867* are carried over in some form to the list that appeared in the 1869 almanac. Four firms apparently had gone out of business. Three new firms appeared in Galveston, two in San Antonio, and one each in Brownsville, Bryan, Corpus Christi, Dallas, Indianola, Jefferson, Lavaca, McKinney, and Nacogdoches. Because of the nature of operation and lack of regulation of these institutions, it is probable that the almanac's list is not all-inclusive. For example, the firms of H. Runge of Indianola and D. & A. Oppenheimer were in operation long before the 1866 list was printed, but H. Runge was omitted from the 1866 list and D. & A. Oppenheimer from both lists. Another firm that was omitted, W. L. Moody & L. F. Moody & Company, is known to have been in business by 1866.

Statistics giving the total number of private banks in existence subsequent to the 1868 *Texas Almanac* list appear to be no more than rough estimates made without a uniform conception of what constituted a private bank. Since banking was frequently combined with mercantile, commission, real estate, and brokerage concerns, notable inconsistency occurs in the estimates of the total number of private banks in the state. To illustrate, George E. Barnett reports in his study "State Banks and Trust Companies," published by the National Monetary Commission, that in 1877 there were 73 private banks in Texas,[5] while another source estimates that there were 140 private banks in 1878.[6] However, in spite of the wide discrepancies in estimates, it is evident that private banking made substantial gains during Reconstruction.

National Banks in Texas during Reconstruction

The first national bank in Texas, chartered under the National Bank Act of 1863, was the First National Bank of Galveston, which was chartered on September 22, 1865. Its president was T. H. McMahan of the private banking firm T. H. McMahan & Company, and one of the directors was George Ball, a partner in the private banking firm of Ball, Hutchings & Company. Capital was $200,000, and by the call date of October 1, 1866, its deposits were in excess of $385,000. In 1958 the First National Bank of Galveston merged with Hutchings-Sealy National Bank, which continues to operate today under the original charter granted in 1865.

Three other national banks were chartered in Texas before 1869. The National Bank of Galveston, Texas, was chartered March 9, 1866, with capital of $100,000. It was voluntarily liquidated on March 19, 1890, and its assets were acquired by the private banking firm of W. L. Moody & Company. The First National Bank at Houston was chartered on March 22, 1866. On May 3, 1933, the bank was granted a new charter and its name was changed to the First National Bank in Houston, which later merged with the City National Bank to form the First City National Bank of Houston. The fourth national bank chartered in Texas was the San Antonio National Bank, which was chartered July 30, 1866, and continues to operate today. In 1945 its name was changed to First National Bank of San Antonio. Other national banks chartered during Reconstruction were the National Bank of Jefferson, in 1871, and the National Exchange Bank, Houston, the First National Bank, Denison, and the First National Bank, Austin, in 1873.

Apparently these banks enjoyed profits that averaged "considerably higher" than the average for national banks in the rest of the United States. From October 1866 to October 1873 their aggregate resources increased from about $1,370,000 to approximately $2,870,000, which indicates that the people of Texas did enjoy some prosperity during this period.[7]

Bank Chartering under the State Constitution of 1869

In the three years following the adoption of the Constitution of 1866, strong sentiment in favor of a state banking system appears to have developed. As a result the Constitution of 1869 omitted the clause prohibiting the chartering of banks by the state. It did not, however, make provisions for the chartering of state banks, but instead remained silent on the subject. Because the Constitutional Convention of 1869 did not keep a reliable journal of debate on the subject, little is known concerning the issues involved. It is probable, though, that the success of the private banks and the beginning of national banking in Texas influenced the convention's decision.

Pursuant to the change in the constitution, the Texas legislature assumed the authority to grant bank charters. These charters were granted by special acts of the legislature at the request of the organizers of the bank. In this manner thirty state banks were authorized in 1870 and 1871 and many more in the following two years. The authorized capital for the institutions ranged from $30 thousand to $5 million. Only eight of these specially chartered banks opened for business.

The first bank ever to receive a valid bank charter granted by the state of Texas was the Texas Banking and Insurance Company, Galveston; the charter was approved on July 1, 1870. The legislation providing for the charter permitted depositors to participate in the bank's profits. Dividends were to be paid annually or semiannually as follows: one fourth of the net profits to the depositors and three fourths to the stockholders; if the capital-to-deposit ratio was one to three or less, one third of the net profit was to go to the depositors and two thirds to the stockholders; if the capital-to-deposit ratio was one to four or less, one half of net profit was to go to each group. Unfortunately, little is known about the Texas Banking and Insurance Company, except that it had capital of $150,000 and operated successfully until 1889, when it was succeeded by the Galveston National Bank.[8]

The first state bank to open its doors for business was the Island City Savings Bank, Galveston, which prospered for many years but was closed by failure in January 1885. It was subsequently reorganized and later succeeded by the Texas Bank and Trust Company. The Texas Bank and Trust Company was converted on January 1, 1924, into the United States National Bank, which today is one of the most prominent commercial banking institutions in Galveston. Other banks to receive charters by special acts of the Texas legislature in this period, listed in order of their charter date, were:

Name of Bank	Location	Date of Charter
City Bank of Houston	Houston	July 21, 1870
The State Central Bank of Waco	Waco	August 8, 1870

Name of Bank	Location	Date of Charter
Citizens Bank of Navasota	Navasota	March 31, 1871
Galveston Bank & Trust	Galveston	December 2, 1871
City Bank of Sherman	Sherman	April 11, 1873
City Bank of Dallas	Dallas	May 31, 1873

The City Bank of Houston was incorporated to take over the banking portion of the Houston Insurance Company. Little is known of the Waco and Navasota banks, since they operated for only a short period of time. The Galveston Bank and Trust Company had the distinction of being the first state bank in Texas with trust powers, but it was liquidated voluntarily in 1882. The City Bank of Dallas was converted on January 27, 1880, into the City National Bank, which was later merged into the First National Bank in Dallas. The City Bank of Sherman opened in 1873 but did not survive. It was authorized to establish branches but never exercised this prerogative.

Many other institutions were authorized by the Texas legislature under the Constitution of 1869 but failed to open for business primarily because they were unable to raise the necessary capital. A number of these were authorized to establish branches. In most cases the authority to branch was not restricted as to total number of offices or geographic location.

In 1871 the Texas legislature passed a general incorporation law providing for the formation of various types of corporations, including savings banks.[9] However, in practice, the savings banks "were given the ordinary and usual powers of banks of discount and deposit and had no savings bank characteristics whatever."[10] This law was later declared unconstitutional but was reenacted in 1874.[11] The 1874 law specified capital of not less than $50,000 or more than $500,000, 10 percent of which was to have been paid in before operations could commence. Any five or more persons were allowed to incorporate.

Thirty-four institutions were chartered by the secretary of state under the unconstitutional law between 1871 and 1874, but none of them opened for business. Under the general banking law of 1874 more than twenty applications for banks were approved; however, the records of the secretary of state are not sufficiently clear to indicate the exact number. The following ten banks are known to have opened under the law:

Name of Bank	Location	Date of Charter	Capital
The Fannin County Bank	Bonham	Jan. 27, 1874	$ 50,000
The Red River County Bank	Clarksville	Sept. 12, 1874	10,000
Merchants & Planters Bank	Sherman	Sept. 28, 1872	150,000
Farmers & Merchants Bank	Paris	May 16, 1874	250,000
The Paris Exchange Bank	Paris	Jan. 28, 1875	300,000
The Exchange Bank of Dallas	Dallas	Unknown	Unknown
State Savings Bank of Dallas	Dallas	Unknown	Unknown
Drovers & Planters Bank	Denison	Unknown	Unknown
Merchants & Planters Bank	Denison	Unknown	Unknown
Citizens Savings Bank	Jefferson	Unknown	Unknown

The Fannin County Bank was nationalized on October 3, 1898, as the Fannin County National Bank; it was reorganized as a state bank in 1918. The Red River County Bank obtained a national charter in 1894. The Farmers and Merchants Bank at Paris failed in 1896. In the same year the Paris Exchange Bank was converted into the Paris National Bank, which merged with the First National Bank of Paris in 1907. The Exchange Bank of Dallas was converted in 1887 into the National Exchange Bank, which, after a series of mergers, became part of the First National Bank in Dallas. The Drovers and Planters Bank and the Merchants and Planters Bank merged during 1876; the resulting organization failed in 1878. Little is known of the State Savings Bank of Dallas or of the Citizens Savings Bank, Jefferson, except that both operated for a relatively short time.

According to Thomas B. Love, commissioner of banking from September 1, 1907, to February 1, 1910,

the formation of banks and banking corporations under the Reconstruction Constitution exhibits the very worst phase of the banking legislation of Texas, and no one can study the results without viewing as unwise, in the light of the times and conditions, the unconditional repeal of the prohibition [of state banks] contained in the prior and subsequent constitutions of the state. . . . There were numerous disastrous failures among these banks within a few years after they began to be organized, resulting in much loss to the public and demoralization of business.[12]

In contrast, Professor Avery Carlson, writing twenty-two years later, stated:

Doubtless these State banks rendered a valuable service to the people of Texas during the last quarter of the 19th century. The official reports indicate that their deposits were relatively large and that they made extensive loans. They usually kept a large cash reserve. While the law made no rule for the conduct of the banking business, and the State exercised little supervision over them, their extensive reports indicate conservative management.[13]

In either case, the delegates to the Constitutional Convention of 1875, with the Panic of 1873 fresh in their memories, restored the prohibition of the chartering of banks by the state.[14] An examination of the journal of the convention suggests that there was little or no opposition to this move, as there is no record of debates on the subject. The clause prohibiting state banks was identical to that originally written into the Constitution of 1845, and it seems to have been accepted without attempt at amendment.[15]

Era of Private and National Banks, 1876-1900

The prohibition of the chartering of state banks, as adopted in the Constitution of 1876, remained in effect until the passage of the Texas State Bank Law of 1905. Thus, with the exception of the few state banks that continued to operate under charters obtained during the 1869-1876 period, banking services in Texas for twenty-nine years were provided by private banks and national banks.

During the period beginning with the adoption of the Constitution of 1876 and ending in 1900 private banking in Texas reached its zenith. The chartering of additional state banks was prohibited and the minimum capital requirement of $50,000 for national banks limited their formation. Consequently, the number of private banks grew at a rapid rate, the trend being interrupted only briefly during 1885 and 1886 and during 1893 because of financial panics in the United States in 1884 and 1893. By 1900 there were 190 private banks in Texas; in 1877, only 73.

Table 1

Private Banks in Texas, 1877-1905

Year	Banks	Year	Banks
1877	73	1892	127
1878	78	1893	133
1879	79	1894	128
1880	85	1895	131
1881	98	1896	153
1882	124	1897	147
1883	123	1898	165
1884	122	1899	187
1885	116	1900	190
1886	112	1901	195
1887	122	1902	168
1888	130	1903	183
1889	138	1904	184
1890	148	1905	197
1891	145		

Source: George E. Barnett, "State Banks and Trust Companies since the Passage of the National Bank Act," *National Monetary Commission, Sixty-first Congress, Third Session*, Senate Document no. 659 (Washington, D.C.: 1911), vol. 2, p. 250.

The heyday of private banking came to an end as the minimum capital requirement for national banks was reduced in 1900 to $25,000, and five years later the Texas State Bank Law was passed.

As for earlier periods, little information is available regarding the finances and operations of private banks between 1877 and 1900. There were still no regulations imposed on these institutions at the time, and the prevailing opinion of the private bankers was that their business affairs were privileged information. However, a few of the more prosperous institutions did designate the amount of their capital, which in some instances was as much as $1 million.

In addition, some of the bankers made yearly reports to the comptroller of the currency on a voluntary basis, and these were consolidated and published each year in the comptroller's annual report. Even though the figures are incomplete, they reveal something of the magnitude of private banking in Texas during the era. The number of banks reporting between 1880 and 1904 varied widely, as did the aggregate resources of these establishments. For example, in 1880 eighty-seven banks reported resources of $5,814,000, whereas in 1904 twelve banks reported resources of $11,550,000.

Undoubtedly most of the private banks enjoyed profitable operations and rendered notable service to Texas during these years. Probably the most valuable service performed by the private banks was to provide banking facilities to small communities that otherwise would have had none. The prohibition on state banks was in effect, and to the small agrarian Texas community the $50,000 minimum capital requirement for a national bank was usually prohibitive. However, to the larger, more developed town or city the private bank was not of such vital importance. Most of the private banks operating in these cities could easily have met the minimum capital requirements and conducted their business as national banks.

The relative importance of the private bank began to diminish in the late 1880s and 1890s. By the late 1880s Texas had completely recovered from the Civil War and its economy was beginning to prosper. U.S. census figures reveal that the Texas population increased from 818,579 in 1870 to 1,591,749 in 1880;

by 1900, 3,048,710 persons lived in Texas. The entire economy of the state was beginning to change. People were moving to Texas in large numbers and gathering in urban areas, which were becoming retail and financial centers. The development of national banking was a natural outgrowth of this new prosperity, since it became less difficult to raise the $50,000 minimum capital required to organize a national bank. Also, as pointed out before, the minimum requirement was reduced to $25,000 at the turn of the new century. Hence national banking was on the upswing.

Table 2

Texas Private Banks Reporting to the Comptroller of the Currency
Selected Years, 1880-1904

Year	Banks	Total resources ($000)	Total capital and surplus undivided profits ($000)
1880	87	5,814	1,762
1888	26	6,230	3,157
1889	21	4,157	1,526
1890	27	9,783	3,990
1892	28	8,034	3,191
1893	22	6,390	2,943
1894	20	6,228	3,085
1895	25	7,296	3,372
1899	33	6,703	1,468
1900	41	4,709	1,554
1904	12	11,550	3,856

Source: *Annual Reports of the Comptroller of the Currency* (Washington, D.C.: Government Printing Office, selected years, 1880-1904).

The sixteen years following the establishment of the first national bank in Texas in 1865 constitute the formative period of national banking in the state. At the end of 1881 there were only twelve national banks in Texas, with total resources of about $8 million. However, beginning in 1882 the number of national banks grew at a rapid rate; by the end of 1890 there were 198 national banks in Texas, with total resources of more than $73 million. This remarkable growth seems to have been undaunted by the May 1884 financial crisis in the United States and related events. From the beginning of 1884 through 1886 the number of national banks in the state increased by twenty-eight and their resources expanded by $10 million.

Table 3

National Banks in Texas, 1865-1905

Year	Banks	Total resources ($000)	Year	Banks	Total resources ($000)
1865	1	100	1885	68	25,237
1866	4	1,369	1886	74	28,254
1867	4	2,017	1887	91	34,260
1868	4	1,921	1888	100	39,415
1869	4	1,779	1889	135	55,560
1870	4	1,891	1890	198	73,240
1871	5	2,656	1891	207	74,293
1872	5	2,782	1892	223	84,765
1873	7	3,334	1893	221	72,723
1874	9	3,537	1894	218	77,061
1875	10	3,617	1895	213	77,831
1876	10	3,622	1896	204	71,835
1877	12	4,171	1897	202	81,007
1878	11	4,103	1898	196	86,737
1879	11	4,373	1899	199	97,689
1880	14	5,741	1900	234	131,557
1881	12	7,948	1901	290	139,016
1882	24	12,246	1902	345	145,860
1883	46	18,132	1903	377	166,644
1884	61	20,652	1904	420	192,723
			1905	440	189,484

Source: *Annual Reports of the Comptroller of the Currency* (Washington, D.C.: Government Printing Office, 1865-1905).

In the 1890s, however, the growth of national banks was significantly affected by the Panic of 1893. Between 1893 and 1896 seventeen national banks were closed and no new ones were organized. From the beginning of 1891 through 1899 there was a net increase of only one national bank in Texas; the aggregate resources of national banks in Texas increased by $24,449,000. In 1900 the rapid expansion in the number of national banks that had characterized the 1880s resumed as the minimum capital requirements for national banks were reduced to $25,000. The conversion of private banks and the organization of new national banks accelerated; from the beginning of 1900 through 1904 there was a net increase of 221 banks operating under national charters in Texas. Thus at the beginning of 1905 there were 420 national banks in the state, with total resources of $192,723,000. National banking had indeed prospered during the prohibition of state-chartered banks and was well established by the time the Texas State Bank Law of 1905 was passed.

Notes

1. *The Texas Almanac for 1867 and Emigrants Guide to Texas* (Galveston: Richardson & Co., 1867), p. 217.
2. Ibid., p. 25.
3. Ibid., p. 24.
4. *The Texas Almanac for 1869 and Emigrants Guide to Texas* (Galveston: Richardson & Co., 1869).
5. George E. Barnett, "State Banks and Trust Companies," *National Monetary Commission, Sixty-first Congress, Third Session*, Senate Document no. 659, (Washington, D.C.: 1911) 2:250.
6. *Texas Bankers Record* 22 (July 1933): 17.
7. Ibid., p. 30.
8. "An Act to Incorporate the Texas Banking and Insurance Company," *Gammel's Laws of Texas* 6:511-513.
9. "An Act Concerning Private Corporations," *Gammel's Laws of Texas* 8:137-139.
10. Love, "Banking Legislation in Texas," p. 27.
11. "An Act Concerning Private Corporations," *Gammel's Laws of Texas* 8:137-139.
12. Love, "Banking Legislation in Texas," p. 28.
13. Avery Luvere Carlson, *A Monetary and Banking History of Texas* (Fort Worth: Fort Worth National Bank, 1930), p. 37.
14. *Texas Constitution of 1876*, Article 16, Section 16.
15. *Journal of the Constitutional Convention of Texas*, 1875.

4

The Texas State Bank Law of 1905

While national banking had begun to develop very rapidly in Texas in the 1880s, many communities in the state were still without banking facilities. In addition, the instability of and lack of control over the many private banks had become a source of growing concern to the people of Texas. It did not make sense to allow unregulated private banking and at the same time prohibit by law the establishment of commercial banks that could be regulated by the state. As a result, sentiment in favor of state-chartered banks began to grow during the latter part of the nineteenth century.

Growing Support for State-Chartered Banking

In 1885 Frank R. Malone and E. M. Longcope (officers of the First National Bank of Lampasas Springs), inspired by the organization of the American Bankers Association ten years earlier, conceived the idea of organizing Texas bankers into an association.[1] The first meeting of the Texas Bankers Association, which was held at Lampasas Springs July 23 through July 26, 1885, was devoted mostly to organizational details. In the following years the annual convention of the association was devoted largely to current topics of concern to Texas bankers, as has been the practice ever since.

At the 1889 meeting of the association E. M. Longcope, one of the founding fathers, presented a paper to the delegates entitled "Should the State Charter Banks, and Under What

Restrictions?"[2] Longcope's answer to the first part of the question was affirmative. He asserted that the prohibition against the incorporation of banks was born in a "so-called spirit of revenge" and that it fostered prejudice and "struck a blow at the vital interests of Texas, a recovery from which it has taken years to effect, and . . . is not wholly effected yet." He cited the success of national and private banks in support of his position favoring state banks and enumerated the advantages of an incorporated bank as follows:

The responsibility of the shareholder is fixed. It provides a means of saving to the poorer classes, equal if not superior to building associations. It identifies large numbers and all classes [of people] with its success. It enables small towns to possess banking facilities which cannot now be enjoyed by them. By enabling small places to have these facilities it creates capital for business purposes, which would before long reduce the heavy rates of interest over the state.[3]

Longcope further asserted that a system of state-chartered banks, paying all its taxes to the state government and subject only to Texas laws, could be made a great "tower of strength" that would in no way be injurious to the banks then in existence.

Longcope, drawing upon the state banking laws of New York, Nebraska, and Missouri, then outlined what he believed should be included in a Texas law. First, according to Longcope, there would be a "Banking Department of Texas" under the direction of an appointed officer, a banker with five years of practical experience. Part of his duties should be the selection of a "suitable" person to examine all banks under the law once each year, to call upon the banks for statements four or five times a year, and to see that these statements are published. Longcope further advocated a legal loan limit of 10 percent of capital and surplus to any single person or business entity; a prohibition against loans secured by the bank's own capital stock; a limit on real estate loans equal to 25 percent of the bank's deposits; a legal reserve of 30 percent of deposits for city banks and 20 percent for country banks (banks in cities with less than 1,000 population); the allocation of 20 percent of yearly net earnings to a surplus reserve until the amount of surplus equaled that of capital; a minimum capital of $25,000 fully paid in; an oath for directors;

stockholder liability for only the amount of stock held; and a guarantee fund for deposits participated in by all chartered banks.

At the close of Longcope's address the convention provided for a committee to consider the recommendations made and deliberate on any legislation found to be advisable. It is a credit to Longcope that most of the provisions that he envisioned were ultimately included in one form or another in the state banking laws that were adopted over fifteen years later.

At the 1889 convention another paper dealing with the same subject as that assigned to Longcope—"Should the State Charter Banks, and Under What Restrictions?"—was presented by Captain Nicholas Weekes, the association's president.[4] Captain Weekes presented several cogent arguments in favor of state-chartered banks. In the first place, to the extent that the constitutional provision was intended to prohibit banking, it was a complete failure, as witnessed by the many national and private banks doing business in the state. Moreover, the exclusion of government-controlled state banks facilitated and encouraged "banking in every objectionable form," including the "five percent per month pawnbrokers who thrived on the starving needs of helpless unfortunates." Second, national banks, due to stringent regulations, did not always meet the requirements of the citizens of Texas, the great majority of whom were farmers. The principal assets of these people consisted of real estate and certain types of personal property not acceptable as security under the national banking laws. Consequently, this class of borrower was compelled to seek assistance from "some foreign loan agency" at the "fearful price" of 12 percent per annum plus innumerable fees or to borrow from "some local usurer" at the exorbitant rate of 2 percent per month. It was thus argued that a third advantage of state banks would be a substantial reduction in the maximum interest rate throughout the state from the then-existing level of 12 percent. Finally, it was believed that a well-regulated state banking system would encourage saving, mobilize capital, and increase the amount of money in circulation. Captain Weekes declared that the reason for the prohibition of state banks had long since passed, that the opposition was one of tradition and not of reason, and that it "smacked" of politics and was based on prejudice.

The issue lay more or less dormant for the next three years. In 1892, though, the convention of the Texas Democratic party adopted a platform containing a plank that favored an amendment to the constitution "permitting the incorporation of state banks under proper restrictions and control for the protection of the depositors and the people." The convention nominated for governor James Stephen Hogg, who was seeking reelection and who had substantial support throughout the state. His opponent, George Clark, the Republican candidate, was opposed to a state banking system. Thus the banking question became one of the issues of the campaign. Although Governor Hogg was reelected and, as he had promised, recommended to the Twenty-third Legislature, in 1893, an amendment to the constitution that authorized state banks, the amendment was not submitted by the legislature to the people until ten years later.

The banking issue apparently did not surface again until the 1898 convention of the Texas Bankers Association, at which D. J. Young, cashier of the Canadian Valley Bank, presented a paper with the title "State Banks."[5] Actually Young's address was an indictment of private banks rather than an endorsement of state banking. Mr. Young, himself a private banker, pointed out that anyone having sufficient funds to buy a safe and rent an office could open a bank and advertise whatever capital he desired regardless of whether it was paid in. People living in rural areas that had insufficient resources to support a national bank were forced to depend on the honesty and integrity of the private bankers for the safety of their money. It was the opinion of Young that in order to protect the people against irresponsible and illegitimate private banks, private banks should be brought under regulation by the state. Hence he proposed that the association should bring the subject before the next legislature.

Although Young's paper actually made little reference to state banks, as a diatribe against private banks by a private banker it was a very convincing argument for a well-regulated state banking system.

After the 1898 convention the state bank controversy appears to have subsided for a while. However, three years later, at the 1901 convention of the Texas Bankers Association, the issue was a very live one indeed. The Honorable Thomas H. Franklin of

San Antonio addressed the convention on "Legislative and Business Interest." The major portion of this speech dealt with the state bank question.[6] Franklin recounted most of the arguments that had been previously advanced in favor of state-chartered banks and exhorted the bankers to take appropriate action to place the issue before the people.

Taking the cue from Franklin, J. N. Brown of San Antonio moved at the close of the speech that the address be referred to the influential newspapers of the state. This proposal carried unanimously, whereupon A. J. Baker of San Angelo took the floor and moved that the legislative committee bring the state bank question to the attention of the governor and that he be requested to make special mention of it in his call for a special session of the legislature that was to be convened that summer. Baker's motion passed, apparently with no opposition, as there is no record of dissenting votes or discussion on the subject in the proceedings of the Seventeenth Annual Convention of the Texas Bankers Association. Presumably the legislative committee acted as instructed by the convention.

The banking issue was placed before the meeting of the Democratic State Convention in Galveston in 1902, and once again the convention adopted a plank in its platform favoring a constitutional amendment to authorize state banks. The party's candidate, Samuel W. T. Lanham, was elected governor and, in compliance with the platform, submitted the question to the legislature in the form of the following proposed constitutional amendment:

The legislature shall by general laws, authorize the incorporation of corporate bodies with banking and discounting privileges, and shall provide for a system of state supervision, regulation and control of such bodies which will adequately protect and secure the depositors and creditors thereof. Each shareholder of such corporate body incorporated in this state, so long as he owns shares therein, and for twelve months after the date of any bona fide transfer thereof, shall be personally liable for all debts of such corporate body existing at the date of such transfer, to an amount additional to the par value of such shares so owned or transferred. No such corporate body shall be chartered until all of authorized capital stock has been subscribed and paid for in full in cash. Such body corporate shall not be authorized to engage in business at more than one place, which shall be designated by its charter. No foreign corporation, other than national banks of the United States, shall be permitted to exercise banking or discounting privileges in this state.[7]

Several members of the legislature opposed the amendment because of the feature providing that state banks "shall not be authorized to engage in business at more than one place, which shall be designated in its charter." These members represented a small minority, however, and the amendment passed the house and the senate by an overwhelming vote. Representative Mays, a prominent lawyer from Corsicana, introduced and successfully urged the inclusion of the clause prohibiting branches.

The 1904 state convention of the Democratic party and the Texas Bankers Association endorsed the amendment to the constitution and it was passed by a substantial majority in the November 1904 general election. Thus the prohibition against incorporated state banks, which had been a part of the constitution since 1845, was removed. Subsequently the Twenty-ninth Legislature enacted the Texas State Bank Law, which became effective August 14, 1905.

Although several bank bills were introduced in the legislature, Senator Thomas B. Love of Dallas authored the measure that ultimately became law. The bill was modeled after the Missouri banking law, which in turn was drawn largely from the New York statute. The New York law, considered to be one of the most effective laws in force, served as the model for many other state banking laws, as well as for the National Banking Act.[8]

Provisions of the New Banking Law

Aside from traditional provisions authorizing the organization and operation of a state bank, the Texas State Bank Law had several distinctive features that set it apart from national bank laws and significantly influenced the structure of banking in the state.[9]

The first of these features was the section providing for the establishment of a bank. Any five persons meeting the capital and residence requirements could incorporate a state bank merely by filing the articles of association with the secretary of state. Upon receipt of a certified copy of the articles of association from the secretary of state, the bank could be opened for business.

This feature of the law, together with minimum capital requirements for banks without trust powers—from $10,000 to $100,000 depending upon the population of the city of domicile—provided an ease of entry for incorporated banks in Texas that had not previously existed. As a consequence a "free banking" period in Texas history commenced with the passage of the Texas State Bank Law and lasted for eight years.

The law of 1905 also provided for the establishment of banking and trust companies and savings banks. A banking and trust company was authorized to operate as a bank of deposit or discount and to have trust powers. Capital stock for a bank with trust powers was required to be no less than $50,000 and no more than $10 million. A savings bank was confined strictly to a savings business, with capital requirements ranging from $10,000 to $50,000 depending on the population of the city of domicile.

No state bank was allowed to "maintain any branch bank" or to "receive deposits or pay checks" except in its own house. Foreign corporations were precluded from operating a bank in the state.

In addition to the provision covering organization and operation, the Texas banking law provided for the supervision of state banks. This responsibility was given to the commissioner of agriculture, insurance, statistics, and history. The commissioner was required, either personally or through examining personnel, to examine every corporation doing business under the act at least once a year. He was given the authority to close any insolvent corporation and was charged to require any corporation with impaired capital to restore the deficiency.

In 1906 the legislature established a separate department of agriculture, changed the name of the Department of Agriculture, Insurance, Statistics, and History to the Department of Insurance and Banking, and named the head of that department the commissioner of insurance and banking.

The Texas State Bank Law of 1905 did not bring private banks under supervision. Although a proposal was made to regulate private banks in the 1905 law, the constitutionality of the proposal was promptly questioned. On January 31, 1905, a public hearing held in Austin was attended by fifty private bankers. At this hearing the private bankers recounted the valuable service provided by their banks to Texas and its citizens and asked to be "let alone."[10] As a result of this well-articulated, though emotional, argument private banks were allowed to continue to operate without regulation alongside state and national banks.

In 1913 a law was passed that required investigation into the necessity for a new bank and into the financial and moral integrity of the incorporators as a process for evaluation of charter applications. Between 1905 and 1913, however, nine hundred state bank charters were granted.

The primary features of the 1905 bank law that set state banks apart from national banks were the greater lending powers accorded the state institutions. State banks, unlike national banks, could lend money secured by real estate provided the bank did not lend more than 50 percent of its capital or more than 50 percent of the "reasonable cash value" of the real estate. Additionally, a state bank could lend an amount not exceeding 25 percent of its capital and surplus to any single individual, corporation, or company, whereas a national bank was limited to 10 percent.

As in the case of national banks, each stockholder of a state bank was personally liable for all defaulted debts of the bank or for any loss that exceeded the capital stock of the bank. The total liability of each stockholder was an amount equal to twice the par value of the stock owned or sold within the previous twelve months. The liability did not extend to persons holding stock in a fiduciary capacity or as collateral.

Notes

1. *The Founding Convention: Texas Bankers Association in 1885* (Dallas: Egan Company, 1959), pp. 1-17.
2. E. M. Longcope, "Should the State Charter Banks, and Under What Restrictions?" (address before the Texas Bankers Association's annual convention, Dallas, May 8, 1889), in *Proceedings of the Fifth Annual Convention of the Texas Bankers Association* (Galveston: Press of Clarke and Courts, 1889), pp. 14-19.
3. Ibid., pp. 16-17.
4. Nicholas Weekes, "Should the State Charter Banks, and Under What Restrictions?" (address before the Texas Bankers Association's annual convention, Dallas, May 10, 1889), in *Proceedings of the Fifth Annual Convention of the Texas Bankers Association*, pp. 66-68.
5. D. J. Young, "State Banks" (paper read before the Texas Bankers Association's annual convention, Austin, May 12, 1898), in *Proceedings of the Fourteenth Annual Convention of the Texas Bankers Association* (St. Louis: Press of Frey Stationery Co., 1898), pp. 113-114.
6. Thomas H. Franklin, "Legislative and Business Interests" (address before the Texas Bankers Association's annual convention, Houston, May 15, 1901) in *Proceedings of the Seventeenth Annual Convention of the Texas Bankers Association* (Dallas: McMath Lithograph and Printing Co., 1901), pp. 78-92.
7. Love, "Some East Texas Banking History," p. 1372.
8. Ibid., pp. 1373-1374.
9. Love, "Some East Texas Banking History," p. 1374.
10. Carlson, *Monetary and Banking History*, p. 50.

5

The First Five Years under the Banking Law of 1905

As early as June 11, 1905, the secretary of state reported that many people had asked how early his office would be open on August 13, the day the Texas State Bank Law was to become effective. In addition, by June 11 four persons had informed the secretary of state that they were going to try to obtain the first charter issued and thus secure the name of the First State Bank of Texas.

August 13 fell on a Sunday. The secretary of state announced that the department would not be open on that day but that charters could be filed after 8:30 a.m. on the next day, Monday, August 14. The secretary also stated that any charter filed under the name of the First State Bank of Texas would not be accepted, since the First State Bank of Texas, located in Hillsboro, had been chartered before the adoption of the Constitution of 1876. Although the First State Bank of Texas in Hillsboro had been chartered, the authors found no evidence that the bank ever opened for business.

On August 14 applications for charters were approved for four banks. The first charter was granted to the Union Bank and Trust Company of Houston, with capital of $500,000. The next three charters were granted respectively to American Bank and Trust Company of Houston, American Bank and Trust Company of San Antonio, and Bank of Somerville. While the first charter granted was to the Union Bank and Trust Company of Houston, the distinction of being the first state bank to commence business is shared by the American Bank and Trust Company of Houston and the Bank of Somerville, each of which opened for business on August 16, 1905. The Union Bank and Trust Company commenced business five days later.

Demand for Charters

As anticipated, the demand for charters was great. By the end of September, only one and one-half months after the law became effective, thirty-one charters had been granted. In the initial six months—August 14, 1905, to February 20, 1906—sixty-five banks were authorized to do business in the state. Of these, thirty-seven had capital of less than $25,000, which indicated that they were domiciled in towns with fewer than 2,500 inhabitants. Only nine were located in cities with a population in excess of 20,000. These facts seemed to corroborate the need for banking facilities in smaller areas where the capital requirement of national banks could not be easily raised or justified.

The first call for a statement of condition was issued by the commissioner on September 30, 1905. Twenty-nine banks answered the call and reported total resources of $4,341,000. By the next call, January 3, 1906, there were forty-three banks in operation with resources of $7,255,000.

The First Five Years of the State Banking System

The growth of the state banking system in Texas during its first five years was spectacular. A total of 636 charters were issued for state banks from August 14, 1905, through August 31, 1910. On August 31, 1910, there were 584 state banks in operation.[1] On June 30, 1910, the 584 banks answering the call had total capital accounts of $21,707,201 and total resources of $69,497,041.

Of the 636 banks chartered during the first five years, 52 surrendered their charters. Twelve of these represented banks never actually opened for business, four were nationalized, four were assumed by or merged into other institutions, and twenty-nine were liquidated. Remarkably, only three banks failed, although

Table 4
State Banks Chartered and in Operation in Texas, 1907-1969

Year ended	Number chartered	Increase from previous year	Voluntary liquidations					Total		Forced liquidations		Banks chartered but not opened	Total banks in operation	Change from previous year
			Dissolved	Nationalized	Sold or assumed	Merged	Never opened	per year	cumulative	per year	cumulative			
August 31														
1907	--	--	3	2	0	0	1	6	6	0	0	0	--	--
1908	375	--	14	2	1	1	2	20	26	3	3	0	--	--
1909	--	--	3	0	2	0	0	5	31	0	3	0	--	--
1910	636	--	9	0	0	0	9	18	49	0	3	0	584	--
1911	765	129	20	4	2	5	3	34	83	1	4	0	678	94
1912	839	74	13	3	1	2	1	20	103	2	6	0	730	52
1913	967	128	8	2	3	2	2	17	120	4	10	0	837	107
1914	1,020	53	6	4	0	6	0	16	136	2	12	0	872	40
1915	1,037	17	16	18	4	8	0	46	182	3	15	0	840	(32)
1916	1,064	27	12	2	5	6	0	25	207	5	20	0	837	(3)
1917	1,116	52	3	5	2	5	0	15	222	2	22	0	872	35
1918	1,143	27	5	1	2	2	0	10	232	0	22	0	889	17
1919	1,203	60	3	1	1	5	2	12	244	3	25	0	924	35
1920	1,310	107	6	3	0	6	1	16	260	2	27	10	1,010	86
1921	1,359	49	2	1	7	11	0	21	281	22	49	13	1,016	6
1922	1,386	27	9	16	4	12	0	41	322	35	84	0	980	(36)
December 31														
1923	1,410	24	7	16	7	5	0	35	357	17	101	2	950	(30)
1924	1,438	28	4	3	14	3	0	24	381	23	124	0	933	(17)
1925	1,490	52	4	80	17	0	2	103	484	47	171	1	834	(99)
1926	1,502	12	8	11	12	0	0	31	515	33	204	1	782	(52)

49

Table 4 (continued)

Year ended	Number chartered	Increase from previous year	Voluntary liquidations					Total		Forced liquidations		Banks chartered but not opened	Total banks in operation	Change from previous year
			Dissolved	Nation-alized	Sold or assumed	Merged	Never opened	per year	cumu-lative	per year	cumu-lative			
1927	1,543	41	2	2	22	3	0	29	544	38	242	9	748	(34)
1928	1,582	39	9	1	34	2	0	46	590	36	278	1	713	(35)
1929	1,617	35	11	1	25	2	0	39	629	11	289	0	699	(14)
1930	1,623	6	7	1	21	2	0	31	660	18	307	1	655	(44)
1931	1,645	22	10	0	26	1	0	37	697	46	353	1	594	(61)
1932	1,660	15	15	1	30	0	0	46	743	23	376	1	540	(54)
1933	1,673	13	25	3	20	0	0	48	791	16	392	1	489	(51)
1934	1,683	10	16	9	11	0	0	36	827	2	394	2	460	(29)
1935	1,687	4	13	0	6	0	0	19	846	3	397	3	441	(19)
1936	1,695	8	7	1	9	0	0	17	863	6	403	3	426	(15)
1937	1,704	9	8	3	5	0	0	16	879	5	408	2	415	(11)
1938	1,704	0	4	0	0	1	0	5	884	0	408	6	406	(9)
1939	1,707	3	4	0	7	2	0	13	897	4	412	3	395	(11)
1940	1,712	5	8	1	1	0	0	10	907	1	413	3	389	(6)
1941	1,716	4	1	1	0	0	0	2	909	0	413	3	391	2
1942	1,724	8	5	1	1	0	1	8	917	0	413	3	391	0
1943	1,728	4	0	0	3	0	1	4	921	0	413	3	391	0
1944	1,735	8	0	0	1	0	0	1	922	0	413	2	398	7
1945	1,754	18	2	0	2	1	0	5	927	0	413	5	409	11
1946	1,766	12	0	2	1	0	0	3	930	0	413	5	418	9
1947	1,788	12	0	0	6	0	0	6	936	0	413	3	436	18
1948	1,799	11	0	0	3	0	0	3	939	0	413	3	444	8
1949	1,805	6	0	1	1	0	0	2	941	1	414	4	446	2
1950	1,810	5	0	2	0	0	0	2	943	0	414	4	449	3
1951	1,815	5	2	0	0	0	0	2	945	0	414	3	453	4

Table 4 (continued)

Year ended	Number chartered	Increase from previous year	Voluntary liquidations							Forced liquidations		Banks chartered but not opened	Total banks in operation	Change from previous year
			Dissolved	Nationalized	Sold or assumed	Merged	Never opened	Total per year	Total cumulative	per year	cumulative			
1952	1,819	4	0	0	0	0	0	0	945	0	414	3	457	4
1953	1,824	5	0	0	0	0	0	0	945	0	414	5	460	3
1954	1,833	9	0	0	2	1	0	3	948	0	414	6	465	5
1955	1,847	14	0	3	0	0	0	3	951	0	414	10	472	7
1956	1,858	11	0	3	0	0	0	3	954	1	415	9	480	8
1957	1,867	9	0	1	1	0	0	2	956	1	416	9	486	6
1958	1,882	15	0	0	0	0	0	0	956	1	417	10	499	13
1959	1,902	20	0	2	0	0	2	4	960	1	418	13	511	12
1960	1,919	17	0	0	0	0	0	0	960	0	418	9	532	21
1961	1,924	5	0	0	0	0	0	1	961	1	419	6	538	6
1962	1,943	19	0	1	0	0	0	1	962	0	419	9	551	13
1963	1,962	19	0	3	0	1	0	4	966	0	419	7	570	19
1964	1,976	14	0	1	0	0	0	1	967	1	420	8	581	11
1965	1,985	9	0	0	0	0	0	0	967	3	423	8	587	6
1966	1,992	7	0	0	0	0	0	0	967	2	425	7	593	6
1967	2,001	9	0	0	0	1	0	1	968	1	426	7	600	7
1968	2,015	14	0	0	0	1	0	1	969	1	427	10	609	9
1969	2,045	30	0	0	0	1	0	1	970	4	431	14	630	21
Total			304	219	322	99	27		970		431		630	

-- Not available.
( ) Decrease.
Source: Compiled from official records of the Banking Department of Texas.

another five institutions were closed temporarily. As far as can be determined, no depositor or creditor of a liquidated state bank lost any money.

The first bank to be closed by the Department of Insurance and Banking was the First State Bank of Skidmore, in South Texas, which was closed on March 23, 1907, because its capital stock was "seriously impaired." On March 28, 1908, the impairment was corrected "by the officer responsible for the same," and the bank was reopened. The other banks that were temporarily closed were the West Texas Bank and Trust Company, San Antonio; the Johnson City State Bank; the Bronson State Bank; and the First State Bank of Weimar. The West Texas Bank and Trust Company and the Johnson City State Bank suspended payment during the Panic of 1907, having closed their doors on October 31 and November 18, respectively.

In each case, the assets and affairs were placed in the hands of the commissioner of insurance and banking who subsequently appointed a "special agent" to take charge as representative of the department. In both instances, the special agent, with the assistance of officers and directors, proceeded to collect the debts owed to the bank and place its affairs in order. As a result, the West Texas Bank and Trust Company reopened on December 31, 1907, and Johnson City State Bank reopened on December 23, 1907.

The Bronson State Bank was closed on February 14, 1908, presumably because of losses on loans that had impaired the capital of the bank. As in the case of the San Antonio and Johnson City banks, a special agent was appointed and through his efforts the bank's "affairs were reorganized"; on April 28, 1908, the bank was reopened with the capital stock reduced from $15,000 to $10,000.

The First State Bank of Weimar was closed on September 22, 1908, because its capital stock of $25,000 had never been fully and actually paid in. It seems that a part of the capital was in the form of notes that were uncollectible. This deficiency was soon corrected and the bank reopened on October 1. Of the foregoing institutions that were temporarily closed, only the Weimar bank survives today.

The first bank failure under the new law involved the First State Bank of Ravenna, which was closed on February 14, 1908, "for persistent and repeated violations of the law endangering the interest of the depositors." Commissioner Love asked the attorney general to apply for the appointment of a receiver and wind up the bank's affairs. The receiver was appointed by the district court of Fannin County on March 12, 1908. Under his direction, the bank was liquidated, and every creditor and depositor paid in full. The other two banks that failed were the Zulch State Bank, Zulch, which was closed February 21, 1908, and American Bank and Trust Company, Temple, which was closed September 28, 1908. The depositors of both of these banks were paid in full upon liquidation. Unfortunately, the reasons for the latter failures were not reported in the second biennial report of the commissioner of insurance and banking.

The Panic of 1907

In the fall of 1907, shortly after the Department of Insurance and Banking had announced that "it comprised 275 banking institutions operating under a law which had never known a bank failure," the Panic of 1907 occurred.[2] The business contraction that accompanied the bank panic actually began in May 1907 and lasted only until June 1908. From May to September the contraction showed no signs of severity, although for some time there had been an unhealthy increase in speculative activity in securities and commodities. By late summer new issues of railroad securities were difficult to sell, copper stocks and other equities were overvalued by conservative standards, production had flattened out, and construction had declined. In October the banking panic occurred, resulting in the suspension of payments by the banking system.

The first direct signs of the crisis appeared during the week of October 14. After a sharp decline in copper prices there was a run on the Mercantile National Bank in New York, which soon spread to other banks. On October 22 the Knickerbocker Trust Company, one of New York's largest institutions, emptied its cash vaults and closed its doors, after the National Bank of Commerce,

New York, announced that it would no longer act as its clearinghouse agent and Charles T. Barney had resigned from its presidency. On the same date a stock exchange firm failed, the average price of Wall Street's principal securities dropped from $50 to $8 per share, and call money rose to 70 percent. Soon runs developed against the Trust Company of America and the Lincoln Trust Company as well. For several days lines of depositors, sometimes two or three blocks long, besieged the New York banks. Unable to stem the tide of distrust, the New York bankers appealed to the secretary of the treasury, George B. Cortelyon, for relief. On October 22 he directed that $6 million of U.S. Treasury funds be deposited with New York banks as soon as collateral could be arranged. However, it was soon realized that this amount would be insufficient, and on October 24, $25 million was deposited in the principal banks. At the same time a committee representing the trust companies of New York agreed to come to the aid of the Trust Company of America by providing such funds as it needed.

By October 26 the panic in New York was under control, but by this time alarm had spread throughout the nation. Country banks that in previous times of crisis had experienced difficulty in obtaining currency from their city correspondents now demanded currency for their demand deposits and call money. In response the New York banks immediately restricted payments, a move that was followed by country-wide restrictions, legally sanctioned in a few states and tolerated in the rest.

In Texas, Commissioner of Insurance and Banking Thomas B. Love issued the following statement on October 23:

The statements of the state banks, numbering about 300, made in response to the August call, show that they are in an unusually good condition. They had 33-1/3 percent more cash on hand than they had a year ago, and this not withstanding the unusual drain upon the banks occasioned by the increased holdings of cotton over former years. There is absolutely nothing in the Texas banking situation, so far as the state banks and trust companies are concerned, which should not inspire the usual degree of confidence in them. None of the state banks were in any way affected by the closing of the Knickerbocker Trust Company and practically none of the state banks have any money borrowed in New York or the East, and the New York and Eastern balances carried by the state banks of Texas are noticeably small.[3]

On October 25 and 26 Texas newspapers carried news that the crisis was subsiding in New York, although a few of the smaller banking institutions were still under pressure. On October 26 President Roosevelt sent a communiqué to Secretary Cortelyon and the New York financiers, congratulating them for their "admirable handling" of the financial crisis. By October 28 it was generally agreed among prominent New York bankers and merchants that the crisis had passed and that constant improvement could be expected thereafter.

However, reverberations from the New York disturbance were being felt throughout the remainder of the country. On Monday, October 28, the governor of Oklahoma proclaimed the remaining days of the week to be bank holidays because of the banking community's inability to secure currency on demand. This proclamation was precipitated by the actions of the clearing houses of Kansas City, Wichita, St. Louis, and Chicago, which had resorted to the use of clearinghouse certificates and refused to ship currency to interior banks.

By this time, Texas bankers began to take precautionary steps. On Tuesday the bankers of Bell County, Texas, adopted measures designed to meet an emergency. With most of their reserve balances frozen by their eastern and other correspondents, the Bell County banks agreed to curtail all loans, to pay out no funds to banks or other financial institutions that would require the shipment of currency out of Bell County, and to limit payment on checks drawn on individual deposits to twenty-five dollars. The Austin bankers were the next to take action. A clearinghouse was formed for their protection, and a resolution was adopted limiting payments to each depositor to 10 percent of his balance and fifty dollars in any one day.[4] During the week the rule of limited cash payments was adopted throughout the state, with the amount of withdrawal limited to twenty-five dollars in most cases.

Another currency-preserving device commonly adopted by the Texas banks was to issue and circulate a money substitute, scrip or I.O.U.'s, secured by a common deposit of high-quality securities. This provided a "life-saving service" during the Panic of 1907, which occurred in the midst of the cotton season. With a dependable and acceptable substitute for money, a market for the cotton was provided.[5]

The first banking suspension in Texas to be attributed to the national monetary disturbance was that of the West Texas Bank and Trust Company of San Antonio, on Thursday, October 31. The bank was closed voluntarily with no semblance of a run, and a sign was placed on its door assuring the depositors that the bank had ample resources to pay all depositors and that it was solvent.[6] Upon receiving the news Commissioner Love released the statement of condition of the bank at the date of the last examination (August 14) and left for San Antonio on the first train. On the following day G. Bedell Moore, president of the bank, released a statement explaining that the bank was closed because of a shortage of cash resulting from the scarcity of money throughout the country and that it would reopen as soon as possible.[7]

The shortage of currency continued well into November. On November 7 the Woods National Bank of San Antonio suspended payment. Three days later the First National Bank of Eagle Lake did the same. Even as late as November 13 the *Dallas Morning News* reported restriction of payments at Brownwood, Granger, and Plainview. However, by November 16 there were signs that the crisis was easing. On that date the Austin clearinghouse announced that money would be made available to cotton buyers in order to allow resumption of normal business.[8]

The closing of the Johnson City Bank on November 18 was not even carried in the Dallas, Galveston, or Austin newspapers. By this time confidence was beginning to be restored, as reports of bank suspensions and restrictions on withdrawals had all but disappeared from the newspapers. Bankers throughout Texas agreed that conditions were improving daily and that there would be an early resumption of business under normal circumstances. Commissioner Love, attempting to maintain the status quo, wisely suppressed the news of the suspension of the small bank in Johnson City. By the end of the year the West Texas Bank and Trust Company and the Johnson City State Bank had reopened, and confidence had been restored.

Impact of the Panic of 1907

From the available evidence it appears that the Panic of 1907 had little lasting effect on the economy of Texas or its banks. According to Commissioner Love, only two of the several hundred national banks closed their doors; one of these closures was temporary, and the closure that was permanent entailed no loss to depositors. Five state banks closed, three temporarily and two permanently, with no loss to depositors resulting from one of the permanent closures and only a slight loss from the other. In addition, "about a dozen" private banks, which were still without regulation or supervision, closed and did not reopen.[9]

Of the twenty-nine liquidations during the two-year period from year-end 1906 to year-end 1908, only six occurred before October 1907. The other twenty-three banks were liquidated during the twelve months immediately following the Panic of 1907 and ending December 31, 1908. Perhaps this is only coincidental, but the timing suggests that those banks that were liquidated subsequent to the crises were weak institutions and represented marginal operations even in times of prosperity. During hard times profit margins would have narrowed, and the likelihood of substantial losses would have become apparent. Under these conditions the logical course of action would have been to liquidate or merge to form a stronger institution.

Though the Panic of 1907 may have precipitated the liquidations of 1908, it only discouraged new charter applications temporarily. For the first nine months of 1907, 147 charters were issued. But from October through December just thirteen new charters were issued and only two of those were issued in November and December. In 1908 charter activity continued below the norm of earlier years, with 59 charters being granted. But in the following 21 months the pre-Panic pace was resumed.

Economic Impact of the State Banking System

Until the middle of the nineteenth century the economic development of Texas was confined almost entirely to the expansion of agriculture. However, during the last half of the nineteenth century Texas industry began to produce a greater variety and quantity of goods.

The period from 1870 to 1900 in Texas economic growth was dominated by the expansion of cotton and livestock production, lumbering, and related industries. This expansion, however, was not caused by an increase in local or Texas demand, but rather by growth in the external demand for these goods. Industrialization increased in west-central Europe and in east-central North America, causing an increase in the demand for wheat and livestock products of the United States. The world demand for cotton products also continued to grow—a phenomenon that had begun with the Industrial Revolution in England.

Not only was Texas dependent upon foreign markets for the sale of her products, she also was dependent upon foreign capital to finance her industrialization. Funds from outside sources were invested on a large scale, particularly in ranching and lumbering. Obviously there were many reasons for the influx of capital, one of which was the inadequacy and immaturity of the Texas banking system. Before the National Bank Act of 1863 there were no formal banking institutions in Texas. By 1880 Texas had only fourteen national banks, with total resources of $5,741,000. In the following twenty years the growth in the number of national banks, albeit impressive, failed to keep pace with the industrial development of the state. By 1900 there were 234 banks with total resources of $131,557,000, but judging from speeches and statements by bankers during the period, the general feeling was that Texas was underbanked.[10]

High minimum capital requirements prevented the establishment of an adequate number of national banks in rural areas. Furthermore, the National Bank Act of 1863 prohibited national banks from making loans secured by land. Farmers were thus precluded from either financing the purchase of land or pledging unencumbered land as collateral at national banks. These provisions of the law undoubtedly inhibited the development of agriculture, the basis of the Texas economy.

The passage of the Texas State Bank Law in 1905 and the subsequent creation of state banks greatly facilitated the economic growth of Texas. The low minimum capital requirements permitted the establishment of state banks in small communities that previously did not have banking facilities. Thus capital was mobilized and credit was provided without the cumbersome prohibition of loans secured by land. By 1910 only 14 out of 249 counties in Texas had neither a state nor a national bank.

The taxable value of Texas property in 1900 was $946.3 million; by 1910 the value had increased to $2,391.9 million, or by 152 percent. In 1900 Texas factories employed 48,153 workers and produced a total valuation of $119 million. The number of employees in 1909 was estimated at 100,000 and the value of production at $249 million. The output of lumber rose substantially in the period, as the number of board feet produced increased from 1.2 billion (with a value of $30 million) to 2 billion feet (with a value of $45 million).

The most significant production gain between 1900 and 1910, however, was in cotton. Among the commercial crops in Texas, cotton had always ranked first. By 1900 Texas led the country in cotton production, accounting for more than 25 percent of the total for the country and more than twice as much as Mississippi, the second-ranked state. In that year, of the 19.6 million acres of land under cultivation in Texas, 7.2 million, or 36.7 percent of the total, was in cotton. The value of the production for the year was not available, but by 1902 it was $117.4 million. By 1910 the total acreage under cultivation had increased to 27.1 million, of which 10.1 million acres, or 37.2 percent, was in cotton. The total value of the cotton crop in that year was $266.0 million.

Perhaps even more significant is the geographic expansion of cotton production. In 1889 the production of cotton was confined entirely to the eastern half of the state. There was virtually no cotton production west of Abilene, and there was little cotton in that area. Further extensions westward were made by 1899, but total cotton production in the western half of the state was still insignificant. By 1909, however, the geographic distribution of cotton acreage had changed considerably. The concentration in the Texas prairies continued to increase, particularly in the middle and northern portions, and the movement into western Texas had become quite definite. Even the Panhandle had some 300,000 acres of cotton in cultivation by this time.

It appears that the creation of the state banking system contributed to the extension of agriculture into West Texas. At any rate, initial development of the banking system in that area more or less paralleled the spread of cotton production.

Before 1889 there was only one bank in existence in the Panhandle, and it was a private bank. The first national bank in the area was organized in 1889 in Amarillo; as far as can be determined, there were only ten banks, both private and national, by 1904. By 1910, however, the only county in the Panhandle that did not have either a state or national bank was Hutchinson County.

Many other factors besides the state banking system contributed to the state's growth between 1900 and 1910: for example, the mechanization of agriculture and industry and the use of the internal combustion engine. The increase in the population of the state was substantial. In 1890 there were 2,235,537 persons in Texas. By 1900 the population had increased to 3,049,710, and in 1910 it was 3,896,542. Immigration contributed significantly to the growth in population and to the state's ability to produce wealth. The pattern of the geographic distribution of the population reflected the geographic expansion of agriculture.

Another important factor affecting the growth of population and the economic development of Texas was the expansion of the railroad system. In 1900 Texas had 9,867 miles of railroads in operation, contrasted with 3,244 miles in 1880 and 8,710 in 1890. During the first decade of the twentieth century this was considerably expanded, to a total of 13,819 by 1910. According to Elmer H. Johnson, industrial geographer, railroad development in Texas has been closely associated with the factors of production, as well as with the potentialities of the various areas concerned.[11] In turn, regional growth of the various sections of the state has conformed rather closely to the extension of railroads. This suggests that one reason for the late development of the western regions of Texas was the belated extension of railroads westward.

The economic growth of Texas from 1900 to 1910 is reflected in the banking statistics. In 1900 there were 234 national banks in Texas, with resources of $131,557,000. In addition, approximately 190 private banks were in operation—with unknown resources. By the call of November 10, 1910, there were 1,141 national and state banks operating in the state, and their combined resources amounted to $422,122,000. Of these, 520 were national banks (with resources of $334,019,000). No estimate of the number of private banks operating in 1910 is available, but the estimate for 1909 was 186, which is probably close to the 1910 figure. The net increase in the number of national and state banks was 907, or 387 percent, and the net increase in total national and state bank resources was $290,565,000, or 221 percent, over the decade.

The creation of the state banking system also had a significant impact on the number of new national banks formed. Before 1905 the number of national banks had increased continuously. The formation of such new banks had accelerated significantly after the reduction in the minimum capital requirement in 1900. Between December 2, 1899, and November 9, 1905, 248 new national banks were formed, an increase of 124 percent. After the prohibition on state banking was abolished there was a net gain of only 73 national banks in the next five years, against a net increase of 621 state banks.

The "Free-Banking Period," 1905-1913

In the twenty-six months ending with the outbreak in October of the Panic of 1907, 311 state banks were chartered in Texas. During this period Texas experienced unprecedented prosperity. In fact, conditions were so favorable that W. J. Clay, the first commissioner of insurance and banking, remarked in his report of December 31, 1906, that "the general prosperity was never so great nor money so unusually plentiful . . ."[12] The economic climate thus facilitated the organization of new banks. But the eruption of the 1907 financial crisis visibly slowed chartering activity. From the middle of October, when the upheaval began, until the end of the year, only six new charters were granted. The 1907 and 1908 cotton crops were good, however, and the slowdown in business activity that accompanied the financial panic did not severely affect Texas. As a result, prosperity soon returned, and in the following thirty-two months (ending August 31, 1907) an additional 340 banks were chartered.

Favorable economic conditions and easy money gave impetus to the early development of the state banking system. However, weaknesses in the law itself sustained the rapid growth of the system, which was in evidence throughout the "free-banking period" from the inception of the system in 1905 until 1913. According to Charles O. Austin, commissioner of banking during the 1920s and a recognized student of banking, the chief weaknesses in the law were the provision permitting the organization of banks with less than $25,000 of capital and the failure to regulate the issuance of bank charters.[13]

As previously stated, the secretary of state was vested with sole responsibility for chartering state banks. Commissioner Austin observed later that during the "free-banking period" apparently the only consideration of consequence in chartering was the amount of income derived from charter fees.[14] Charters were thus granted with no regard for need or for the number of banking institutions already serving the area, and as history later revealed, many new banks were either undercapitalized or located in communities without adequate business to support a bank. It was not uncommon for a community that could barely support one bank to have three or four banks, including state, national, and private institutions. As a result, during times of economic stress the weaker institutions that found continued existence unprofitable would either fail, liquidate, or merge to form larger and stronger banks.

Most of the commissioners in office during the "free-banking period" recognized that too many banks were being formed. In 1908 Commissioner Thomas B. Love officially recommended the establishment of a state banking board to pass on new state charters.[15] His proposal did not mention the tendency toward overbanking. Love proposed to transfer the chartering function from the secretary of state to the Department of Insurance and Banking. In 1909 such a state banking board was created, but it had little power to restrict charters.

B. L. Gill, who assumed office on January 17, 1911, was the first commissioner to officially propose that the number of new charters granted be restricted. Commissioner Gill was acutely aware that too many banks were being formed, and he strongly advocated that the State Banking Board be given control over the chartering function. In his official report for the 1910/1911 fiscal year Commissioner Gill stated:

I am forced to ask where will the formation of new banks end, and should there not be a limit placed on small, weak banks? Their rapid organization is a source of anxiety to this Department, and it is a matter of regret that the Banking Board is not vested with more power to restrict their organization. The fact that a bank can be chartered with so small a capital as ten thousand dollars is a temptation for rival factions in a community to start a bank, or for real estate promoters to ask for a permit with the sole object of using it for advertising purposes, and sundry other reasons are found for the organization of the small bank, because of the limited capital required.[16]

The concern evidenced above was reiterated in Commissioner Gill's report for the following year, in which he stated that many banks had been chartered and opened contrary to his judgment.[17]

Shortly after this report was released the subject was taken up by the Thirty-third Legislature and reforms were finally enacted. An increase in the minimum capital requirements, as recommended by Commissioner Gill, was not considered; however, during the regular session, which lasted from January 14 to April 1, 1913, a bill was passed that gave the State Banking Board the authority to exercise its judgment on charter applications. Unfortunately, by this time over 900 banks had already been chartered, many of them located in areas where there was little demand or business to support a bank or where too many banks already existed.

Review and Reform of the Texas State Bank Law

Most new laws, from the time they become effective, are subjected to constant review and criticism and, as a result, are revised and amended. Such was the case with the Texas State Bank Law. There was general agreement that the law was one of the best state banking laws in force in the country, and most of the remarks directed to it were laudatory. Most of the criticism was not directed at provisions of the statute, but rather at what it failed to include.

The commissioners of insurance and banking, who had responsibility for administering the law, were in the best position to observe its effectiveness and, as a result, were its most perceptive critics. Also, as might be expected, most legislation pertaining to the banking law emanated from the commissioner's office.

The first official pronouncement concerning the banking statute, as far as can be determined, appeared in the biennial report of the commissioner of insurance and banking covering the first sixteen months. Commissioner Clay commented in this report that the law had not been given sufficient time to "test itself" and that it should not be altered.[18] Partly because of Clay's report, the Thirtieth Legislature, which convened shortly after the report was released, only considered a few minor changes in the law. It also considered, but did not approve, a bill that attempted to provide protection for bank depositors (forerunner of a similar measure passed by the Thirty-first Legislature that established the Depositors Guaranty Fund and the Bond Security System).[19]

Upon the retirement of W. J. Clay on August 31, 1907, Thomas B. Love was appointed commissioner of insurance and banking. It is not surprising that Commissioner Love, author of the Texas State Bank Law, was its most ardent supporter and perspicacious critic. Shortly after assuming office, on June 5, 1908, Commissioner Love addressed the annual convention of the Texas Bankers Association. The topic of this speech was "Banking Legislation in Texas—Past, Present, and Future."[20] As expected, he praised the law very highly, but he was not hesitant to note its weaknesses. He made specific recommendations for its amendment and for improvements in its administration.

Commissioner Love strongly urged that the law be amended to provide for state supervision of private (unincorporated) banks. He pointed out that Texas was the only "leading" state in the union without such a provision and that it was the duty of the government to require any institution that invites the public to deposit funds with it to submit to "safe and stringent regulations," "rigid and effective" supervision, and periodic examinations. The experience of private banks during the Panic of 1907 had been far less favorable than that of national and state banks in Texas. While only three national and state banks were closed permanently during the upheaval, with no loss to depositors, approximately twelve private banks failed; in practically every case these closures involved "serious loss to their depositors and demoralization and distress to the communities in which they were located."[21] There were more than two hundred private banks in Texas at this time. These banks contained substantial deposits, and it was considered imperative that they be brought under control to ensure the public welfare. He also argued that those banks that had received state charters before the Constitution of 1876 should be subject to regulation by the state. In short, Commissioner Love felt that the public welfare demanded that either the state or federal government should "know definitely and constantly the financial condition of every bank."[22]

Commissioner Love also strongly recommended that the state of Texas adopt a law that provided for the insurance or guaranty of bank deposits. This recommendation was formally proposed in the form of a bill that was presented in the second biennial report of the commissioner of insurance and banking; it was substantially the same as the bill that was passed by the Thirty-first Legislature and enacted into law.[23]

The regular session of the Thirty-first Legislature met from January 12 to March 13, 1909, and was followed by four special sessions, the last of which ended September 10, 1910. The banking legislation introduced was voluminous, most of it dealing with the guaranty of bank deposits, which became a reality with the passage of Senate Bill Number 4 during the second called session.[24] In addition to providing protection for bank depositors, Senate Bill Number 4 created the State Banking Board, consisting of the attorney general, the commissioner of insurance and banking, and the state treasurer. The board was empowered to regulate, control, and supervise all state banking corporations and trust companies and to have charge of the Depositors Guaranty Fund and Bond Security System.

The accomplishments of the Thirty-first Legislature with regard to banking legislation were significant. Not only did it pass a statute creating the ill-fated Depositors Guaranty Fund and the Bond Security System, but it also passed other legislation that strengthened the state banking system. Much of the achievement of the Thirty-first Legislature in regard to banking must be attributed to Commissioner Love. He was a former state senator, an avid student of banking, and the man primarily responsible for the creation of the state banking system. With his intimate knowledge of banking and banking law, and his profound concern for the public welfare, it is not surprising that during his tenure as commissioner of insurance and banking much legislation was proposed by the department.

Thomas B. Love served a two-year term and retired from office on January 31, 1910, shortly after the closing of the Thirty-first Legislature. Unfortunately, neither of the men who followed Love possessed his awareness of banking or his legislative acumen. William E. Hawkins, who was Love's immediate successor, served only briefly and resigned under criticism from the governor's office on August 1, 1910.

The next commissioner was F. C. Von Rosenberg, who held the office until January 17, 1911. He was the fourth and last person to serve as commissioner during the first five years of the state banking system. In the third biennial report of the commissioner of insurance and banking, issued on August 31, 1910, Von Rosenberg recommended that no changes be made in state laws affecting banks and banking.[25] The Thirty-second Legislature, which convened on January 11, 1911, failed to pass a single bill of significance to banking.

During the initial five years of the system at least one "voice in the wilderness" outside the Department of Insurance and Banking suggested the need for banking reforms. Speaking before the annual convention of the Texas Bankers Association on May 30, 1907, W. F. McCaleb, one of its most prominent members, criticized the minimum capital requirement of $10,000 for state banks and suggested reforms in the position of commissioner of agriculture, insurance, history, and banking. He stated that the tenure of the office was too short and that it depended upon the whims of politics; in addition, he questioned the wisdom of encumbering one person with such diverse duties.[26]

The Thirtieth Legislature, which had convened in January 1907, created a separate department of insurance and banking, as suggested by McCaleb. Unfortunately, however, it was many years before action was taken to increase the minimum capital requirements for state banks or to bring stability to the office of commissioner by divesting the governor of the responsibility for the commissioner's appointment.

Notes

1. *Third Biennial Report of the Commissioner of Insurance and Banking for the Years 1909 and 1910, Pertaining to Banking* (Austin: Von Boeckmann-Jones, 1910), pp. 3-13.
2. Love, "Some East Texas Banking History," pp. 1375-1376.
3. *Dallas Morning News*, October 23, 1907.
4. *Dallas Morning News*, November 1, 1907.
5. Love, "Some East Texas Banking History," p. 1377.
6. *Dallas Morning News*, November 1, 1907.
7. *Dallas Morning News*, November 2, 1907.
8. *Dallas Morning News*, November 17, 1907.
9. Love, "Some East Texas Banking History," pp. 1377-1378.
10. *Proceedings of the Twentieth Annual Convention of the Texas Bankers Association* (Dallas: McMath Lithograph and Printing Co., 1904), p. 45, and Duane F. Guy, *A History of the Panhandle Bankers Association*.
11. Elmer H. Johnson, *The Basis of the Commercial and Industrial Development of Texas: A Study of the Regional Development of Texas Resources* (Austin: Bureau of Business Research, 1933), pp. 13-23.
12. *Biennial Report of the Superintendent of Banking of the State of Texas* (Austin: Von Boeckmann-Jones, 1907), p. 4.
13. Charles O. Austin, "Our State Banking System," *Texas Bankers Record* 15 (June 1926): 36-39.
14. Ibid.
15. *Second Biennial Report of the Commissioner of Insurance and Banking for the Years 1907 and 1908, Pertaining to Banking* (Austin: Von Boeckmann-Jones, 1908), p. 5.

16. *First Annual Report Following Third Biennial Report of the Commissioner of Insurance and Banking for the Year 1910-1911, Pertaining to Banking* (Austin: Austin Printing Company, 1912), p. 5.
17. *Second Annual Report Following Third Biennial Report of the Commissioner of Insurance and Banking for the Year 1911-1912, Pertaining to Banking* (Austin: Von Boeckmann-Jones, 1912), p. 25.
18. *Biennial Report of the Superintendent of Banking of the State of Texas*, p. 4.
19. *House Journal, Texas, Thirtieth Legislature, Regular Session, 1907* (Austin: Von Boeckmann-Jones, 1907), pp. 56 and 1347.
20. Love, "Banking Legislation in Texas," pp. 37-38.
21. Ibid., p. 38.
22. Ibid.
23. *Second Biennial Report of the Commissioner of Insurance and Banking for the Years 1907 and 1908*, pp. 7-36.
24. *General Laws of Texas, Thirty-first Legislature, Regular, First, and Second Called Sessions, 1909* (Austin: Von Boeckmann-Jones, 1909), p. 406.
25. *Third Biennial Report of the Commissioner of Insurance and Banking for the Years 1909 and 1910*, pp. 5-6.
26. W. F. McCaleb, address before the Texas Bankers Association annual convention, Corpus Christi, May 28, 1907, in *Proceedings of the Twenty-third Annual Convention of the Texas Bankers Association* (Dallas: M. P. Exline Company, 1907), pp. 205-207.

6

Insurance of Bank Deposits in Texas

History of Deposit Insurance in the United States

The first application of the bank deposit-guaranty concept in the United States was the Safety-Fund Banking System, which was established in New York in 1829. At that time deposit banking was so limited that the framers of the law failed to recognize that bank debts were incurred by a bank's acceptance of deposits. Consequently, the New York law, which guaranteed all debts of the bank, unknowingly guaranteed deposits as well as outstanding note issues. The importance of this oversight was soon realized. During the Panic of 1837 and the years immediately following, widespread bank failures occurred in New York. By 1842 the Safety-Fund faced a crisis because of the large amount of claims levied against it, a substantial portion of which were imposed by depositors rather than noteholders. Although the crisis was averted through the sale of bonds, the difficulties encountered induced the legislature to restrict protection under the fund to noteholders only. This restriction remained in force until the Safety-Fund law was repealed in 1866.

In addition to the Safety-Fund of New York, five other states operated bank insurance systems prior to 1866. The states and the period of operation were: Vermont, 1831-1866; Indiana, 1834-1866; Michigan, 1836-1842; Ohio, 1845-1866; and Iowa, 1858-1865. As in New York, the plans of Vermont, Indiana, and Michigan—all of which were established before the financial difficulties of 1837—protected all creditors of the bank, both noteholders and depositors. In the case of the two plans established after the 1837-1842 difficulties, only noteholders were protected.

Most of the state funds existing before 1866 had outstanding records. Only in Michigan was the system unable to meet any of the claims made against it; consequently, it failed in 1842. The deposit-guaranty plans in the other states were terminated only because the participating banks had become national banks or, in the case of New York, Ohio, and Iowa, the note issues of state banks had contracted after the 10 percent federal tax on the circulation of state-chartered bank notes became effective on July 1, 1866.

After the termination of the state systems that existed before 1866, there were no further attempts to guarantee bank liabilities until the end of the nineteenth century. The efforts at that time seem to have been associated with the Panic of 1893. In 1893, Congressman William Jennings Bryan from Nebraska introduced a bill in the U.S. House of Representatives that would have provided protection to depositors of national banks through an insurance fund administered by the comptroller of the currency. Also in 1893, Senator Eppa Hunton from Virginia sponsored a similar bill in the U.S. Senate. In addition to the Bryan and Hunton proposals, twelve other such bills were introduced in Congress before 1900. These unsuccessful bills represented the first attempts in American history to insure deposits of national banks against loss.

The Panic of 1893 also precipitated efforts at the state level to provide for deposit guaranty. However, these seem to have been confined to the west-central states and were associated with the Populist movement that was under way at the time. The depression that began in 1893 was particularly hard on the Midwest. Between 1893 and 1897 crop failures occurred in rapid succession. As a result, banks of the area, which were heavily laden with crop loans, suffered numerous failures, thus causing further hardship to the populace. The deposit guaranty proposals reflected the adversities suffered during this period.

Although the Populist movement was short lived, some of the ideas that it germinated lived on with its former devotees. One of these was Judge J. T. Dickerson, who had been a Populist in Kansas during the effort to guarantee bank deposits in 1898 but who later moved to Edmond, Oklahoma. When the Oklahoma constitutional convention met in 1906, Judge Dickerson urged a provision guaranteeing bank deposits. Although he was supported by Charles N. Haskell, who was later to become governor, the proposal never got out of committee. In spite of this defeat, the concept of deposit insurance had been presented, and it only took the Panic of 1907 to revive it and accord it new appeal. The Panic began on October 28, 1907, and on December 17, the Oklahoma legislature, with scarcely any debate, passed a law guaranteeing bank deposits.

Shortly thereafter, Kansas and Nebraska, the two states where earlier attempts to pass such legislation had been made, followed Oklahoma's example. The Panic of 1907 provided the impetus in both of these states. However, in Kansas there was another motivating factor. Banks in the southern part of the state, near the Oklahoma state line, were fearful of the competition from Oklahoma banks, which were advertising throughout a wide area that their deposits were guaranteed. The Kansas bankers felt they needed a law in order to keep their depositors from transferring funds to the Oklahoma banks.

The sentiment in favor of bank deposit guaranty was not confined to the state level in the early 1900s. In 1905, one year before Judge Dickerson made his plea to the Oklahoma constitutional convention, C. F. Allis, vice-president of the Second National Bank of Erie, Pennsylvania, recommended to the American Bankers Association that a law be enacted to guarantee the deposits of national banks. He later wrote and brought about the introduction of a bill in Congress that would have created a guaranty fund by a tax on national banks. This bill received little attention. In the Sixtieth Congress, following the Panic of 1907, approximately thirty bills proposing deposit-guaranty legislation were introduced. Most of these applied only to national banks, but in a few cases other banks were eligible for participation. In 1908 the Democrats, in their attempt to elect William Jennings Bryan, added a bank deposit-guaranty plank to their platform. This, of course, forced the Republican national organization into opposition. Bryan lost, the National Monetary Commission was formed, and only a few bills pertaining to bank deposit guaranty were introduced in Congress in the next five years. It is probable that many more recommendations concerning bank deposit guaranty were made to the commission, but no record of them exists.

Agitation for Deposit Insurance in Texas

Sentiment in favor of deposit insurance in Texas began as early as 1889. In that year E. M. Longcope of Lampasas, one of the founders of the Texas Bankers Association, advocated a guaranty fund for bank deposits. In an address before the annual convention of the Texas Bankers Association, Longcope set forth what he felt should be included in a state banking law in Texas. An integral part of his proposal was a guaranty fund for deposits—the "capstone" of a state banking system.[1]

When Texas finally adopted a state banking law, more than a decade and a half later, deposit insurance apparently was not considered along with it. In fact, the available evidence suggests that deposit insurance was not seriously considered in Texas until the latter part of 1906 or early 1907. The efforts that took place then seem to have been inspired by the events that were occurring in other states. In Oklahoma Judge Dickerson had presented his proposal, and in February 1907 it was receiving a favorable response from the banking committee of the legislature (although it was later tabled). At the same time in Kansas a bill had been prepared providing for the guaranty of deposits in state banks, and it was to be introduced with the strong endorsement of the banking commissioner at the next session of the legislature. The subject of bank deposit guaranty, according to the February 1907 edition of the *Texas Banker*, was receiving attention across the country.[2]

The same edition of the *Texas Banker* reported that W. L. Blanton had introduced a bill in the regular session of the Thirtieth Legislature providing for the guaranteeing of deposits of the state banks in Texas. Although the bill was reported favorably by the Committee on Banks and Banking, sufficient support on the floor of the house was lacking, and it died. The subject of bank deposit guaranty, however, did not die.

Since the question of deposit guaranty was being so widely aired, it was only natural that considerable space on the program of the 1907 Texas Bankers Association Convention was devoted to the topic. M. E. Guynn, cashier of the Eagle Lake State Bank, presented the negative aspects,[3] and H. K. Boatwright, vice-president of the First National Bank, Bryan, discussed the positive side of the subject.[4]

Guynn and Boatwright discussed deposit insurance in general and referred specifically to the Blanton bill pending before the Texas legislature and the Allis proposal being considered by Congress. Boatwright suggested that deposit insurance would improve the image and prestige of the entire banking business and system, that the threat of "runs" would be removed, and that a vast accumulation of funds being hoarded because of a lack of confidence in banks would be brought into the banking system.

Guynn argued that it was unjust to tax the conservatively run banks to pay for the mistakes of the weaker and more speculative banks. In addition, he felt that conditions existing at the time did not warrant the enactment of a deposit-guaranty law. Instead, he advocated more rigid controls and supervision and more stringent forms of punishment for bankers who violated the law.

The speeches made by Guynn and Boatwright marked the beginning of open debate over the deposit-guaranty question in Texas. During the summer of 1907 the *Texas Banker* and the *Texas Bankers Journal* devoted considerable space to the subject. Progress in the other states, particularly Oklahoma, was reported, and numerous editorials and articles appeared in support of the movement.

In 1907 two events occurred that were critical to the ultimate passage of deposit insurance legislation. One was the appointment on August 31 of Thomas B. Love as commissioner of insurance and banking; the other was the Panic of 1907, which began in October.

Influence of Thomas B. Love and William Jennings Bryan

Thomas B. Love, "father" of the Texas state banking system, was also the father of the law enacted in 1909 to protect bank depositors against loss. This is one of the great ironies of Texas banking history—the man responsible for the creation of the system also was responsible for the creation of the Depositors Guaranty Fund, the instrument that would have caused the system's downfall had legislative reforms not been enacted beginning in 1925. It is also ironic that Love was a member of the Texas senate when the Depositors Guaranty Law was repealed in January 1927.

It is not really surprising that Commissioner Love was an ardent advocate of the concept of bank deposit insurance or that he wrote and guided through the legislature the bill that created the Depositors Guaranty Fund and Bond Security System in Texas. Love's stand on deposit insurance was strongly affected by its leading supporter, William Jennings Bryan, whom Love greatly admired. In fact, Love originally came to Texas in 1899 to organize and run Bryan's presidential campaign in the state. After Bryan lost Love stayed in Texas to pursue a career in law and public service.

Bryan not only provided spiritual and moral support for advocates of deposit-guaranty legislation in Texas, but he also addressed the Texas legislature at an important time in the evolution of the deposit insurance bill, on April 5, 1909.[5] While Bryan's contribution was significant, Love must receive more credit for the passage of the legislation. He was an acknowledged student and authority on banking and as commissioner of insurance and banking he was in a position to exert considerable influence. Perhaps more important, however, was the fact that Love was a skilled legislator. Before becoming commissioner of insurance and banking he had served three terms in the Texas House of Representatives and had been its speaker from January 1907 until his appointment as commissioner of insurance and banking.

Though Love and, to a lesser extent, Bryan did occupy critical roles in securing the passage of deposit-guaranty legislation in Texas, even without them Texas might well have passed a deposit-guaranty law in time, as there was wide support for bank deposit insurance in many parts of the United States during the first two decades of the twentieth century.

Influence of the Panic of 1907

The Panic of 1907 provided impetus to the deposit-guaranty movement in Texas as well as in Oklahoma, Kansas, and

Nebraska. The effects of the Panic in Texas, though not severe if compared with subsequent disturbances, were felt throughout the state. Depositors of defunct private banks suffered losses, many farmers were unable to sell their cotton crops at harvest, and the emergency measures adopted by banks and clearinghouse associations inconvenienced everyone. In addition, Texans were constantly reminded through the newspapers of the difficulties experienced during the crisis in other parts of the country. Perhaps the loudest and most influential voice calling for protection was that of the *Dallas Morning News*. The first of a series of editorials, which urged deposit insurance for state, national, and private banks, appeared on November 14, 1907. The campaign in favor of deposit insurance was continued by the newspaper during the remainder of 1907 and into 1908. Because of these editorials Governor Thomas Mitchell Campbell became convinced of the desirability of deposit insurance, as did Commissioner Love, and both of them campaigned in its behalf.[6]

Division of Opinion between State and National Bankers

When the annual convention of the Texas Bankers Association convened in Fort Worth on June 4, 1908, bankers in the state were divided into two distinct camps on the deposit-guaranty question. J. W. Hoopes, secretary of the Association, submitted the following question to all of the members: "Are you in favor of guarantee of bank deposits through the state or governmental agency?"[7] A vote revealed that 210 favored, while 282 opposed deposit insurance. Of the affirmative votes, 109 were cast by state bankers, 90 by national banks, and 11 by private banks; of the negative votes, 69 were cast by state banks, 175 by national banks, and 38 by private banks. The capital and surplus of the banks voting "yes" aggregated $1,570,000; of those voting "no," $5,334,000. The smaller rural banks predominantly favored the bill, judging from the aggregate capital and surplus figures reported. They expected to benefit the most from such legislation because they were the most vulnerable to "runs." The larger banks, regardless of the method of calculation, would have borne a greater portion of the expense; they objected to being taxed to protect the smaller and weaker institutions.

The *Texas Bankers Journal*, from its own informal poll, concluded that the division between state and national bankers was far more distinct than reported by Hoopes. In fact, they did not find "a single national banker" who favored the law. The primary reason given for opposition on the part of the national banks was the fear that deposits would be lost to the state banks after the passage of a state deposit insurance law. It was claimed that the national banks in Oklahoma had lost deposits because of the operation of the law in that state.[8]

Sentiment among state bankers was so strongly in favor of deposit insurance that there was a movement to organize a "State Bankers Association," separate and distinct from the Texas Bankers Association, solely for the purpose of promoting such a law. Commissioner Love was in favor of a "State Bankers Association"; he believed that it would be organized and would prove to be quite useful in securing the desired legislation. The commissioner was aware of the division of opinion that existed on deposit insurance and the strong opposition that he faced. However, he believed that after the passage of a state law the national bankers would be forced to adopt a similar form of deposit insurance to ensure their preservation.[9]

Shortly after the 1908 Texas Bankers Association Convention in Fort Worth, the Democratic National Convention was held in Denver. The Democrats blamed the Panic of 1907 on the incumbent Republican administration. They charged that during the preceding decade the Republicans had linked the country to Wall Street and had brought on a panic that was injurious to the common people and favorable to the "money trust." They suggested that deposit insurance would remedy this and adopted a bank-guaranty plank in their platform.[10]

The Texas Democratic party, at its state convention in San Antonio, August 11-13, 1908, followed the precedent of the national convention. Governor Campbell, who had just been nominated for a second term, led a successful campaign for a platform supporting bank deposit insurance. The following resolution was adopted: "In harmony with the National Democratic platform, pledging the party to legislation for the guaranty of national bank deposits, we favor the prompt establishment of a system under the supervision and control of the state for the guaranty of deposits in the state banks of Texas."[11] Governor Campbell sent a message to the Thirty-first Legislature on January 14, 1909, two days after it convened, asking for legislation to insure bank depositors against loss. However, opposition among bankers seemed to be intensifying.

After the negative vote was cast on the question of bank deposit insurance at the 1908 Texas Bankers Association Convention, the *Texas Banker* openly revealed its opposition. In the words of the editor, Colonel W. J. B. Patterson, "it became the manifest duty of this publication to oppose that view of the question which the association believed would be detrimental to the welfare of the banking interest of Texas and depositors."[12] The columns and the time, influence, and personal energies of the editor (who, incidentally, was a national banker) were devoted to an attempt to mold public opinion against bank deposit insurance.

On January 17, 1909, Colonel Patterson, in an interview published by the *Austin Statesman*, observed that most state bankers were in favor of deposit insurance because of the belief that it would give them a competitive edge over the national banks.[13] He further remarked that the only excuse for proposing deposit-guaranty legislation was that it was mentioned as a platform demand in the previous election. Moreover, he said, the question had never been submitted to the people.

Shortly before the Depositors Guaranty Law became a reality in the spring of 1909, the *Texas Banker* attacked Commissioner Love personally. In its March 1909 edition the magazine charged that Commissioner Love was using the deposit-guaranty question as a political lever:

It is no secret—for Mr. Love has so declared—that the Commissioner of Banking believes if he could get credit for the enacting of a Guaranty Law, the people in their gratitude would hasten to elect him Governor of this state; and therein lies the inspiration for his dramatic enthusiasm and semblance of solicitude for the depositor classes of the community . . . [14]

The *Texas Banker* also contended that the other reason for support for deposit insurance in Texas was that it was desired by

William Jennings Bryan. An editorial in the March 1909 issue insisted that the state should be permitted to

determine its local policies without the interference of outsiders, and especially of one who has thrice been rejected in national elections because of the dangerousness of every doctrine with which he has attempted to illuminate the realm of finance. The San Antonio Platform would have contained no reference to the guaranty of bank deposits, irregularly and unlawfully incorporated therein, but for the hypnotic influence that this gentlemen persists in exercising. Can "Bryanism" not be relegated to the graveyard once and for all without hope of resurrection?[15]

Deposit-Guaranty Legislation

In spite of the strong opposition organized against deposit insurance, during the regular session of the Thirty-first Legislature, which convened in January 1909, four bills involving guaranty of bank deposits were introduced in the house and one in the senate. Two of the house bills only incidentally involved deposit insurance, while the other two were fundamentally guaranty bills. The bill prepared by Love was sponsored by Representatives Baker, Jennings, Cureton, and Mobley and introduced as House Bill Number 143.[16] The bill was referred to a committee and a public hearing was scheduled for January 25. The first session of the hearing was actually held on February 5, and it was concluded on February 9. At the latter session, Senator R. M. Roddie, the author of the Oklahoma law, testified at the invitation of the House Committee on Banking. He asserted that the principles of bank deposit insurance had been thoroughly proved in Oklahoma and that the law was not being amended because of its failure, as suspected by some committee members, but merely because he had been forced to accept unsuitable amendments to the bill when it was initially passed.[17] Regardless of the support furnished by Senator Roddie, the bill died on the speaker's table. This may have been partly due to the inundation of the legislature with bills, since over one thousand were introduced during the regular session. The principal reason, however, was Speaker Marshall's objection to the part of the bill that provided for the guaranty of interest-bearing deposits.

The day after the adjournment of the regular session, Governor Campbell, in accordance with his campaign promise to keep the legislators' "nose to the grindstone" until platform demands were enacted into law, reconvened the legislature for the purpose of considering guaranty legislation. In his message of March 13, 1909, proclaiming the first called session, he strongly urged the prompt enactment of laws providing for an effective system of deposit guaranty.[18]

In this session three guaranty bills were introduced in the house and one in the senate. A revised version of the bill written by Commissioner Love was introduced as House Bill Number 1. This new bill did not contain the clause providing for the guaranty of interest-bearing deposits. The bill was reported favorably from committee and became known as the Cureton bill because of the active part Representative Cureton took in its progress through the house. On April 2 the measure was finally passed by a vote of ninety to seventeen and was referred to the senate.[19]

In the meantime Senate Bill Number 4, known as the Alexander bill, had run into opposition. The Committee on Insurance, Statistics, and History offered a substitute in the form of the Senter-Hume bill, which provided that each state bank should protect its depositors by obtaining a bond, insurance policy, or other guaranty of indemnity and filing the same with the Department of Insurance and Banking. The bill passed the senate on April 3 by a vote of twenty-two to three and was sent to the house.[20]

Despite the eloquent endorsement of the legislation by William Jennings Bryan in his address to the joint session of the legislature on April 5, 1909, the Cureton bill failed in the senate and the Senter-Hume bill failed in the house. It is true that each house had approved a form of deposit protection, but each was so adamantly in favor of its own measure that the chance for the enactment of a law was lost during the first called session.

In an attempt to complete the program of legislation recommended by Governor Campbell, the legislature remained in session through Easter Sunday. It was on this day that the governor issued his famous "Easter Egg" message, calling for a second extra session. In the section pertaining to banking, he said:

A law providing for the guaranty of deposits in state banks was demanded and the people mean it. The national platform and the state platform demanded this legislation, because the people demanded it and have a right to demand it. The depositors have asked for a bank guaranty law. Not a bond law, with only the right to bring a suit. Such a plan as proposed is, I believe, a sham and a fraud that would liquidate every state bank in Texas.
As the law now stands, nobody is protected but the banker, and we will fall short of our duty to the people, if we fail to protect the depositors and their savings by an effective law. The system proposed by the Democratic platforms would make our banking system better and stronger, it will give stability and confidence, and stimulate development all along the line. I have taken the Democratic party at its word, and have reason to believe that legislators holding Democratic commissions, are in duty bound to keep the faith.[21]

This message created a furor in the senate; however, it brought results. Five bills providing for bank-deposit guaranty were introduced in the senate and an equal number in the house during the second called session. The most significant of these bills was the Meachum-Greer bill, which was introduced in the senate.[22] It provided for a dual system under which banks could choose the guaranty plan advocated by the House or the bond plan favored by the senate. The bill was passed by the legislature, sent to the governor on May 11, and signed into law on May 12, 1909.

Provisions of the Texas Guaranty Law

The principal provisions of Senate Bill Number 4, passed in the second called session of the Thirty-first Legislature, providing for bank deposit protection, are summarized below.[23]

General Provisions

The act provided for a depositors' guaranty fund and fixed the terms by which banks could provide their depositors with the benefits of the fund. It also provided for a bond for securing depositors.

Each existing state bank and each such institution chartered thereafter was required to protect its depositors either by the

Depositors Guaranty Fund or by the Bond Security System. National banks transacting business in the state likewise could protect their depositors under either alternative. Private banks could, under certain conditions, protect their depositors by the Bond Security System, but they were not eligible for the Depositors Guaranty Fund.

The State Banking Board created under the act was charged with control and management of the Depositors Guaranty Fund and general supervision and control of the Bond Security System. All state banks were required to exercise their option on or before October 1, 1909, and to secure their deposits by one of the plans beginning on January 1, 1910.

Depositors Guaranty Fund

Banks that chose the Depositors Guaranty Fund were required to pay to the State Banking Board on January 1, 1910, 1 percent of their daily average deposits for the preceding year ending November 1, 1909. Annually thereafter, each bank was to be assessed one fourth of 1 percent of its daily average deposits for the year ending November 1 of the preceding year until the fund reached $2,000,000, at which time the commissioner was to notify each bank not to pay any more. However, if the fund fell below $2,000,000, or in the event of an emergency, further assessments were allowed in an amount sufficient to restore the fund to the $2,000,000 maximum. No bank was required to pay more than 2 percent of average daily deposits for any one year. Twenty-five percent of each payment was to be in cash, with the remainder being paid by crediting a demand deposit account in the name of the State Banking Board.

National banks were eligible to participate under the same terms as state banks. If a federal law should be enacted to protect depositors of national banks, the national banks could withdraw and have the unused portion of their assessments returned to them.

The commissioner of insurance and banking had the responsibility for liquidating insolvent banks. Depositors were to be paid in full out of the cash immediately available from the insolvent bank, with the remainder paid out of the Depositors

Guaranty Fund. Interest-bearing deposits were not eligible for insurance under the act. The commissioner could enforce the double liability of stockholders.

If the solvency of a suspended bank could be restored, the bank could resume business, with the written approval of the commissioner.

Bond Security System

Banks that chose the Bond Security System were required to file with the commissioner of insurance and banking on January 1, 1910, and annually thereafter, a bond insurance policy or other guaranty of indemnity for the benefit of all depositors in an amount equal to the bank's capital stock.

Any private bank could voluntarily elect to file a bond, insurance policy, or other guaranty of indemnity in an amount fixed by the commissioner of insurance and banking but not less than one half the amount of the average of the daily deposits for the preceding year.

If any bank, private or incorporated, defaulted in the payment of a deposit, the commissioner of insurance and banking was required to take charge of the bank if the examination found it to be insolvent. The commissioner was further required to notify the maker of the bond, insurance policy, or other guaranty of indemnity, and within sixty days after notice the full amount demanded was due and payable to the commissioner. The funds in turn were to be paid promptly by him on a pro rata basis to unpaid depositors.

The protection furnished under the Bond Security System was not limited to unsecured deposits or to deposits on which no interest was paid, as it was under the Guaranty Fund section of the law. The deposits protected were those that were held when the bond was filed and all deposits made during a period of twelve months thereafter. The bond or other form of guaranty could be made by any entity authorized to carry on a bonding business in Texas.

Whenever the deposits of any incorporated bank operating under the Bond Security System exceeded six times its capital and surplus, the bank was required to furnish additional security equal to the total amount of the excess. If at any time it appeared to the State Banking Board that the security was insufficient, it was compelled to require the bank to file new or additional security in an amount sufficient to protect its depositors.

In an effort to counteract any tendencies toward more reckless banking that the guaranty system might have engendered, the 1909 law imposed more stringent regulation upon banks. It provided that no state bank could own more than 10 percent of the capital stock of any other banking corporation. It also levied additional penalties for bank defalcation and limited the amount of indebtedness of any officer or director to the bank.

The Texas law represented one of the first attempts in American banking history to establish a required statutory relationship between deposits and capital of banks. With a capital of $10,000, the deposits of a bank were restricted to five times its capital and surplus; with a capital from $10,000 to $20,000, to six times its capital and surplus; from $20,000 to $40,000, to seven times; from $40,000 to $75,000, to eight times; from $75,000 to $100,000, to nine times; and if the capital exceeded $100,000, the deposits were restricted to ten times its capital and surplus. If these amounts were exceeded, within sixty days the bank was required to increase its capital by 25 percent.

Preference for the Guaranty Fund

From the outset the state bankers of Texas expressed a preference for the Guaranty Fund rather than the Bond Security System. The commissioner's report dated August 31, 1910, the first report following the required choice of a plan by a state bank, stated that as of that date 541 banks had chosen the Guaranty Fund, whereas only 43 banks had chosen the Bond Security System. The law originally did not contain a provision to allow a bank to change from one plan to the other. New banks coming into the state banking system continued to favor the Guaranty Fund. Consequently, the largest number of banks in the Bond Security System reported at any one time before 1925 was sixty-two on August 31, 1914. In 1925 the law was changed to allow a bank to switch from one plan to the other; as a result, there was a mass exodus from the Guaranty Fund to the Bond Security System.

There are several plausible reasons for the initial preference for the Guaranty Fund. In the first place, the principles behind the Guaranty Fund had been backed by Governor Campbell, Commissioner Love, and most of the members of the banking community who had agreed to deposit insurance. It embodied the same concepts as the laws that previously had been enacted in Oklahoma, Kansas, and Nebraska. It was, therefore, a system that had been tried and tested and that was reasonably familiar to the bankers of Texas. The bond plan, on the other hand, originated in the Texas senate and was included in the bill that finally passed as a compromise. It had no support from the banking community.

Second, it is probable that some banks chose the Guaranty Fund under the misapprehension that they would be able to advertise that their deposits were guaranteed by the state. This deceitful practice had been widespread in Oklahoma, and it was consequently forbidden by the Texas law. Advertisements in Texas were limited to the following words: "The non-interest-bearing and unsecured deposits of this bank are protected by the Depositors Guaranty Fund of the State of Texas." In the beginning this provision of the statute was violated in numerous instances.

Banks might have been influenced to join the Guaranty Fund by the fact that the amount contributed to the Fund by any one bank could be carried on that bank's books as an asset. Under the Bond Security System, on the other hand, premium payments on insurance were expense items. Such was not the case, however, if a personal bond was posted, with the directors and stockholders as guarantors. Then there was no liability until the capital and surplus were lost and the stockholders had been assessed 100 percent on their capital stock. The extent to which this latter procedure was used is unknown.

National banks were prevented by national law from entering any mutual assessment system of state bank guaranty, yet they were at liberty to join the Bond Security System. There was at least one national bank in Texas that availed itself of this protection. On January 1, 1910, the Commercial National Bank of Sherman gave a personal bond to the banking commissioner in the amount of $100,000, the equivalent of its capital. Apparently no private banks chose to protect their depositors under the Bond Security System, because they did not want to be subjected to state examination and supervision.

Summary

With the passage of Senate Bill Number 4 in the second called session of the Thirty-first Legislature, Texas joined Oklahoma, Kansas, and Nebraska in the establishment of a bank depositors' insurance system. The Panic of 1907, the passage of depositors' insurance laws in other states, the national Democratic platform demand of 1908, and the oratory skills of William Jennings Bryan all exerted significant influence upon the deposit-guaranty movement in Texas. However, the most persuasive forces proved to be the initiative and determination of Commissioner of Insurance and Banking Love and the leadership of Governor Campbell. In the face of what must have seemed like overwhelming opposition from the national bankers, some state bankers, and the *Texas Banker*, these men had the courage to stand by their convictions and carry the fight for deposit insurance. Following its adoption in Texas, state deposit insurance for banks was also adopted in Mississippi, South Dakota, North Dakota, and Washington.

Notes

1. E. M. Longcope, "Should the State Charter Banks, and Under What Restrictions?" p. 19.
2. *Texas Banker* 6 (February 1907): 13.
3. M. E. Guynn, "Guarantee of Bank Deposits: Is It Desirable that Bank Deposits Be Protected by a Guarantee Fund Supervised by Nation or State" (address before the Texas Bankers Association's annual convention, Corpus Christi, May 28, 1907), in *Proceedings of the Twenty-third Annual Convention of the Texas Bankers Association* (Dallas: M. P. Exline Company, 1907), pp. 109-118.
4. H. D. Boatwright, "Guaranteed Deposits" (address before the Texas Bankers Association's annual convention, Corpus Christi, May 28, 1907), in *Proceedings of the Twenty-third Annual Convention of the Texas Bankers Association* (Dallas: M. P. Exline Company, 1907), p. 119.
5. Carlson, *Monetary and Banking History*, p. 62.
6. Love, "Some East Texas Banking History," p. 1378.
7. *Texas Banker* 7 (August 1908): 7.
8. *Texas Bankers Journal*, July 1908, p. 8.
9. Ibid.
10. *Dallas Morning News*, January 10, 1909.
11. *Platforms of Political Parties of Texas* (Austin: University of Texas, 1916), p. 521.
12. *Texas Banker* 8 (March 1909): 12.
13. Ibid., January-February 1909, p. 28.
14. Ibid., March 1909, p. 13.
15. Ibid., pp. 13-14.

16. *House Journal, Texas, Thirty-first Legislature, Regular Session, 1909* (Austin: Von Boeckmann-Jones, 1909), p. 96.
17. *Dallas Morning News*, February 10, 1909.
18. *House Journal, Texas, Thirty-first Legislature, First Called Session, 1909* (Austin: Von Boeckmann-Jones, 1909), p. 2.
19. Ibid., pp. 45-47.
20. *Senate Journal, Texas, Thirty-first Legislature, First Called Session, 1909* (Austin: Von Boeckmann-Jones, 1909), p. 387.
21. *Senate Journal, Texas, Thirty-first Legislature, Second Called Session, 1909* (Austin: Von Boeckmann-Jones, 1909), p. 327.
22. Ibid., p. 407.
23. *General Laws of Texas, Thirty-first Legislature, Regular, First, and Second Called Sessions, 1909* (Austin: Von Boeckmann-Jones, 1909), p. 406. The summary of Senate Bill No. 4 is partly quoted and partly paraphrased.

7

Banking under the Guaranty Fund

Growth of the State Banking System

The first ten years of state banking under the Guaranty Fund, September 1, 1910, through August 31, 1920, could be characterized as the "quiet before the storm," considering the unsettling events that were to follow during the 1920s. The growth of the system, both in number of banks and in capital structure and resources, continued at an impressive pace, though not as rapid as during the system's initial years. Economic conditions were conducive to growth, while the establishment of the Federal Reserve System and a revision of bank chartering procedures were constraining but constructive factors. Twenty-four bank failures and 211 voluntary liquidations occurred during the period and were recognized by some as signs of structural weaknesses in Texas state banking. In recognition of these weaknesses, modifications in the law were suggested by the banking commissioners and a few others.

In the first ten years under the Guaranty Fund, Governor Colquitt attempted to establish the "Bank of Texas" as an alternative to the Federal Reserve System, Governor James E. Ferguson was impeached, and Commissioner Charles O. Austin was indicted. From September 1, 1910, to August 31, 1920, 674 state banks were chartered, bringing the total number of banks chartered since the inception of the system to 1,310. However, 235 state banks were liquidated during the ten-year time span just referred to, and 13 that had been chartered had not opened by the end of the period; so that the total number of banks in operation on August 31, 1920, was 1,010 (see table 4, page 49).

Although the growth in the number of banking offices during the decade was less impressive than during the previous five years, the absolute or dollar-volume growth in capital funds and total resources was considerably more impressive. On June 30, 1910, the 584 banks then in operation had capital, surplus, and undivided profits of $21,701,201 and total resources of $69,497,041. By the call of September 8, 1920, there were 1,014 state banks in operation, reporting capital, surplus, and undivided profits of $71,968,842 and total resources of $419,967,594.

Effect of Economic Conditions, 1910-1920

Changes in economic conditions, some of them rather dramatic, molded the development of the state banking structure during that portion of its formative years spanning the decade from September 1, 1910, to August 31, 1920. At the beginning of the decade the United States entered the initial phase of a prolonged recession following a sharp rebound from the 1907-1908 depression. From January 1910 to December 1914 the country experienced recession, except during one period from January 1912 to January 1913.

In July 1914, however, World War I began; it was the controlling influence on the American economy from the middle of 1914 to 1920 and produced the greatest prosperity experienced to that time. The war in Europe had scarcely begun when both sides found it necessary to purchase their wartime needs from the United States. Within a short time, a large part of America's productive resources were engaged in wartime production. Exports to Europe increased six times, plants were operating at capacity, and unemployment disappeared.

From the outbreak of the war the United States followed a policy of neutrality and isolation, but in December 1915 President Wilson exhorted Congress to increase the country's military preparedness by increasing allocations to the armed services. Within six months legislation was passed increasing the authorized enlistment in the armed forces and the Council of National Defense was established. On April 6, 1917, the United States declared war.

Financing of the war and the prewar buildup required a tremendous expansion of credit. To accomplish this, the Federal Reserve followed a policy of making reserves easily available to banks. In the period of greatest economic activity, June 1916 to June 1919, total bank deposits in the United States increased from $21.9 billion to $34.4 billion, and total loans and investments from $21.2 billion to $37.2 billion. Price controls were initiated during the conflict, but only at the point of marketing of raw materials. Despite these efforts, the wholesale price index in May 1920 had risen two and one-half times the level in September 1915. The gross national product, in current dollars, increased from $36.3 billion in 1914 to $75.2 billion in 1919; in constant dollars, however, the increase was only from $36.3 billion to $41.8 billion in 1919.

Wartime prosperity and inflation had a profound impact upon the Texas economy and banks. Both the national and the state banks benefited greatly from the war effort, but the state banks received more than a proportionate share of the growth.

Table 5

Growth of State and National Banks in Texas, 1914-1919

Year ended Dec. 31	Banks	Increase from 1914	Total resources ($000)	Increase from 1914 ($000)	Increase from 1914 (percentage)	Percentage of total resources
National banks						
1914	533		373,516			74.3
1919	552	19	965,855	592,339	158.6	70.4
State banks						
1914	872		129,053			25.7
1919	924	52	405,130	276,077	213.9	29.6

Source: *Annual Reports of the Comptroller of the Currency* (Washington, D.C.: Government Printing Office, 1914 and 1919); official records of the Banking Department of Texas.

Table 6

State Bank Liquidations in Texas, 1907-1939

Year	Liquidations			Average number of banks*	Liquidation rate†
	Voluntary	Involuntary	Total		
Year ended August 31					
1907	6	--	6	213	2.82
1908	20	3	23	308	7.47
1909	5	--	5	418	1.20
1910	18	--	18	513	3.39
1911	34	1	35	627	5.58
1912	20	2	22	704	3.13
1913	17	4	21	784	2.68
1914	16	2	18	855	2.10
1915	46	3	49	856	5.72
1916	25	5	30	839	3.58
1917	15	2	17	855	1.99
1918	10	--	10	881	1.14
1919	12	3	15	907	1.65
1920	16	2	18	967	1.86
1921	21	22	43	1,008	4.27
1922	41	35	76	998	7.62
Year ended December 31					
1923**	35	17	52	965	5.38
1924	24	23	47	942	4.99
1925	103	47	150	883	17.10
1926	31	33	64	808	7.92
1927	29	38	67	765	8.75
1928	46	36	82	730	11.23
1929	39	11	50	706	6.94
1930	31	18	49	677	7.24
1931	37	46	83	624	13.30
1932	46	23	69	567	12.17
1933	48	16	64	515	12.43
1934	36	2	38	475	8.00
1935	19	3	22	451	4.88

Table 6 (continued)

Year	Liquidations			Average number of banks*	Liquidation rate[†]
	Voluntary	Involuntary	Total		
1936	17	6	23	434	5.30
1937	16	5	21	421	4.99
1938	5	--	5	411	1.22
1939	13	4	17	401	4.24

*The arithmetic mean of the number of banks in operation at the beginning of the year and the number of banks in operation at the end of the year.
[†]Percentage of total banks liquidated each year.
--Zero.
**The figures for the year ended December 31, 1923, include the period from the close of the fiscal year ended August 31, 1922, through December 31, 1922.
Source: Compiled from the official records of the Banking Department of Texas.

Even though the dollar increase in total resources of national banks in Texas far exceeded that of state banks during the war, the percentage increase in state bank resources was greater. Furthermore, during the war the state banks were able to increase their proportion of total resources in Texas (exclusive of private banks) from 25.7 percent to 29.6 percent; the state-chartered institutions were ultimately able to retain more of their growth. Between December 1919 and December 1920 the total resources of Texas national banks decreased from $965.9 million to $780.2 million. During the same period the total resources of Texas state banks only decreased from $405.1 million to $391.1 million. Consequently, on December 29, 1920, the percentage of total Texas bank resources accounted for by state banks had risen to 33.4 percent, from 29.6 percent one year earlier.

The effects of wartime prosperity on the state banking system are even more discernible when certain facts are considered. Eighty-three percent of the growth in total state bank resources between September 1, 1910, and August 31, 1920, occurred during World War I. The lowest level of liquidations since 1909 occurred during the fiscal years between 1917 and 1920, when the United States was directly engaged in the war and economic activity was at its highest. In fiscal 1920, for the first time since 1913, over one hundred charters for new state banks were granted.

Economic conditions during the 1910-1920 period also exerted some distinct negative effects on the state banking systems. The timing of the 211 voluntary and 24 involuntary liquidations strongly suggests that they were influenced by economic events and conditions (see table 6). For example, liquidations increased sharply from 1909 to 1910 and peaked in 1911 at the zenith of the recession that began in January 1910 and ended in January 1912. During the brief recovery that followed, liquidations declined and bottomed out in 1914, before rising again the following year. The increase in liquidations in 1915 and 1916 was undoubtedly precipitated by the disruptions and uncertainties associated with the outbreak of World War I. The 49 liquidations that occurred in 1915, the highest in any year since the establishment of the system, were partially due to the change by many banks from state to national charters after the establishment of the

Federal Reserve System. Even after discounting conversions, however, there were still 25 liquidations, more than in any other year except 1911.

Revision of the State Bank Chartering Procedure

Ben L. Gill, commissioner of insurance and banking from January 17, 1911, to July 10, 1913, was the first commissioner to campaign extensively for more rigid controls over chartering activities. In the biennial reports for the years ending August 31, 1910 and 1911, Commissioner Gill recommended that responsibility for chartering be placed in the hands of the State Banking Board. A precedent for Gill's action had been established by decisions of the supreme courts of Kansas and Wisconsin in 1911; these courts held that it was constitutional for the banking board to determine whether an additional bank would be justified in a community. In reporting their decision, the *Texas Bankers Record* editorialized as follows:

There is nothing so necessary in the interest of safe banking as this authority and yet [neither] the Texas Commissioner, nor the Bank-Board, have any such authority. If it were possible to do so, enough evidence could be furnished by our state department to convince any man, banker or street cleaner, that such regulation is absolutely necessary. This is true now, more than at any other time. Our rapidly growing commonwealth is attracting all sorts of businessmen. They are coming and they are trying to establish banks along with other business enterprises. Kansas has ruled that every stock proposition has to be submitted to the Bank Commissioner before promoters are allowed to undertake the sale of them; This, together with unsatisfactory developments in banking in other states, has started many an erstwhile banker toward Texas. While our Banking Board is very careful to see that we have the right kind of men in the organization, and is making very rigid requirements along all lines, it is a serious matter to overcrowd the banking business in any city, even though it be done by excellent bankers with sufficient capital. The Texas Banking Department should have authority placed in some manner to govern this great need.[1]

When the Thirty-third Legislature convened on January 14, 1913, Commissioner Gill was instrumental in introducing and having passed into law a bill to provide for examination of and investigation into the necessity for a new bank and into the financial and moral integrity of the incorporators. It required that the incorporators apply for a bank charter to the State Banking Board. The board was then expected to verify the financial integrity of the incorporators and require each to show that his net worth was at least twice the amount of the par value of the stock for which he subscribed. Also, the board was required to determine that there was a need for a new bank in the town in which the bank was to be located and that the incorporators were acting in good faith.[2]

This amendment to the Texas State Bank Law had a definite and immediate impact upon the number of charters granted for new state banks. From the inception of the state banking system in 1905 to the end of January 1913, 900 charters had been issued, an average of 130 per year. After the amendment, from January 31, 1913, to August 31, 1920, only 410 new charters were granted, an average of 54 per year. Naturally other explanations could partially account for this trend. The earlier period represented the formative years, when a more rapid growth rate was to be expected. During most of the latter period the United States was engaged in World War I, which significantly affected its economy. Finally, the establishment of the Federal Reserve System in 1913 induced some banks to seek national instead of state charters. It seems reasonable to assume, though, that the decrease in the growth rate in the number of banks chartered was primarily due to the deliberate actions of the State Banking Board under the new authority given them. The fact that the change was so drastic in the year immediately after the amendment was passed, when only 53 charters were issued compared with 128 the previous year, seems to corroborate this conclusion.

Federal Reserve Act

The Federal Reserve Act, passed on December 23, 1913, was an outgrowth of the Aldrich-Vreeland Act, which had been enacted after the Panic of 1907 to provide relief during future upheavals. The Federal Reserve Act provided the nation with central banking facilities. Because of the geographical expansiveness of the United States, the traditional aversion to concentration of financial power in this country, and other reasons, the country was divided into twelve districts with a Federal Reserve bank located in each. Texas came within the boundaries of the Eleventh Federal Reserve District, which also included northwest Louisiana, southeast Oklahoma, southeast Arizona, and the southern half of New Mexico. The Federal Reserve bank serving the Eleventh District was located in Dallas and branches were later established in El Paso, San Antonio, and Houston. Every national bank was required to become a member of the Federal Reserve System and to subscribe for an amount of capital stock in its district Federal Reserve bank equal to 6 percent of its own capital and surplus (the actual purchase required was one half of the subscription).

The Federal Reserve Act provided for the admission of state banks to the Federal Reserve System; however, initially the terms upon which admission was to be granted were left to the discretion of the Federal Reserve Board. On June 21, 1917, regulations covering admission that had been issued by the Board in June 1915 were officially enacted into law by amendment to the Federal Reserve Act. Under these amendments all banks admitted to membership were required to comply with the reserve and capital requirements of the act (as they pertain to national banks) and a state bank was allowed to withdraw from membership in the Federal Reserve System after six months' written notice, the paid-in cash subscription by the bank to be refunded with interest at the rate of one half of 1 percent per month from the date of the last dividend.

The initial reaction of the state bankers in Texas to the passage of the Federal Reserve Act was favorable. The commissioner of insurance and banking, W. W. Collier, in an address before the Dallas district meeting of the Texas Bankers Association on February 5, 1914, stated that the Federal Reserve Act was the "very best piece of constructive legislation that had been enacted by the Congress of the United States."[3] He remarked upon the advantages the act would afford to state banks and urged that the state banks subscribe.

On September 10, 1914, in his message to the Thirty-third Legislature, which was in its second special session, Governor Colquitt called for legislation allowing state banks to join the Federal Reserve System.[4] The bill that was passed and enacted into law during the third special session allowed all banks and bank and trust companies incorporated under the laws of Texas to become members of the Federal Reserve System,[5] subject to the rules for membership in the system. The amendment also provided that the reserve requirements of those state banks joining the Federal Reserve System be reduced to conform to the reserve requirements of national banks.

The Dallas Federal Reserve Bank opened on November 16, 1914, and oddly enough, one of its charter members was the First State Bank of Dallas. In fact, this pioneering institution was the first state-chartered bank in the United States to join the Federal Reserve System.[6] The management of the First State Bank must have joined with some misgivings, though, because at the time no provisions had been made to permit a state bank to withdraw and the Federal Reserve Board was still debating the state bank question.

Other state banks in Texas did not rush to follow the precedent established by the First State Bank of Dallas. Even after the Federal Reserve Board issued regulations governing membership in June 1915, the state banks showed no inclination to join in significant numbers. By the end of 1916 only ten Texas state banks had become members.

The reasons that the Federal Reserve System failed to attract more state members from Texas in these initial years are varied. A large portion of the state banks could not meet the minimum capital requirements for membership in the system, requirements that ranged from $25,000 in the smallest communities to $200,000 in cities of 50,000 and over. At first many bankers feared that they would be subjected to four state and two federal examinations each year, causing a considerable expenditure of time and money; however, this objection was removed by the

June 1915 regulations. The main objection to joining the system voiced by most Texas state bankers was that no interest was allowed on the reserve balances carried with the Federal Reserve Bank.[7] This was a valid argument, but by joining the system a bank's legal reserve requirement was reduced from 25 percent, as required by state law, to 15 percent.

There were also serious doubts with regard to the advantages of the rediscount privilege.[8] This reservation seems to have been well founded, as much of the paper carried by the state banks was ineligible for rediscount. Either their notes were too small, too long in maturity, or not self-liquidating in nature. The Federal Reserve was prohibited from discounting any note that represented a loan in excess of 10 percent of the capital and surplus of the member bank. In Texas the legal lending limit was 25 percent of capital and surplus. Consequently, many of the notes held by state banks exceeded the federal limit. The eligible-paper problem assumes even greater significance when it is noted that before 1920 banks did not carry the large amounts of U.S. government securities that are commonly used today by member banks as collateral for loans from the Federal Reserve. Thus most state bankers believed that their borrowing needs could be handled more efficiently by their city correspondents.

A feeling of general antagonism toward the Federal Reserve developed among the Texas state bankers in 1916 when the Federal Reserve Board announced its plan to collect checks at par on all member banks. Collection charges at the time were an important source of income to the state banks. At the annual meeting of the Texas Bankers Association in 1916 a resolution was passed demanding that the "incoming officers organize a nation-wide opposition to the clearance plan." As a result the new president, J. W. Butler of Clifton, called a meeting in St. Louis, Missouri, on June 10, 1916, which was attended by bankers from nineteen states. The efforts of Mr. Butler and the other state bankers continued throughout the summer but drew to an end at the American Bankers Association Convention in September. Although the par collection plan went into effect and organized opposition disappeared, the bitterness created undoubtedly hindered the Federal Reserve's campaign to enlist state banks as members.

Statistics compiled from Texas Banking Department records show that a considerable number of the state bankers who wished to enjoy the advantages of the Federal Reserve System converted their banks to national charters. From the inception of the state banking system until the passage of the Federal Reserve Act in December 1913, only eleven state banks had surrendered their charters to become national banks. During 1914 and the first half of 1915 twenty-four banks converted to national charters. There seems to be little question that these conversions were directly connected with the Federal Reserve since the majority occurred during November 1914, the month in which the Federal Reserve System became operative.

Most of the Texas bankers who decided to convert to a national charter did so during the initial years that the Federal Reserve law was in effect. This observation is supported by the fact that the number of conversions was drastically reduced in fiscal 1916, when only two banks gave up their state charters. Between September 1, 1915, and August 31, 1920, only twelve conversions occurred (see table 4).

With the initial campaign to recruit state banks a virtual failure, the Federal Reserve Board intensified its efforts in the fall of 1917, after amendments to the act concerning state banks had become law. A letter was sent to each state bank urging it to join. Even President Woodrow Wilson appealed to the state banks, saying that "the duty of the hour is to co-ordinate the banking resources of the country into one great system, and put their resources into a great common reservoir."[9] A meeting of the state bankers in Texas was called in Dallas in December 1917 to consider the subject. In May of the following year Judge W. F. Ramsey, the Federal Reserve agent, spoke to the state bank section at the Texas Bankers Association annual convention.[10] He urged every bank to join the system. Before the beginning of this campaign only 15 state banks from Texas were members, but by May 1918 an additional 55 applications had been received, bringing the total to 70. These 70 banks furnished about 20 percent of the capital of the Dallas Federal Reserve Bank. Of the 425 state member banks in the entire system, Texas accounted for about 16 percent of the total. This was considered by banking leaders of the state to be an excellent showing.[11]

The impact of the Federal Reserve Act on the state banking system was probably much greater than the few conversions that it precipitated. There is no way to determine from available records, for instance, the number of banks that would have been chartered under state law but chose instead to obtain a national charter because of the benefits afforded by the Federal Reserve System, together with the prestige of being a national bank.

State Bank Failures

Of the twenty-four state banks that failed in Texas between August 31, 1910, and August 31, 1920, fifteen were closed due to the fraudulent actions of management; one was closed due to losses on loans; another was closed because of its inability to meet a large withdrawal; and for the remaining seven bank failures the causes are not known. All of the banks, except for the West Texas Bank and Trust Company in San Antonio and the First State Bank in Chillicothe, were closed by the Department of Insurance and Banking. The banks in San Antonio and Chillicothe were closed by the boards of directors of the banks.

The first bank to be closed and taken charge of by the department after the operation of the Guaranty Fund went into effect was the Harris County Bank and Trust Company of Houston. The bank failed because of fraud perpetrated by its president, who put fictitious loans on the bank's books and forged checks on depositors' accounts. The bank was suspended on September 7, 1911, and on the following Monday, September 12, the Guaranty Fund had on deposit in Houston a sufficient sum to pay all non-interest-bearing and unsecured depositors. The Guaranty Fund provided $111,649 for this purpose.[12]

One of the more interesting bank failure cases involved the second institution to fail under the Guaranty Fund—the First State Bank of Kopperl, which was closed on December 6, 1911. In the summer of 1911 controlling interest in the bank had been acquired by S. J. Spotts and his father, brothers, and brothers-in-law. They promptly elected themselves officers and directors and proceeded to use the bank's funds. Meanwhile the department was investigating them, but with little success. On November 28, 1911, a department examiner riding on a train happened to overhear a conversation disclosing that S. J. Spotts had served a term in the federal penitentiary for embezzlement of funds from a national bank (at Petty, Texas) for which he was cashier. Upon inquiry, the facts were confirmed by the office of the comptroller of the currency in Washington. The examiner was sent to Kopperl at once, only to find the cashier gone and the bank closed. A few days later the cashier returned with his attorney and was arrested. After several months of investigation by the Bosque County sheriff, Spotts was finally located in Los Angeles, arrested, and returned to stand trial.

Since the State Bank Law had gone into effect there had been many serious violations of the criminal sections of the law. But before the Spotts case no prosecutions had been attempted by county authorities, in spite of Commissioner Gill's strong recommendations. The commissioner was required to report violations of the law to county or district attorneys, who were under the threat of criminal penalties if they did not initiate legal action. Yet the commissioner had encountered many officials who failed to carry forth their duties. He had pleaded with these officers to be more active and in some instances he had retained private counsel to secure indictments. An important outgrowth of the failure of the First State Bank of Kopperl was that on December 6, 1911, Governor Colquitt authorized the funds needed to employ counsel to assist in the prosecution of these cases.[13]

The largest state bank to be closed during the 1910-1920 period was the West Texas Bank and Trust Company of San Antonio. Only two months before being closed, the bank had merged with the Alamo Trust Company, and two years before that with the American Bank and Trust Company. The West Texas Bank and Trust was seemingly managed by extremely capable men. Nonetheless, inadequate management was the cause of the bank's ultimate downfall. The immediate cause of the closing of the bank on April 3, 1916, was a demand made by the mayor of San Antonio for payment of the entire city fund of $527,000 on deposit there. This demand apparently stemmed from the general knowledge that the bank was having difficulties resulting from unwise loans and an undercapitalized position. The banking commissioner had been aware of the bank's condition and efforts under his supervision to better its affairs had been so successful that its capital was approximately $250,000 greater at the time of closing than it had been the year before. Had the bank not been forced to close, it is conceivable that its affairs would eventually have been restored to a satisfactory condition.[14]

The failure of the West Texas Bank and Trust Company demonstrated the value of the Depositors Guaranty Fund. Although hundreds of depositors had congregated in front of the bank during the morning of April 3, 1916, the uneasiness that had normally attended bank failures was absent. The reason for this was reported to have been that the depositors generally realized that they were protected by the Guaranty Fund.[15]

One of the most unfortunate events in the entire history of the Banking Department occurred with the closing of the Farmers and Merchants State Bank of Teague in 1916. In these early years the department was understaffed, and it was quite common for the commissioner to go into the field to aid in closing an insolvent bank. At the time of the closing of the bank in Teague on August 28, 1916, the commissioner was John S. Patterson, who had succeeded W. W. Collier on January 23, 1915. Commissioner Patterson had traveled to Teague in order to assist Bank Examiner J. Eldred McKinnon in closing the defunct Farmers and Merchants State Bank. After banking hours, when Patterson and McKinnon were putting up a notice announcing that the bank was being placed in charge of the commissioner, T. R. Watson, who was president of the bank, drew a pistol and opened fire on Patterson and McKinnon, killing Patterson. As far as can be determined, the Teague tragedy represents the only incident in which an official of the state or federal government lost his life or was injured while examining or closing a bank in Texas.[16]

Criminal actions of dishonest bankers were the principal cause of bank failures during the decade ending August 31, 1920. Fifteen of the twenty-four banks that failed during the period were closed because of dishonest management. Seven other banks, officially classified as voluntary liquidations, were actually victims of "inside robberies." (These were state banks located in Avoca, Gainesville, Gunter, Llano, Silverton, Spur, and Winters.)

The passage of strict laws in Kansas, Nebraska, and Oklahoma had forced promoters and swindlers to flee to safer and more lucrative areas. The lax laws, the low incidence of prosecution, and the fertile economic environment attracted many of these unscrupulous people to Texas, where they found the banks to be particularly vulnerable. They would either gain control of the bank, or they would work in a critical position, such as cashier, that would give them access to the cash and books of the bank. Lack of adequate internal controls, bookkeeping techniques, and sophisticated machinery aided them in their duplicity. Because of the many state banks in Texas, the lack of an adequate number of examiners, and the number of examinations required (four per year), it is probable that the examinations were often superficial. When a violation of the law was discovered, the commissioner's office often was unable to obtain a conviction or even an indictment because of lack of cooperation from city and county officials with jurisdiction over the cases.

Between 1910 and 1920 the Department of Insurance and Banking compiled a list of dishonest bankers and their crimes. Of the ninety-two persons involved, sixty-two were cashiers of banks, sixteen were presidents, five were vice-presidents, six were tellers, and three were bookkeepers. The predominance of criminal acts committed by cashiers can be attributed to the fact that the cashier was responsible for the cash and books of the bank. Where internal controls were inadequate, the cashier was undoubtedly subjected to great temptation, and the weaker cashiers often succumbed.

Sample cases from the department's list of dishonest bankers are summarized below:

1. *A convicted president of one bank and director of three banks in Longview* was guilty of "kiting" drafts on a very large scale with numerous banks and signing, without authority, the name of the bank of which he was president to telegrams authorizing payment of drafts; later, in 1916, together with the cashier of another bank, he used about $120,000 of the bank's funds to speculate in cotton futures.

2. *A convicted cashier of a small bank in South Central Texas* embezzled between $700 and $800 of the bank's funds by

charging customers' accounts with $5 and $10 at a time on the individual ledger, appropriating the proceeds of such charges and covering up the charge on the customers' monthly statement by adding that amount in the total adding machine list without showing the charge in the list of checks (by throwing the carriage of the adding machine back and inserting the amount in the machine before throwing the carriage back in its place).

3. *A convicted cashier of a small bank in the Panhandle* embezzled in various manners, one of which was to accept deposits and enter them on passbooks but not credit proceeds to the depositor's account; another was charging correspondent banks with various amounts, the proceeds of which he used himself.

The department list of criminal violations and their perpetrators was not maintained after 1920, probably because of the substantial reduction in the incidence of criminal violations after that year. Between 1910 and 1920 the department, through its diligence, was successful in removing from the state banks many of the habitual criminals. This, together with more extensive examinations and refinements in examining techniques, apparently accounts for the reduction in the incidence of bank embezzlements after 1920.

Modifications of the Texas State Bank Law

Although many recommendations were made for reforms in the Texas State Bank Law, no significant legislation was passed between 1910 and 1920. The most important measures to become law were the revision in the chartering rules and the amendment that allowed state banks to become members of the Federal Reserve System.

Other changes of significance in the banking law, some of which had been urged for years by the commissioners, established a salary scale for state bank examiners based on tenure; shifted the place for the filing of bank charter applications from the secretary of state's office to the Department of Insurance and Banking; required bank directors to take an oath in which they pledged to perform certain duties in fulfillment of their office; required all bank employees handling cash to be bonded, instead of just the cashier and treasurer; and changed the law to allow depositors ninety days, instead of forty-five, to present claims to the commissioner when a bank was liquidated.

Governor Colquitt's Bank Bill

One outgrowth of the passage of the Federal Reserve Act by Congress—an incident unique in Texas banking history—was the effort of Governor Colquitt to secure the passage of state legislation creating the "Bank of Texas." On September 15, 1914, Governor Colquitt sent a message to the legislature requesting the creation of such a bank.[17] The organization of the Bank of Texas was to be in many respects similar to that of the Federal Reserve banks. The Bank of Texas was to perform basically the same services for the state banks of Texas and the state government that the Federal Reserve banks were to perform for their members and the U.S. government. The bank was to have nine directors, divided into three classes representing different economic interests, as in the Federal Reserve System. One primary difference from the Federal Reserve was that part of the capital of the Bank of Texas was to be provided from the Permanent School Fund of the state. The entire Permanent School Fund, amounting to $17.8 million, was to be used as the capital base, with subscriptions from member banks providing additional amounts. All state banks were to be required to subscribe to and purchase stock in the bank in an amount equal to 5 percent of their own capital and surplus.[18]

The initial reaction of the banking community to the governor's proposal was one of solid opposition. James E. Ferguson, a banker from Temple and Democratic nominee for governor, was not opposed to the idea of the bank, but he was against capitalizing the Bank of Texas out of the Permanent School Fund. He said that he would rather endure the hardships that such a bank might eliminate than "take the risk of the permanent misfortune of not being able to educate the boys and girls of Texas."[19] George T. Jester, president of the First State Bank of Corsicana, a well-known banker, asserted that there was no need for the bank and that the state should not engage in the banking business with its funds or the school funds.[20] Other prominent Texas bankers who were called before the committee of the house and senate considering the "Bank of Texas" bill were, without exception, opposed to the concept.

In the second session of the Thirty-third Legislature bills were introduced in the house and the senate to establish the "Bank of Texas." The senate bill died, although it received a favorable report from the committee. The house bill also died; it received an unfavorable report from the Committee on Banks and Banking.[21]

In spite of the judgment of the Committee on Banks and Banking, Governor Colquitt continued to pursue legislation to create the "Bank of Texas" in the Thirty-third Legislature. He called a third special session, and in several messages to the legislature during that session he urged the passage of his bill. The governor also obtained an opinion from the attorney general supporting the constitutionality of the bank, and he sent the opinion to the legislature. House Bill Number 1 was introduced in accordance with the governor's wishes, but it finally died by a vote of 81 to 35.[22] With this last effort the Thirty-third Legislature ended and, for all practical purposes, so did the effort to establish the "Bank of Texas." Governor Colquitt was succeeded by James E. Ferguson on January 13, 1915, one day after the Thirty-fourth Legislature convened. In his final message to the legislature on January 13 Governor Colquitt again recommended that the "Bank of Texas" be chartered. In deference to his wishes, a joint resolution was introduced to amend the Texas constitution to permit the establishment of the bank, but it did not receive serious consideration.[23] This was the last attempt to create a central bank solely to serve the needs of Texas.

Indictment of Commissioner Charles O. Austin and Impeachment of Governor James E. Ferguson

It was alleged in the indictment of Commissioner of Insurance and Banking Charles O. Austin, which was returned on July 27, 1917, that Commissioner Austin and Governor Ferguson misapplied public funds in the amount of $5,985.50. In a letter addressed to the banks and insurance companies of Texas, dated July 30, 1917, Commissioner Austin explained the circumstances of the indictment.[24]

According to Mr. Austin, one of the procedures inherited by the commissioner was that of depositing checks received from banks for examination fees in some bank or banks so that they might be collected and the funds subsequently transmitted to the state treasury, as prescribed by law. The examination fees, ranging from $12.50 to $200.00, were collected by the examiners and transmitted in the examination report to the Department of Insurance and Banking. Upon receipt by the department, the drafts were then verified by a clerk and turned over to the bookkeeper. He then made the proper entries in his books and prepared them for a deposit, which was made every other day.

Because some of the department records were either destroyed or removed during a political feud between Commissioner William E. Hawkins and Governor T. M. Campbell (which led to the resignation of Commissioner Hawkins on August 3, 1910), the procedure followed in making the deposits during and before Mr. Hawkins's tenure cannot be determined. From the appointment of Commissioner F. C. Von Rosenberg on August 4, 1910, until the resignation of Commissioner W. W. Collier on January 23, 1915, the drafts were deposited in the Central State Bank of Austin and later in the American National Bank of Austin, after the two institutions were merged on July 2, 1915. The collected funds were turned over monthly to the state treasurer during this period. However, shortly after the appointment of Commissioner John S. Patterson on January 24, 1915, the procedure was changed. Department records indicate that on July 24, 1915, the drafts, instead of being deposited by Commissioner Patterson in the American National Bank for his account as commissioner, were deposited in the American National Bank of Austin for credit to the Temple State Bank, Temple, which passed the credit to the commissioner. This change in procedure was reported to have been prompted by the solicitation of the account for the Temple State Bank by its president, H. C. Poe. It was also reported that as part of the agreement it was understood that the Temple State Bank was not to draw on the funds but was to allow them to remain in its name on the books of the Austin bank.

Another change that was instituted as a matter of convenience during Commissioner Patterson's term was the practice of turning the funds over to the state treasurer quarterly instead of monthly.

Upon assuming office on September 1, 1916, after Mr. Patterson's murder, Commissioner Austin was initially inundated with matters growing out of the trial of Mr. Patterson's murderer. It was not until January 1917 that Commissioner Austin was able to begin making changes in some of the methods of handling department business. One of the first things decided was that it would be less complicated and there would be less work involved if the bookkeeper were to manage one bank account instead of two. Therefore, the bookkeeper was instructed to close out the account kept with the Temple State Bank, to open one with the American National Bank of Austin in the name of the commissioner, and thereafter to deposit all examination fees in that account.

Governor Ferguson was one of the organizers of the Temple State Bank, which was opened on April 24, 1906. He originally subscribed for 89.8 percent of the bank's capital stock and served as its president until he was inaugurated as governor of Texas on January 13, 1915.[25] One of Governor Ferguson's first official acts after inauguration was to appoint his long-time friend John S. Patterson as commissioner of insurance and banking. During his second term of office, on August 25, 1917, Governor Ferguson was impeached by the Thirty-fifth Legislature during the third special session. The house of representatives, sitting as a grand jury, indicted Governor Ferguson on twenty-one counts, of which ten were confirmed by the senate.

The articles of impeachment included the following charges:

1. Governor Ferguson was responsible for depositing state funds in the Temple State Bank, in which he owned over one fourth of the capital stock. The governor and the Temple State Bank used the funds and received profit and benefit from them.

2. State funds on deposit at the Temple State Bank were used by the governor to pay his note due to the First National Bank at Temple in an amount of $5,000 plus interest, and the amount was never refunded to the state.[26]

Governor Ferguson was also charged with misapplying and diverting other state funds, receiving cash totaling $156,500, for which he refused to account, and attempting to assert his "autocratic will" over the Board of Regents of the University of Texas (including the attempted unlawful removal of some of its members). Actually the misapplication charges were brought as a result of the conflict with the University of Texas; had it not been for that, it is likely that the governor would have escaped investigation of his handling of state funds. The Senate Committee on Civil Jurisprudence pronounced the judgment of the court: "Now, therefore, it is adjudged by the Senate of the State of Texas sitting as a Court of Impeachment . . . that the said James E. Ferguson be and he is hereby removed from the office of Governor and be disqualified to hold any office of honor, trust or profit under the State of Texas."[27]

Commissioner Austin maintained that he was innocent throughout the ordeal, and his innocence was attested to by the committee of the house that was appointed to investigate the activities of the Department of Insurance and Banking. The subcommittee appointed to conduct the examination made the following report to the committee:

We, the sub-committee, know that there were charges made against Mr. Austin in his official capacity, all of which have been closely investigated, and each and every one of them was without merit. It was only a slanderous attack upon an able and worthy servant of the whole people of Texas. We recommend C. O. Austin to this committee, as well as to the whole people of Texas, for his ability and for the faithful discharge of his duty.[28]

Following this report, Commissioner Austin was completely exonerated and the charges were dismissed by the district court of Travis County.[29]

James E. Ferguson was apparently not guilty of using state funds to pay his note at the First National Bank at Temple. According to Banking Department records, Mr. Poe, aided by cashier C. A. Hughs, was guilty of misappropriating the funds for his own use. He issued a draft on the Temple State Bank account at the American National Bank of Austin for $5,000, obtained cash, and used the funds in payment of a personal note at a Kansas City bank.[30]

Some Concluding Observations on the 1910-1920 Era

The decade of 1910 to 1920 was a critical time for the U.S. economy. From the outbreak of the war in July 1914 until its end in June 1919 great stress was exerted on the national economy and that of Texas as well. Texas supplied much of the food stock and raw cotton needed by the Allied countries. As a consequence, agricultural production increased substantially, and the demand for credit also rose sharply. The need for a far-reaching and responsive banking system became critically important. The state banking mechanism played an integral role in fulfilling that need.

While the state banks played a major role in financing the war economy in Texas, the war itself had a profound impact upon the state banking system. The uncertainties surrounding the conflict tended to retard the growth in the number of banks, since there was a net increase of only fifty-two state banks from December 31, 1914, to December 31, 1919. During the same period, however, the system experienced unprecedented growth in total resources, which increased from $129.1 million to $405.1 million. As a consequence, the proportion of total Texas bank resources accounted for by state banks increased from 25.7 percent to 29.6 percent.

The establishment of the Federal Reserve System had a permanent, though immeasurable, influence on the Texas state banking system. State bankers in Texas did not join the system in great numbers in the early years of the Federal Reserve; however, a large number apparently did convert their institutions to national charters in order to take advantage of the act. It is probable that other banks that might have been chartered under state law were instead chartered as national banks because of the benefits afforded by the Federal Reserve System and the prestige associated with a national charter. More important, though, the Federal

Reserve System greatly strengthened the banking system and financial structure of the United States and thus of Texas as well.

The Texas state banking system was also strengthened by the passage in 1913 of a law giving the State Banking Board discretion in the granting of charters for new state banks. The board was charged with the responsibility of investigating the financial and moral integrity of the incorporators and of determining that there was need in the community for a new bank.

The chartering power given to the State Banking Board should have been granted when the Texas State Bank Law was initially passed in 1905. As the experiences of the 1920s clearly demonstrate, too many state banks had already been chartered by 1913.

Notes

1. *Texas Bankers Record* 1 (November 1911): 46.
2. *Texas General Laws, Thirty-third Legislature, Regular Session, 1913* (Austin: Von Boeckmann-Jones, 1913), p. 211.
3. W. W. Collier, "State Banks and Federal Reserve Act" (address before the Dallas District Meeting of the Texas Bankers Association, February 5, 1914), in *Texas Bankers Record* 3 (February 1914): 18-20.
4. *House Journal, Texas, Thirty-third Legislature, Second Called Session, 1914* (Austin: Von Boeckmann-Jones, 1914), p. 138.
5. *House Journal, Texas, Thirty-third Legislature, Third Called Session, 1914* (Austin: Von Boeckmann-Jones, 1914), pp. 29 and 46.
6. Dabney Day, "Why State Banks Should Join Federal Reserve System" (address before the Texas Bankers Association's annual convention, Houston, May 1916), in *Texas Bankers Record* 5 (May 1916): 39-40.
7. Ibid.
8. P. A. Murray, "Why State Banks Remain Outside the Federal Reserve System" (address before the first district meeting of the Texas Bankers Association, Houston, February 20, 1918), in *Texas Bankers Record* 7 (March 1918): 23-25.
9. W. F. Ramsey, address before the state bank section of the Texas Bankers Association's annual convention, Galveston, May 15, 1918, in *Texas Bankers Record* 8 (June 1918): 50.
10. Ibid., pp. 49-52.

11. Howell E. Smith, "Address of the President" (address before the Texas Bankers Association's annual convention, Galveston, May 14, 1918), in *Texas Bankers Record* 8 (June 1918): 13.
12. John S. Patterson, "Six Years of the Guaranty Fund: Its Operation and Effect" (open letter to the Guaranty Fund Banks of Texas from the commissioner of insurance and banking, undated but written between December 1, 1915, and Commissioner Patterson's death on August 28, 1916). Available in Texana Collection, University of Texas at Austin.
13. "Interesting History of the Spotts Case," *Texas Bankers Record* 1 (June 1912): 50-51.
14. *Texas Bankers Record* 5 (April 1916): 33-34.
15. Ibid.
16. *Texas Bankers Record* 6 (September 1916): 26-28.
17. "The Governor's Bank Bill," *Texas Bankers Record* 4 (October 1914): 22.
18. *House Journal, Texas, Thirty-third Legislature, Second Called Session, 1914* (Austin: Von Boeckmann-Jones, 1914), pp. 214 and 315.
19. "The Governor's Bank Bill," pp. 22-23.
20. Ibid.
21. *House Journal, Texas, Thirty-third Legislature, Second Called Session, 1914*, p. 254.
22. Ibid., p. 4.
23. *House Journal, Texas, Thirty-fourth Legislature, Regular Session, 1915* (Austin: Von Boeckmann-Jones, 1915), p. 122.
24. *Texas Bankers Record* 6 (August 1917): 21-24.
25. Banking Department of Texas, official records.
26. Wilbourn E. Benton, *Texas: Its Government and Politics*, 2d ed. (Englewood Cliffs: Prentice-Hall, 1966), pp. 223-224.
27. Ibid., p. 225.
28. Charles O. Austin, "State Banking System in Texas" (address before the state bank section of the Texas Bankers Association's annual convention, Galveston, May 15, 1918), in *Texas Bankers Record* 8 (June 1918): 45.
29. *Texas Bankers Record* 7 (December 1917): 33.
30. Banking Department of Texas, official records.

8

The Troubled Twenties

Some important changes in the scope and composition of banking services in Texas, as elsewhere in the United States, occurred during the 1920s. The prominence attained by the automobile exemplifies a rise in incomes and living standards, a change that induced bankers to evince more interest in consumer lending and to reevaluate the significance of personal deposits—both demand and savings deposits—as sources of operating funds. Loans to finance the purchase of automobiles were the main, but not the only, type of consumer loan that many banks, particularly the more urban ones, became interested in making. Business and agricultural lending remained dominant in banking, but the relative importance of consumer lending showed a rise that was to gain momentum in later decades. Beginning in the 1920s banking gave important support to the rise in consumer well-being in Texas as in the nation at large. The discovery of oil in East Texas and the rapid exploitation of sizable oil reserves coincided with the rise of the automobile and for a time exerted profound influence on the character and behavior of many Texas banks, both state and national. Certainly the level of oil production that was achieved would not have been possible without the active financial participation of the Texas banks.

Many of the banks prospered, in the short run, from these changes in commercial banking activities, and the entire banking industry benefited, in the long run, from the broader dimensions of service to the economy that began in the 1920s. However, the net effect of all the changes affecting banking performance and structure in the twenties was to produce a decline for that decade in the number, resources, and total capital accounts of commercial banks.

Decline of the State Banking System

During the period beginning September 1, 1920, and ending December 31, 1929, the Texas state banking system entered the first phase of a protracted decline that did not abate until World War II began in Europe in 1939.

From its inception through August 31, 1921, the state banking system was a remarkable success. In the first sixteen years of its existence the average yearly increase in the number of banks in operation was 63, and in only two years, 1915 and 1916, was a decrease recorded. By the end of the 1920 fiscal year, there were 1,010 state banks in operation. One year later the figure rose to 1,016, primarily because of the relatively large number of new charters granted during the year. After 1921, however, the number of banks in Texas began a sharp and continuous decline. From August 31, 1920, to December 31, 1929, the total number of banks in operation and chartered but not open decreased from 1,023 to 699, or by 324. During this period 307 new banks were chartered, but 631 were liquidated—369 voluntarily and 262 involuntarily. (See table 4, page 49.)

With a net decrease of 324 banks it is natural that there was also a decrease in capital and resources during the period. At the call of September 8, 1920, there were 1,014 state banks in operation, with capital, surplus, and undivided profits of $71,968,842 and total resources of $419,967,594. On December 31, 1929, 699 banks answered the call, with capital, surplus, and undivided profits of $52,437,164 and total resources of $332,534,359. The number of banks answering the call decreased by 31.1 percent, capital accounts and undivided profits decreased by 27.1 percent, and resources decreased by 20.8 percent.

The Economic Climate of the Twenties

From its origin through 1919 the Texas state banking system had never been tested by a severe economic recession. The Panic of 1907 had occurred during the system's infancy, when less than three hundred banks had been organized; it was not accompanied by a severe economic disturbance; and its full impact was never felt in Texas. After the 1907 reversal the Texas economy enjoyed relative prosperity through World War I and until the 1920-1921 recession. During this time the state banking system realized extraordinary growth. However, beginning with the 1920-1921 recession the Texas economy suffered adverse economic conditions, which led to banking difficulties throughout most of the 1920s. As a result, the demand for new charters was dampened; a large number of "voluntary" liquidations, including mergers, acquisitions, conversions, and dissolutions, ensued; and an inordinate number of failures occurred.

Economic Conditions in the United States

After World War I there was a brief decline in business activity and prices from the peaks established in September 1918. By the spring of 1919, however, conversion to a peacetime economy had been completed, and a postwar upward spiral of credit and prices began. This was spurred by both external and internal demand for American goods. The immense demand for American goods, together with a continuation of the permissive credit policies followed by the Federal Reserve during the war, fueled the inflationary fires. An intense boom was under way, marked by a rapid accumulation of inventories and commodity speculation. In the eighteen months between November 1918 and June 1920, wholesale prices increased by 22 percent.

The Federal Reserve policy until just a few months before the peak of the expansion in January 1920 was basically one of inaction. This policy was followed even though the Federal Reserve Board was aware that the discount rate was far below money market rates throughout 1919 and that this was contributing to monetary expansion and thus inflation. The board attributed its quiescence to an alleged necessity to facilitate U.S. Treasury sales of "victory bonds" and to support prices of government securities, which the commercial banks held in substantial amounts. When the treasury finally withdrew its opposition to the Federal Reserve's pursuit of a tighter credit policy and the discount rate was progressively raised at the New York Reserve Bank from 4 percent in December 1919 to 6 percent the following month and then to 7 percent in June 1920, the action was too late and too much.

The contraction following the peak of business and economic expansion that occurred in January 1920 was at first mild. There was little sign of any severe decline throughout the first half of the year. The money supply and wholesale prices had continued their advance through May. After peaking in January, industrial production, employment, and payrolls had declined only moderately. However, in the summer of 1920 the contraction began to intensify, beginning with a precipitous decline in wholesale prices. Between May 1920 and June 1921 wholesale prices declined 56 percent; three fourths of the decline occurred between August 1920 and February 1921. This is the *sharpest decline in prices on record* in the history of the United States.[1]

Although the recession was under way by mid-1920, the Federal Reserve continued to follow deflationary policies well into 1921 because of the strong loan demand that was still in evidence in 1920. Even with the discount rate at 6 percent, it was profitable for member banks to borrow from the Federal Reserve to make additional loans. Consequently, in June 1920 the New York Federal Reserve Bank raised its discount rate to 7 percent. This increase occurred about six months after the cyclical peak, roughly coincided with the peak in wholesale prices and money supply, and preceded the collapse in prices by a few months. Apparently in an effort to protect its own position, the New York Federal Reserve Bank kept the June discount rate in effect until May 1921, when the rate was lowered to 6.5 percent. This decrease was followed by subsequent reductions until, in the early fall of 1921, it reached 4.5 percent.

As a result of the relaxed credit conditions, business began to return to normal and vigorous expansion was soon under way. From the nadir of the contraction in July 1921 to the expansionary zenith reached in May 1923, industrial production rose 63 percent, wholesale prices rose 9 percent, and the money supply rose 14 percent. The next six years, 1923 to 1929, were marked by relatively stable growth, with only two mild interruptions—from May 1923 to July 1924 and from October 1926 to November 1927. During most of the period, or until early 1928, when the Federal Reserve became concerned about stock market speculation, it followed an easy-money policy. From the end of 1921 until mid-1928 the discount rate at the New York Federal Reserve Bank never exceeded 4.5 percent.

While conditions in the United States were generally good after the 1920-1921 recession, there was one soft spot in the economy. The recovery that had occurred resulted principally from increased industrial production; the consequent prosperity was confined primarily to the most industrialized regions of the nation. As Paul Studenski and Herman E. Krooss (authors of *Financial History of the United States*) have stressed, from 1920 through 1929 agricultural communities never enjoyed appreciable prosperity.[2] During most of the period crop and livestock prices and farm values were depressed. Even when farm prices peaked, in August 1925, they recovered only 33 percent of the loss sustained during the 1920-1921 recession.

Economic Conditions in Texas

The economic conditions that prevailed during the 1920s in the United States had a pronounced impact upon the Texas economy. During this period the farm population of the state was approximately 45 percent of the total population. This figure, however, did not reflect the full importance of farming, since the farm population census enumerated only those people actually living on farms and excluded the many thousands of farm laborers living in villages and towns and the large group of landlords who derived their income directly from agricultural operations though they lived in cities. According to the *Economic Survey of Texas*, published in 1928 by Southwestern Bell Telephone Company, agriculture was the "background and support" of the great majority of cities and towns in the state in spite of the presence of lumbering, oil, and manufacturing industries.[3]

Cotton accounted for about 70 percent of the total crop acreage and approximately the same percentage of farm cash income of the state as a whole. By 1900 Texas led the country in cotton production, accounting for more than one fourth of the national total. At that time some 36.7 percent of all land under cultivation was in cotton. By the 1920s Texas had assumed an even more prominent position: the state then produced about one third of the nation's cotton and one fifth of the world's output. The *Texas Almanac* for 1928 assessed the significance of cotton in the Texas economy as follows: "It is a guess, but a conservative guess, that 70 percent of the population of the state are dependent primarily upon cotton for a living."[4]

Table 7

Approximate Farm Cash Income in Texas from Specified Products
Selected Years in the 1920s
(In millions of dollars)

	1923-1925	1925-1926	1926-1927	1927-1928
Cotton	599.0	478.0	409.0	466.5
Wheat	14.5	5.9	31.0	19.5
Other cereals	22.2	14.4	22.5	17.6
Fruits and vegetables	21.0	22.3	24.0	25.5
Other crops	12.7	11.4	12.0	16.0
Cattle	70.3	73.7	67.0	70.0
Other livestock	38.3	35.8	41.3	40.0
Animal products	50.0	52.4	53.5	59.5
Total	828.0	693.9	663.3	714.6

Source: Southwestern Bell Telephone Company, *Economic Survey of Texas, 1928.*

Most of the people deriving their living from agriculture other than cotton production were dependent upon cattle, other livestock, and animal products, which in aggregate accounted for about 20 percent of total farm income from 1923 through 1928. Beef cattle alone accounted for about 10 percent of all farm income, and slaughtering and meat packing was the eighth largest manufacturing industry in Texas, employing some 4 percent of the wage earners. Because of the dominance of cotton and cattle and other livestock and animal products, the Texas economy was extremely vulnerable to fluctuations in their prices.

Though the total decline in wholesale prices in the United States during the 1920-1921 recession was 56 percent, in Texas the decline in the average prices received by farmers was much more severe. Cotton prices, which had reached a high point in March 1920 of 36.2 cents per pound, fell to 9.2 cents per pound by April 1921—a precipitous decline of 74.6 percent. The decline in cattle prices was nearly as severe. From its high in May 1919 of $8.40 per hundredweight the price fell to a low of $3.60 per hundredweight in December 1921, or by 57.1 percent. The index of prices received by Texas farmers for all crops fell 71.4 percent from April 1920 to April 1921, while the index for all livestock and livestock products decreased 47.3 percent from December 1919 to July 1921 (see table 8).

A. J. Lewis, attorney and chairman of the board of the Jefferson State Bank, San Antonio, and former office counsel in the Department of Banking in the 1920s, provided the authors with the following recollection of the break in cotton and cattle prices in 1920:

My uncle Bud Barrett owned a small cotton farm on the west bank of the Brazos River about 15 miles up the river from Waco, Texas. He was conservative and saving in his way of life. Prior to World War I, he had been accustomed to selling his cotton each year when it was picked from the fields. But in 1914 the prices went down to new lows (around 7 cents per pound), below production costs, and he decided to hold his bales of cotton from the market by leaving them in the family farmyard; then the clouds of war appeared, and the prices began to soar. In 1919 cotton reached the staggering price of nearly 45 cents per pound. However, after 1919 the price of cotton fell and fell and fell; yet Uncle Bud still held on, hoping (and probably praying) that the price would again turn upward. Alas, in despair and desperation, he finally sold in 1921 for less than 8 cents per pound.

My father, who owned a six-hundred-acre farm and ranch in the Bosque River Valley, free and clear of debt, had a large number of steers which he hoped to sell at the end of the feeding season for a nice profit; he suffered the saddest financial experience of his life. The fat cattle market also drastically broke in 1921, when his steers were not quite ready for market, and his hope for a nice profit suddenly changed to a staggering loss, so great that he turned his farm over to the bank to pay his feed debts. Thousands of small operators like Uncle Bud and my father suffered the same fate, and many were wholly unable to pay their bank debts. There were also great numbers of wealthy livestock operators (like the Dobies, the Russells, the Jenningses) who had for years been accustomed to raising and/or buying steers in Texas by the thousands and then shipping them to the Osage and Blue Stem grazing pastures in Oklahoma and Kansas for fattening, experiencing

Table 8

Average Prices Received by Texas Farmers, 1919-1939

Year	Cotton	Wheat	Rice	Corn	All crops	Beef cattle	Hogs	Sheep	All livestock and livestock products
1919	34.40	2.04	5.58	1.34	252	7.90	15.50	9.70	193
1920	17.30	1.09	2.47	0.90	242	7.20	12.40	9.10	181
1921	16.80	1.03	2.18	0.60	106	4.70	6.90	4.65	120
1922	22.00	0.98	2.22	0.84	155	4.35	7.10	5.50	116
1923	27.80	1.14	2.49	1.04	209	4.25	6.80	6.20	120
1924	23.00	1.57	2.98	1.21	207	4.15	7.00	6.30	122
1925	20.30	1.15	3.36	1.14	183	4.70	10.10	7.40	137
1926	12.70	1.26	2.56	0.70	133	5.30	11.50	7.00	143
1927	20.10	1.16	1.98	0.76	133	6.40	9.60	7.20	145
1928	17.60	1.21	2.02	0.85	153	8.00	8.10	8.10	167
1929	16.90	0.94	2.31	0.90	145	8.00	8.30	7.70	167
1930	9.60	0.73	1.78	0.73	108	6.10	7.80	3.95	135
1931	5.60	0.36	1.20	0.35	66	4.50	6.20	3.30	97
1932	6.20	0.33	0.98	0.30	50	3.30	3.40	2.35	71
1933	9.90	0.74	1.80	0.55	67	3.10	3.25	2.55	72
1934	12.50	0.78	1.84	0.83	97	3.15	3.90	3.10	81
1935	10.00	0.84	1.60	0.53	101	4.90	7.30	3.00	110
1936	11.80	1.00	1.93	0.91	95	5.00	8.30	4.80	117
1937	8.40	0.96	1.58	0.65	96	5.70	8.60	5.30	124
1938	8.20	0.57	1.53	0.44	69	5.40	7.20	4.10	111
1939	8.70	0.76	1.73	0.55	73	6.20	6.20	4.55	116

Note: Cotton—cents per pound; wheat—dollars per bushel; rice—dollars per hundredweight; corn—dollars per bushel; all crops—index numbers (1910-1914=100); beef cattle, hogs, and sheep—dollars per hundredweight; all livestock and livestock products—index numbers (1910-1914=100).

Source: *Prices Received by Texas Farmers and Price Index Numbers, 1910-1958* (College Station, Texas: Texas Agricultural Experiment Station, December 1958).

good profits each year from 1910 to 1920. But steer prices likewise tobogganed in 1921, almost overnight as it were. These big operators perhaps fell harder than the smaller operators, because they had farther to fall and more money to lose, and had more deficit indebtedness thrust upon them. Bankruptcies and debt compromises were rampant in 1921 and 1922; and of course the banks and loan companies suffered greatly too because they were holding the deficit bags.[5]

Although conditions were severe in Texas during the latter part of 1920 and all of 1921, in the spring of 1922 there were signs that the economy was recovering. As a result of the improved economic climate and renewed confidence, the Texas economy was stronger in 1923 and 1924. By January 1924 crop prices, as measured by the index of prices received by Texas farmers for all crops, were only 16 percent below their prerecession high. Livestock prices had not fared as well, but nevertheless the general economic climate was improved. Unfortunately, this improvement was short-lived.

Cotton prices peaked in 1923 and then declined gradually through 1926. From a level of 32.3 cents per pound in January 1924, the price fell persistently until it reached a low in December 1926 of 9.6 cents per pound, only 0.4 cents per pound above the 1920-1921 nadir.

The price collapse in 1926 was the result of overproduction—the 1926 crop being the largest on record before or since. The ultimate effect of the price collapse was to reduce the value of the crop to $304 million from $385 million in 1925 and $554 million in 1924. With the majority of the people of Texas dependent upon cotton for their livelihood, the overproduction of 1926 was a disaster.

Conditions improved in some sections of the state in 1927. The cotton crop was 1.3 million bales less than in the previous year and prices rebounded to the 1925 level. Much of the reduction in the crop, however, was due to disease and insect infestations in the blackland belt, the most productive and highly concentrated cotton-growing region in Texas. The 1928 crop was second in yield only to that of 1926, and as a result prices declined to disappointing levels. The 1929 crop, on the other hand, was the poorest on record since 1921, yet prices were even lower than in 1928.

The averages for cattle prices moved somewhat contrary to the cotton averages. In relation to the highs of 1919 and 1920, cattle prices remained extremely depressed even during the economic recovery that occurred during 1923 and 1924. Some improvement was evident in 1925 and 1926, but the 1926 average was still only about two thirds that of 1919. However, in 1927 the average price rose almost 21 percent from the previous year, and in 1928 and 1929 beef cattle prices were approximately equivalent to the prerecession levels.

The price indexes of all crops and all livestock and livestock products indicate that Texas agricultural prices were generally depressed from 1921 through 1929, in spite of the crop index improvement in 1923 and 1924 and the livestock index improvement in 1928 and 1929. The 1920-1921 recession, persistent depression of agricultural prices, and localized adverse economic conditions in some sectors of the state created a generally unfavorable business and economic climate during much of the 1920-1929 period in Texas. As a result, many Texas banks experienced substantial hardships, and sizable numbers of them did not survive.

State Bank Liquidations in the Twenties

The sharp break in crop and livestock prices during the 1920-1921 recession had a severe impact upon Texas banks, particularly the state banks, most of which served rural areas. The majority of the banks found their portfolios laden with frozen crop and livestock loans, and in most cases substantial losses were sustained. As a result, a rash of liquidations, both voluntary and involuntary, occurred in the bank fiscal years ending on August 31 of both 1921 and 1922 (see table 6, page 94).

The impact of the 1920-1921 recession was not felt until the fall of 1920, the beginning of the 1921 fiscal year in banking. Consequently, the liquidation rate (percentage of total banks liquidated each year) for fiscal 1921 shows a sharp rise from that of the previous year. The full impact of the recession on state bank liquidations did not occur until fiscal 1922, when the liquidation rate reached an unprecedented high of 7.62 percent.

Most of the liquidations reflected in this calculation, however, occurred during the first half of fiscal 1922, which ended February 28; only six of the thirty-five failures during 1922 took place after that date.

By the spring of 1922 banking conditions were considerably improved in Texas. This improvement continued throughout 1923. In May 1923 Commissioner J. L. Chapman remarked:

During the past twelve months we have had only ten banks to close that really failed. About one and one-fourth percent of the whole number, and today the banks are in stronger position than for three years. But very few, less than one-half of them, have failed on account of economic conditions; and as the weak and inefficient bankers, together with the dissipater and defaulter, are rapidly being eliminated, we hope to soon purge the system of all the objectionable elements that tend to weaken and embarrass the system. With strenuous efforts and cooperation from the good bankers and with continuous supervision, already in vogue, carried out to completion, within a year failures should seldom occur.

Out of 980 banks, we only have 18 that are under severe criticism, and they are under strict surveillance. Out of the 18 referred to, we hope, with the good prospects now in sight, that practically all of them will stand and not be in our hands for liquidation. Less than a half dozen are in immediate danger, and with the nursing we are giving them, we hope to keep them all going.[6]

The reduction in bank failures referred to by Commissioner Chapman is evidenced in the lower liquidation rates for 1923 and 1924. In spite of the reduction, however, the rates in 1923 and 1924 still remained considerably higher than during prerecession days. The liquidation rate rose sharply in 1925, from 4.99 percent in 1924 to a historical high of 17.10 percent in 1925, and in 1926 it still remained above all pre-1925 levels. In fact, the average number of liquidations per year during the "prosperous" years, 1923-1929, was seventy-three, considerably higher than the average of thirty per year recorded during the 1920-1921 recession.

Table 9

Commercial Bank Failures in the United States and Texas, 1920-1939

Year ended December 31	United States—all banks			Texas—state banks		
	Failures	Banks as of June 30	Failure rate[a]	Failures	Average number of banks[b]	Failure rate[a]
1920	155	28,485	0.54	8	967	0.83
1921	505	29,201	1.73	33	1,008	3.27
1922	366	28,704	1.28	21	998	2.10
1923	646	28,531	2.26	14	965	1.45
1924	775	27,745	2.79	23	942	2.44
1925	618	27,258	2.27	47	883	5.32
1926	967	26,622	3.67	33	808	4.08
1927	669	27,061	2.47	38	765	4.97
1928	498	26,213	1.90	36	730	4.93
1929	659	25,330	2.60	11	706	1.56
1930	1,350	24,079	5.61	18	677	2.66
1931	2,293	22,071	10.39	46	624	7.37
1932	1,453	19,163	7.58	23	567	4.06
1933	2,428	14,624	17.29	16	515	3.11
1934	57	15,894	0.04	2	475	0.42
1935	34	16,053	0.02	3	451	0.67
1936	44	15,803	0.03	6	434	1.38
1937	59	15,580	0.04	5	421	1.19
1938	55	15,341	0.04	--	411	--
1939	42	15,146	0.03	4	401	1.00

[a] Percentage of total banks that failed each year.
[b] Arithmetic mean of the number of banks in operation at the beginning of the year and the number of banks in operation at the end of the year (as of June 30).

Sources: *Board of Governors of the Federal Reserve System, Banking and Monetary Statistics* (Washington, D.C.: Government Printing Office, 1943), p. 283; official records of the Banking Department of Texas.

Bank Failures

Between September 1, 1920, and December 31, 1929, 262 state banks failed in Texas—an average of about 31 per year. From the inception of the state banking system in August 1905 through August 31, 1920, only 27 state banks had failed, approximately 2 per annum.

Although bank failures in Texas between September 1, 1920, and the end of 1929 were at shockingly high levels and the failure rate in Texas was somewhat higher than in the entire United States, the trends in Texas and the country as a whole showed striking similarities. In both the United States and Texas the failure rate (percentage of total banks that failed each year) rose significantly in 1921, then declined somewhat in 1922. In Texas the decline from the 1921 level continued into 1923 and a reversal began in 1924, whereas in the United States the upturn occurred a year earlier. During the "prosperous" 1923-1926 period the average failure rate in the United States and Texas was actually higher than the average rate for the 1920-1922 period. For the United States the average rate for 1923-1926 was 2.73 percent, while the rate for 1920-1922 was 1.19 percent. For Texas the average rates for the respective periods were 3.25 percent and 2.09 percent.

Undoubtedly the sharp increase in failures that occurred in 1921 and 1922 in both the United States and Texas was induced by the brief but pronounced economic recession of 1920-1921. According to Studenski and Krooss, the depressed agricultural prices occurring concurrently with the recession were the most significant causative factor in the failures.[7] In their opinion it was the persistence of unfavorable agricultural conditions after the recession and during most of the 1920s that accounted for the high failure rates from 1923 to 1926. This conclusion is corroborated by the statistics for failures, which indicate that the majority of the commercial-bank suspensions in the United States during the 1920-1929 period involved smaller banks concentrated in the agricultural areas of the West and South. Towns of less than 2,500 inhabitants suffered 80 percent of the total failures, and approximately one half of these were in towns of less than 500 people. The observed trends are not surprising, since in the West and South chartering restrictions had been lenient and supervision was generally lax. This laxity had allowed far too many banks, as well as banks with inadequate capital, particularly in the rural areas.

As previously noted, farm conditions in Texas during the decade of the twenties were at least as unfavorable as in the nation generally, and perhaps worse. It is noteworthy, though, that over 20 percent of the total failures of state banks in Texas between 1919 and the end of 1926 involved banks in the oil fields. These failures, induced by adverse local conditions, partially explain the higher failure rate experienced in Texas than in the United States between 1920 and 1929.

State bank failures in Texas during the 1920s usually did not occur from a single cause but instead resulted from a combination of factors. These factors or causes of failure may be separated into three categories of influence. First, underlying factors—such as laws, policies, and the economic structure of the state—that were indigenous to Texas or to the Texas state banking system tended to debilitate or increase the vulnerability of the system. Second, adverse economic conditions indirectly caused bank failures. These conditions affected the entire economy, one or more sectors of the economy, or a local area. Finally, internal problems or heavy deposit withdrawals or both were usually the immediate causes of bank failures. The internal problems that caused failures were mainly incompetent management and dishonest management and employees; both of these maladies existed in some of the banks that failed.

Underlying Regulatory Factors and
Structural Conditions Debilitating the State Banking System

As in other states, early chartering laws and policies, along with frequently lax supervision of state banks, created in Texas a banking system with some extremely weak institutions.

Too Many Banks

As noted previously, the banking laws in Texas before 1913 did not provide adequate means to restrict the number of new banks chartered in the state. This was clearly recognized by some of the most prominent bankers, and, largely through the efforts of Commissioner Ben L. Gill, the law was changed in 1913.

Before the revision of the law, the chartering function was the responsibility of the secretary of state, and the State Banking Board was vested with little power to restrict the organization of new banks. The only function that the board exercised was to inquire into the worth and character of those who would be the initial stockholders and the ability, reputation, and previous record of the individuals who would be the initial officers of the new bank if it were, in fact, chartered. When the State Banking Board was given the power in 1913 to exercise its judgment on charter applications and public necessity was required as a prerequisite for a new state bank, a legacy of problems arising from the authorization of far too many banks already existed: nine hundred bank charters had been granted by them.

The Depositors Guaranty Law

Among the bankers and officials who held that the Depositors Guaranty Law also encouraged the organization of too many banks, as well as unsound and illicit banking practices, was R. L. Thornton, president of the Mercantile Bank and Trust Company of Dallas. In 1925, while he was also serving as president of the Texas Bankers Association, he wrote in an article appearing in the September issue of the *Texas Bankers Record*:

It is my judgment and opinion, based upon a pretty close-up view and study of its operation, that the system created too many banks and too few bankers. Many men had engaged in the banking business, because the Guaranty Fund would assist them in getting deposits, but the test showed that, while that was to some extent true, it did not endow them at the same time with the ability and experience necessary to handle and properly conduct the business of banking. So, failure after failure occurred. It also showed that many unscrupulous men had entered the business for numerous reasons, the principal one of which was that the public was protected by the good and solvent banks and this offered a splendid opportunity to embezzlers and pilferers . . . [8]

Low Minimum Capital Requirements

While the Guaranty Fund Law may have encouraged the organization of too many banks, it was the $10,000 minimum capital requirement that enabled persons of quite limited means to organize banks.

As early as 1907 some prominent bankers recognized that the minimum capital requirement of $10,000 was too low. W. F. McCaleb, in a speech before the 1907 Texas Bankers Association convention, vigorously attacked the low capital requirement for state banks. The dangers enumerated by McCaleb were soon widely acknowledged by important Texas bankers and by regulatory officials. According to the March 1912 edition of the *Texas Bankers Journal*, Commissioner Ben L. Gill had concluded that the minimum capital requirement should be $25,000.[9] He asserted that the small banks with capital funds of only $10,000 were a constant source of concern to the department, largely because such institutions found it impossible to attract and retain first-class managers.

In the same year, Texas banker M. L. Riddle suggested in a speech to the Panhandle Bankers Association that the $10,000 minimum capital requirement threatened the entire system.[10] Riddle believed that the low minimum capital requirement had allowed in earlier years the establishment of banks in settled, economically sound communities that needed a bank but that could not afford the $25,000 capital required for a national bank. But in his opinion times had changed. All the communities needing banks had now been provided with them. He voiced concern that the low capital requirement in Texas was attracting undesirable individuals—mostly promoters—from other parts of the country.

Unfortunately, the minimum capital requirement was not increased until 1923, when it was raised to $17,500. As in the case of the revision of the chartering procedure, by the time the capital requirement was raised most of the damage had been done.

Inefficient and Lax Supervision

While Texas bankers generally believed that the state possessed one of the better banking departments and examining forces in the country, they were aware of some weaknesses. One already noted was that the department of insurance and the department of banking were combined under a single administrative head. Moreover, the commissioner was appointed by the governor for a term of two years coinciding with the governor's term. By the time a commissioner became conditioned to the job, a new governor would come into office and a new commissioner would be appointed. These factors caused a high turnover in the office. Commissioner J. L. Chapman criticized the frequent changes in the office as "very detrimental to the administration of the law."[11]

The records of the Department of Insurance and Banking revealed frequent changes not only in the commissioner's office but also in the examining staff. The turnover in the examining staff caused the most serious problems. According to Ed Hall, commissioner from January 20, 1921, to August 31, 1922, the constant turnover in that position "seriously handicapped" the efficiency of the department.[12] He felt, however, that this condition could be overcome by sufficient remuneration. Commissioner Hall also stated that the physical handicaps under which the department worked were substantial. The departments occupied cramped quarters, and the equipment available to them was inadequate in both quantity and quality.

Most of the deficiencies of the Department of Insurance and Banking and in the supervision of the state banks were ultimately attributable to the same basic cause—inadequate appropriations from the state legislature. Even at its birth the state banking system was victimized by the parsimony of the legislature. It was for reasons of economy that the supervision of state banks was delegated to the Department of Agriculture, Insurance, Statistics, and History instead of to a separate department of banking. The lack of foresight displayed by the legislature in failing to fund adequately the Department of Insurance and Banking most certainly hampered its effectiveness and thus rendered the state banking system more prone to sizable numbers of failures than it would have been otherwise.

Lack of Diversity in the Texas Economy

While there were basic weaknesses in the banking laws and the administration of those laws, the condition that made the state banks of Texas extremely sensitive to economic adversity in the 1920s was the dependence of the economy upon agriculture in general and cotton in particular. General business conditions in the state from year to year were determined primarily by the return that the farmer received from the cotton crop, a return that was subject to extreme fluctuations. Since the dominance of cotton in the Texas economy was at its high point during the 1920s, the problems associated with the preponderance of one crop were also more severe then than at any other time in the history of the state. In every year during the 1920s except for 1923 and 1924 the cotton industry in Texas experienced difficulties.

A basic problem in Texas, and for that matter in the entire South, was the overproduction of cotton, which adversely influenced its price and thus the return to the farmer. Under these conditions, anything that tended to reduce the total crop—disease, insects, or drought—was generally considered a blessing. However, these destructive forces were disastrous for the individuals directly affected and, instead of improving the situation, tended to result in the long run in larger crops and lower prices. This was true because of the necessity to plant larger crops in future years in order to compensate for the loss sustained as a result of these calamities. It apparently did not occur to the cotton farmers that they were thereby increasing their losses.

The solution to the farmers' problem, in the opinion of most experts, was acreage reduction through diversification. Perhaps more than any other group, including the agricultural interests, the bankers of Texas strongly urged diversification of the farming industry. For many of the bankers, there was hardly a

Table 10

Texas Cotton Acreage, Production, and Value, 1920-1940
(Thousands)

Year	Acres harvested	Bales produced	Value
1920	12,323	4,345	$286,770
1921	10,426	2,198	176,939
1922	11,963	3,222	378,585
1923	14,851	4,340	659,680
1924	17,049	4,949	554,228
1925	17,336	4,163	385,007
1926	17,749	5,628	303,912
1927	15,689	4,352	419,968
1928	16,887	5,105	446,687
1929	16,875	3,940	315,200
1930	16,138	4,037	189,739
1931	14,754	5,320	148,960
1932	13,334	4,500	139,500
1933	11,069	4,250	195,500
1934	10,097	2,401	150,062
1935	10,657	2,950	161,102
1936	11,597	2,933	173,487
1937	12,539	5,154	217,490
1938	9,153	3,125	129,688
1939	8,520	2,846	124,104
1940	8,523	3,285	147,825

Source: *The Texas Almanac and State Industrial Guide, 1941-1942* (Dallas: A. H. Belo, 1940), p. 207.

phase of their operations that was not affected by adverse cotton conditions. The impact was particularly severe in the case of the state banks, since most of them served rural Texas.

The endeavors of Texas bankers to secure agricultural reforms-crop diversification in particular—typically involved group action, usually under the direction of the Texas Bankers Association. In addition, however, occasional attempts to promote reform were initiated by individual banks and bankers of their own volition and were confined to local areas.

Economic Conditions As Factors That Induced Bank Failures

While the establishment of too many banks, low minimum capital requirements, laxity in supervision, and a lack of diversity in the economy tended to weaken the state banks, failures were usually induced by economic adversity that affected either the entire state, some sector of the economy, or a localized area.

During the 1920s, the state banks failed in all parts of the state, but there were particularly heavy concentrations of failures in five areas. These areas comprised the following counties:

1. Stephens, Eastland, Comanche, and Young counties in North Central Texas;
2. Grayson, Hunt, and other counties in the northeast;
3. Matagorda, Harris, Brazoria, and Chambers counties on the Gulf Coast;
4. Hidalgo and Cameron counties in the lower Rio Grande valley; and
5. The counties in the blackland belt in Central Texas.

Between November 1920 and January 1927, seventy-two failures, or about 41 percent of all failures, took place in the first four areas listed above. Most of these were caused by adverse conditions in the oil fields, crop failures, and depressed farm prices, together with a general lack of diversity in the loan portfolios of the banks.

Bank failures in 1927, 1928, and 1929 were heavily concentrated in the blackland belt, North Central Texas, and

Northeast Texas. In fact, over 75 percent of all state bank failures in Texas during the late twenties occurred there. The principal disturbances that induced these failures were the overproduction of cotton in 1926 and the consequent precipitous decline in cotton prices; the poor cotton crop in 1927, resulting from insect infestations and disease; the depressed cotton prices of 1928; and the low-yielding cotton crop of 1929, which was caused by a combination of drought, disease, and insect activity.

Another factor that accounted for a large number of bank failures after September 1, 1927, was a change in banking department policy concerning the closing of insolvent banks. Upon assuming the office of commissioner of banking on September 1, 1927, James Shaw was distressed to find numerous insolvent banks open and operating. To remedy the situation, he instigated a "clean-up campaign" that resulted in the closing of a large number of state banks during the 1928 fiscal year and the fall of 1929. During Commissioner Shaw's first year in office 30 banks were reorganized, with new capital of $1,575,500, and 40 more were either taken over by other banks or liquidated. In aggregate, $7.6 million of losses was written off and $3.2 million in capital was paid into 449 banks during the year.[13]

Decline in Farm Prices

In four of the five areas of the state in which there were heavy concentrations of state bank failures, the failures were precipitated by the depressed price and the poor condition of one or two agricultural products that dominated the economy of that particular area. The banks involved had one common shortcoming: a failure to diversify their loans, or at least to diversify them as fully as they could have.

One of the areas referred to above with a heavy concentration of bank failures consisted of the counties of Northeast Texas; they formed a rectangle with Johnson County in the southwest corner and the Red River and the Texas-Louisiana border as the northern and eastern boundaries. This area was predominantly cotton country and included six of the seventeen most productive cotton counties in the state—Collin, Dallas, Grayson, Fannin,

Kaufmann, and Hunt. Of the thirty counties located in this part of Texas, all but eight had more than 100,000 acres planted in cotton in 1925, and six of the eight—Freeman, Titus, Morris, Camp, Marion, and Gregg counties—had little land area. The region had the lowest concentration of livestock per county of any section of the state except for the far west and southwest.

There is a relatively close correlation between the incidence of state bank failures in Northeast Texas and fluctuations in the price of cotton. The first state bank to fail in this area was the First State Bank of Beattie, in Upshur County, which closed on December 1, 1920. The price of cotton also fell to a five-year low in this month, having declined from 34.0 cents per pound in July 1920 to 12.1 cents per pound. In the twenty months beginning December 1920 and ending July 1922, during which the price of cotton was depressed, sixteen banks failed in this area. This represented 29.6 percent of all state bank failures in Texas during the period. From July 1922 to November 1925, or for forty months, the price of cotton remained relatively high. During this period there were seventeen state bank failures in Northeast Texas, but this only accounted for 20.9 percent of the state total. In November 1925 the price of cotton began to decline, and the decline continued into the next year.

The "misfortune of 1926"—the largest cotton crop in the history of the state—caused the decline in cotton prices to accelerate after late summer of 1926, and by December of that year the price reached a low of 9.6 cents per pound, the lowest level since April of 1921. On November 15, 1925, the First State Bank of Campbell, Hunt County, closed and in the next twelve months another fifteen banks failed in the area. These failures represented 41.0 percent of all state bank suspensions during the thirteen months.

The combined state bank failures that occurred in Northeast Texas during the two periods of depressed cotton prices accounted for 34.4 percent of total state bank failures in Texas during the corresponding months. Perhaps more significant, however, is the fact that, of these thirty-two failures, twenty-one (or 65.6 percent) were in the six counties that had planted over 300,000 acres of cotton each in 1925.

Another area of Texas where there was a concentration of state bank failures was Hidalgo and Cameron counties in the lower Rio Grande valley. In Hidalgo County, truck farming was the principal industry, with tomatoes, lettuce, cabbage, and spinach being the main products. Citrus fruits were gaining importance but at this time could not have been considered one of the principal industries. Cameron County, on the other hand, was one of the most productive citrus areas in the United States, with grapefruit being the dominant crop. Truck farming was also important in Cameron County, though second to citrus fruits. Livestock was not important in either county, but cotton was a significant crop.

The first bank failure in Hidalgo County occurred on March 14, 1921, and it was followed by two more failures that year. There was another failure in Hidalgo County in 1923 and one in each of the following two years in Cameron County. Unfortunately, reliable data on the prices of truck crops and citrus fruits, which might help to explain the circumstances of the bank failures, are not available for the years before 1925. However, a study by Findley Weaver in 1926 concluded that the concentration of failures in Hidalgo and Cameron counties was caused by "rapid land development of that section" and "the dependence of the section on truck farming and the production of citrus fruit, an industry that requires a large capital investment in land."[14] Although Weaver did not elaborate on his conclusion, it is probable that much of the land development had been bank-financed when land prices were extremely inflated. During the 1920-1921 recession, prices broke and borrowers were unable to liquidate their crop production loans to make payments on their land. As a result, the banks, which were forced to foreclose and take possession of land that was worth far less than its original loan value, incurred severe losses. The failures in 1923, 1924, and 1925 cannot be so easily explained, since data on price movements of the principal commodities are not available and since nothing about the prices can be concluded from the composite index of crop prices (their relative influence upon the index would have been negligible). It is possible, of course, that these bank failures stemmed from the effects of the depressed prices during the 1920-1921 recession.

A concentration of state bank failures also occurred in Matagorda, Brazoria, and other coastal prairies counties. In these

Table 11

Causes of State Bank Failures in Texas, 1920-1925

Cause	\multicolumn{6}{c}{Number of failures per cause by years}	Total failures per cause	Percentage of total to banks in group, 1920-1925
	1920	1921	1922	1923	1924	1925		
I. Adverse economic conditions								
1. Decline in cotton price and poor cotton crops	--	1	4	6	4	17	32	35.6
2. Decline in cattle or wool price	1	2	1	1	4	5	14	15.5
3. Decline in rice price	--	--	--	2	--	3	5	5.5
4. Decline in land values	--	1	--	--	1	1	3	3.3
5. Oil deflation	--	8	3	--	3	2	16	17.8
6. Town too small to support bank or too much competition	1	3	1	2	1	9	17	18.9
II. Poor management								
7. Excessive credit extensions to certain individuals or interests	--	2	2	2	1	5	12	13.3
8. Poor credit policies	1	7	7	6	16	20	57	63.3
III. Mismanagement								
9. Defalcation by officers	4	6	7	7	6	8	38	42.2
10. Illegal loans to officers or directors	1	1	--	--	3	3	8	8.8
11. Speculation by officers	2	10	3	3	8	3	29	32.2
IV. Other problems								
12. Heavy withdrawals	--	--	--	--	--	1	1	1.1
13. Death or sickness of officers	--	--	--	--	--	1	1	1.1
Failed banks used in study group	5	15	12	10	17	31	90	
Actual failures each year	8	33	21	14	23	47	146	

Source: Findley Weaver, "State Banking in Texas" (M.A. thesis, University of Texas, 1926), p. 189. Numbers of failures for each cause are derived from Weaver's presentation of percentages for each cause of total bank failures per year. More than one cause of failure was listed for each bank.

counties rice and beef were the dominant agricultural products and cotton was of negligible importance. Beef cattle and rice prices, like the price of cotton, plummeted during the 1920-1921 recession; unlike the price of cotton, they failed to show any significant recovery at any time through 1926. During the entire period, sixteen state banks failed in the coastal prairies. All but one of the banks were located in rural areas and were thus heavily dependent on the rice and beef cattle industries. Undoubtedly the failures were in large measure induced by the sharp decline and continued low price of these products. Another contributory factor was the decline of the West Columbia and Damon Mound oil fields in Brazoria County and the Humble and Goose Creek fields in Harris County. The problems in the Brazoria County oil fields probably had a greater impact since the decline of West Columbia and Damon Mound began in the early 1920s, whereas the dissipation of the fields in Harris County was already well under way at the beginning of the decade. Depressed beef cattle and rice prices only aggravated the deterioration of local economies in the oil towns of Humble, Goose Creek, West Columbia, and Damon, and that in turn created the environment that spawned several bank suspensions during the period between 1920 and 1926.

Banks located in all of rural Texas in the 1920s felt the strains of the poor economic conditions that prevailed, and the areas discussed above were undoubtedly not the only ones affected by depressed agricultural prices. If material in Findley Weaver's study is accurate, as many as half of the state bank failures from the beginning of 1920 through 1925 may have been induced by depressed agricultural prices and poor crops (see table 11). This figure does not seem unreasonable since at the time Texas was heavily dependent on agriculture and the great majority of the state banks had rural locations.

Oil-Town Adversities

One factor that led to many bank failures in 1920-1921 and for several years thereafter was the oil boom, which was at its zenith in Texas during these years. Between 1918 and 1925 Texas advanced from a very low-ranking position in the production of oil to the position of third among the states in the union. During this time there was a rush to the oil fields of Texas analogous to the gold rush to California in the previous century. With this rush, economic and social problems inconceivable today developed in the boom towns.

Before oil was discovered in November 1920 Mexia was a typical country town with a population of about 4,000, according to a speech in 1925 by the Mexia banker Noel Hollingsworth.[15] There were two banks, with aggregate capitalization of $100,000 and aggregate deposits of $1,000,000. In May 1921 the first large gusher was brought in. On August 31, 1921, a Western Oil Corporation well spouted a geyser that rose more than one hundred feet into the air and produced 18,000 barrels per day. Within one week the population of Mexia increased from 4,000 to 40,000. Business boomed. Actually, the oil rush was preceded by a leasing campaign, which had brought a great deal of new money and a considerable measure of prosperity to the town. This in itself had been overwhelming to the simple townfolk of Mexia. In addition the influx of people brought on a fivefold to tenfold increase in business. The banks and business houses did not have time to adjust to the new conditions, for as soon as they had increased their facilities and employment the boom was over. It must be remembered that there was no control over drilling or production of oil at this time in Texas. In the Mexia field about 575 wells were drilled within six months, and production of oil peaked at 35.1 million barrels in 1922. Although production had hit a new high, the frantic drilling of new wells had all but ended by January 1922; as a result, the boom also ended. The people disappeared just as quickly as they had come, and business returned to its normal level. It was estimated that the great crowds stayed from 120 to 140 days. During the cycle the deposits of the Pendergast-Smith National Bank had increased from $500,000 to $3,000,000 and then declined to $1,200,000. In 1923 oil production declined to 20.1 million barrels, and in 1926 only 5.6 million barrels were produced in the Mexia field.

Some of the serious problems encountered by the typical oil-town bank, any one or any combination of which could have led to its insolvency, were outlined by Hollingsworth. To begin with, the vast increase in business occasioned by the boom necessitated new bank employees. Good, competent employees were hard to find, and many banks suffered "very disastrous experiences" in hiring helpers without proper inquiry into their character and past connections. Once new help was found, it was necessary to install new procedures in order to accommodate the increased volume of business. Failure to adopt a system accounting for every detail of the business resulted in the closing of numerous banks in the oil towns in the early 1920s.

The increased volume of business did not always result in increased profits for the bank. The adjustments required to handle the new business resulted in notably higher expenses. To offset this it was necessary for the bank to increase revenue by using the new deposits to acquire relatively high-yielding new loans and/or investments suitable for its portfolio. Unfortunately, the development of an oil field often did not give rise to sufficient demand for legitimate loans. The large majority of people following the oil boom were not worthy of credit, and those who were worthy had usually prearranged for financing elsewhere. In addition, oil field equipment once it left the warehouse proved practically worthless as collateral. To make matters worse, the established borrowing customers of the bank, in their sudden prosperity, did not need to borrow as heavily as before. And many of the old customers who did wish to borrow were found to have been afflicted with speculative fever. The only alternative left to the bank was to seek short-term, highly liquid investments such as call loans. Whatever avenue was sought, it had to provide adequate revenue and at the same time allow for almost immediate conversion to cash in order to meet heavy and sudden withdrawals should they occur.

In addition to the problems incidental to banking operations and management, bank officers and stockholders faced many temptations. The officers were all too often coaxed into making high-risk loans. The usual proposition provided that the bank officer would receive 50 percent of the profits. Another temptation with which the officers and stockholders were confronted was to sell the bank. Usually the offer came from "raiders" who misrepresented themselves as people of substantial means and adequate managerial skills. Upon securing control, the manipulator would place his notes and the notes of his friends in the bank, and they would all speculate in oil properties. Of course, when the boom ended and deposits began to decline, many of these notes could not be paid. The bank would fail and the former stockholders would be assessed by the state banking authorities (the twelve-month liability that existed from the date of sale of their stock was still in force at that time).

Fortunately, neither of the banks in Mexia failed. Banks in other oil-boom regions, however, did not enjoy the same good luck. From late 1920 through 1922 banks in Eastland and Stephens counties in West Texas were particularly hard hit. The first bank in the area to fail was the Leeray Guaranty State Bank on December 31, 1920. Banking department records reveal that an additional fifteen banks in these counties failed and were either reorganized or liquidated. These sixteen failures accounted for 29 percent of the total state bank failures in Texas during the period. The town of Ranger had had three state banks, one national bank, and one private bank, all of which closed. Every bank in Eastland failed, and there were other failures in the now practically unknown towns of Desdemona, Olden, Wayland, Necessity, and Caddo. In Eastland County only the First National Bank of Cisco and in Stephens County only the First National Bank of Breckenridge weathered the storm.

C. B. Sullivan, assistant general liquidating agent of the Department of Insurance and Banking from 1921 through 1924, described for the authors his experience as a young banker in the Stephens and Eastland county area:

After nearly two years of varied country bank experience (bookkeeper, messenger and janitor) in Oklahoma, I migrated to Texas in February of 1920 to accept employment in a newly organized national bank in the "boom town" of Necessity (originally called Cottonplant), between Ranger and Breckenridge, which then had 8,000 to 10,000 people within a radius of three or four miles; numerous "wide-open" saloons, dance halls, gambling halls, etc., and a Colt 38 or 45 in the belt under a crepe de chine or silk shirt was standard equipment. Rig builders, drillers, and "tool dressers" were paid $14 to $30 daily, and what a night was Saturday night! But, ham'n'eggs were a buck or more; "chock" beer (home brew) was four bits a bottle; a small "bowl and pitcher" room in a frame or galvanized 2-story hallway was $5 nightly, and other "necessities" were at corresponding levels. The boom in Necessity was short-lived and "my" bank (I was Cashier and managing officer, and the only active officer—several months before the vice president had walked out on me) was absorbed by First National Bank, Ranger, in early 1921, and that bank closed several months later. After about two weeks, I resumed my banking career (I was still a minor) in a Breckenridge bank which closed about 90 days thereafter. I don't think I was responsible because I was in the collection and exchange cage. This bank was merged with another local State bank in about 60 days, with the aid of the State Guaranty Fund (an advance of $300,000-$400,000); the merged bank closed late that year. After this fiasco I was fortunate enough to become an employee of the State Banking Department in Austin in the Liquidating Division. This was about the beginning of the end of the State Guaranty Fund.[16]

For the years 1918 through 1921 oil production in Eastland and Stephens counties exceeded that of any other field in Texas. From no production at all in 1916, aggregate production rose to 36.9 million barrels in 1921 but drastically declined to 19.7 million barrels the following year. Actually, the decline in the field began in 1920. Compounding the problems caused by the decline in production was the fall in the price of crude oil, which also began in 1920. The drop in agricultural prices brought on by the 1920-1921 recession was, of course, an aggravating influence in the severe business downturn in Eastland and Stephens counties.

Table 12

Oil Production in Eastland and Stephens Counties, 1917-1926
(Barrels)

Year	Eastland County	Stephens County
1917	93,053	36,219
1918	3,107,120	790,243
1919	22,396,665	10,514,216
1920	10,141,385	23,852,050
1921	5,887,420	31,037,710
1922	4,787,315	14,924,988
1923	3,764,085	10,062,055
1924	2,627,475	7,120,230
1925	3,710,990	5,729,035
1926	2,133,000	4,414,000

Source: *The Texas Almanac and State Industrial Guide, 1928* (Dallas: A. H. Belo, 1928), p. 182.

Table 13

Price of Crude Oil, United States, 1919-1924

Year	Average annual price (dollars per barrel)
1919	2.25
1920	3.44
1921	1.86
1922	1.78
1923	1.71
1924	1.84

Source: *Commerce Year Book, 1924* (Washington, D.C.: Government Printing Office, 1925), p. 194.

Some notable secondary factors contributed to the problem environment. In the first place, the Stephens-Eastland oil field was developed during the height of the war inflation, when credit was generally easy and prices rising. This condition caused great speculation and overdevelopment and as a result the readjustment process was very severe. Second, Eastland and Stephens counties were not really important producers of agricultural products, nor did they possess any other industries of significance. Consequently, there was no "secondary industry" to rely upon when oil production and oil prices began to decline.

The importance of the state bank failures in the "oil-towns," particularly with regard to the future of the Guaranty Fund, cannot be overestimated. This concentration of casualties occasioned "the beginning of the end of the State Guaranty Fund."[17]

Crop Failures

Crop failures have already been identified as a factor that contributed to some bank suspensions during the 1920s. Crop failures were generally caused by one or more of the following circumstances: drought, disease, and/or insect infestations. In addition to drought, the boll weevil, the bollworm, and root rot were the principal causes of cotton crop failure. Crop failures were generally not serious threats to banks, except in those areas where a single crop was dominant. There was only one year during the 1920s in which crop failures created serious economic problems throughout Texas—1921, when the cotton crop was greatly reduced by the boll weevil.[18] Total production fell from 4,345,282 bales in 1920 to 2,198,158 bales in 1921, or by about 50 percent. While some of the decrease in production was caused by a reduction in cotton acreage from 11,898,000 acres in 1920 to 10,745,000 acres in 1921, it was mainly caused by a poor crop, as indicated by the 43 percent reduction in yield per acre.

The bank-failure experience of four major cotton-producing counties in the blackland belt during and immediately following the 1921 crop failure is perhaps noteworthy. Between July 1921 and March 1922 four banks failed in Grayson County, and in April 1922 one bank failed in Johnson County. There were no failures during this period in Red River and Fannin counties. From the production figures and the statistics on bank failures, it appears that Grayson County suffered more severely than the other three counties. The reason for this was a pink bollworm infestation that ravaged the cotton crop in the county. Since the details of the failures in Grayson and Johnson counties in 1921 and 1922 are unknown, one cannot conclude that the bank suspensions were induced solely by the failure of the cotton crop. On the contrary, the extremely low price of cotton was certainly a contributing factor.

In addition to the cases noted, there were undoubtedly a few other isolated instances of crop failures leading to bank failures during the 1920s.

Other Economic Conditions That Induced Bank Failures

Other types of local economic crises occasionally led to bank failures in Texas. An illustration is provided by the case of the State Bank of Ratcliff, which closed on January 9, 1926, after the shutdown of the local sawmill.[19] A few years earlier, the town had been prosperous, but with the closing of the sawmill (owing to factors operating from outside the community) the citizens gradually departed until there was little business left for a bank.

Immediate Causes of Bank Failures

Incompetent Management and Dishonesty

Excerpts from speeches made by banking department officials and the results of one statistical study made in 1930 provide evidence that incompetent management and dishonesty were the major ultimate causes of bank failures during the 1920s.

Speaking before the state bank section of the Texas Bankers Association at the Association's annual convention in 1923, W. L. Peterson, general liquidating agent in the state Department of Insurance and Banking, identified the primary causes of bank failure from November 1, 1920, to that time as follows:

First, in importance, I should say that outright thievery, corrupt, illicit, and illegitimate banking practices are to blame. Second, I should say that economic conditions are responsible. Third, I think that reckless, injudicious advances of credit are to blame. Some of you may question the correctness of the first important cause as given by me. I tell you, however, ladies and gentlemen, that something must be done to stop these corrupt practices of high financing on the part of state bank officials.[20]

In a review of the effects of the Guaranty Fund, James Shaw, the banking commissioner in 1928, attributed bank failures to one or more of the following causes:

(1) incompetence of officers and directors; (2) excessive lines of credit to a few customers; (3) carrying speculative lines; (4) embezzlement by officers or employees.[21]

A report prepared by the banking commissioner in 1930 for the Federal Reserve Committee on Branch, Group, and Chain Banking specified the primary and contributing causes of 188 state bank failures in Texas between 1921 and 1930. Clark Warburton of the Federal Deposit Insurance Corporation noted in 1955 that incompetent management was either a primary or contributing cause of more than 90 percent of the failures included in the 1930 sample and that defalcation was a primary or contributing cause of almost a third of the failures.[22]

Incompetency and defalcations undoubtedly would have caused even greater casualties during the twenties had it not been for the substantial efforts of the Department of Banking to remove incapable and dishonest bankers from the state banking system. Commissioner J. L. Chapman described the measures taken in a talk before a state bankers' meeting in 1923.[23] To begin with, he said, the State Banking Board made a thorough investigation into the personnel associated with each new bank application in an effort to prevent undesirable persons from ever entering the banking business. Second, the examiners were instructed to investigate the management during examinations. Each examiner was required to report on a special sheet his opinion of the bank's management. If he found the management to be incompetent or inefficient, he was expected, before he left the bank, to suggest to the directors or demand of the directors the resignation of the officer. If he found irregularities, he was to require immediate removal of the man. If the irregularities, weaknesses, and inefficiencies were of minor importance, he was to make a full report, upon which appropriate action would be taken by the department "in the most discreet way." In Chapman's opinion most of the assessments levied against the Guaranty Fund banks were attributable to the "looter," "weak banker," and "inefficient banker" and once the system had been purged of these people, the heavy assessments would end.

The problem of removing the weak and dishonest bankers from the system was also a source of great concern to the bankers themselves. This was evidenced at the 1923 meeting of the state bank section of the Texas Bankers Association. At the suggestion of R. L. Thornton, president of the Mercantile Bank and Trust Company of Dallas, a "Guaranty Fund Association" was organized to aid the Department of Banking in its efforts to purge the state banking system of its undesirable elements.[24] The specific purpose of the establishment of the association was to raise $10,000 per year through assessment of the Guaranty Fund banks, to be used by the banking commissioner in the "prosecution of the law."

Commissioner Chapman declared that one of the obstacles with which the Department of Banking sometimes had to contend in attempting to remove an inept or even a dishonest bank official was the objection of the directors of the bank.²⁵ Usually their argument was that the official in question was a "drawing card" or a "money getter," and they feared that if he were removed deposits and business would slip away.

Another problem encountered by the department was the objection of some bankers to "rigid" examinations. Commissioner Chapman explained that in an effort to expel undesirable bankers from the system in 1923, they had conducted "very rigid examinations." As a result the department received much criticism, especially from the good bankers who complained that the examinations were "too exacting." In deference to the wishes of the strong bankers, the commissioner instructed the examiners to be more lenient with respect to the bankers who were above suspicion. But this proved unsatisfactory, since two or three of the banks believed to possess such management almost failed. Consequently, the policy was changed and all of the banks were subjected to "rigid" examinations.

Though the existence of some uncooperative bank officers and directors impaired the efforts of the Department of Banking to eliminate unscrupulous and incompetent bankers, the main problem appeared to be that the Guaranty Fund Law encouraged unsound and illicit banking practices. This view of the Guaranty Fund was taken by the prominent Dallas banker, R. L. Thornton, as indicated in another context. Banking Commissioner Austin's criticism of the Guaranty Fund in this regard was expressed as follows at the 1926 convention of the Texas Bankers Association:

The existence of the law has in itself invited weak and vicious banking methods. A number of banks have built up their business almost solely through the exploitation of the protection afforded the depositors by the Guaranty Fund. Many bankers have engaged in reckless and unsafe business methods of banking, upon the theory that if their banks should get into trouble, the Guaranty Fund would come along and contribute enough fresh capital to absorb their losses. A number of dishonest bankers have systematically stolen from their banks year after year and used the funds for personal transactions and speculative deals, knowing that if their banks failed, the Guaranty Fund would pay the depositors and there would be no demand upon the part of the depositors that these dishonest officials be punished. No stretch of the imagination is required to assess that the Guaranty Fund as it has been administered in Texas has been a constant premium upon dishonesty and criminal recklessness, and carelessness in the management of some of the banks.[26]

In *A Monetary and Banking History of Texas*, published in 1930 (just three years after the repeal of the Depositors Guaranty Law), Professor Avery Luvere Carlson also blamed the law for encouraging reckless banking methods. He wrote that "the immediate cause of these failures was the depression in the prices of cotton and other agricultural products. The fundamental cause was doubtless the unsound banking policies encouraged by the existence of the Depositors Guaranty Law, which provided a sort of mental insurance for depositors and encouraged reckless methods on the part of the management of numerous state banks."[27]

If the Depositors Guaranty Law did attract weak and unscrupulous bankers into the system, then its repeal would partially account for the alleged decrease in defalcations from the 1920s to the 1930s. That such a decrease did in fact occur cannot be confirmed by available statistics; however, according to the recollections of some of the individuals employed in the Department of Banking in the 1920s, a substantial decrease did occur. While it may be argued that the abolition of the Guaranty Fund was partially responsible, the primary reason for reduced defalcations was undoubtedly the diligence and persistence of the Department of Banking.

Heavy Deposit Withdrawals

In a few instances false rumors (emanating either from within or outside the banks affected) and ensuing runs precipitated bank failures, as illustrated by the following case history provided to the authors by W. A. Sandlin, former state bank examiner:

The Guaranty State Bank of Fort Worth was operated by its president, Ron Rhome. The principal loans of the bank were on automobiles, which were dubious security in those days. President Rhome was one of the first to recognize that this was a type of very profitable business. His loans were principally on Model T Ford cars, in amounts ranging from $200 to $400 with ten percent added-on interest, payable every two weeks and to be paid out no longer than ten months. In my first examination of this bank, I was concerned about this type of security, as it was not considered a good type of business at the time; however, in observing the manner in which the payments were made and the profit derived and also the minimum amount of losses sustained, I concluded that this, evidently, was a good form of financing.

Unfortunately, another bank in town—which has now long been liquidated—was quite jealous of his operation and of him personally and was largely responsible for starting some rumors about the Guaranty State Bank. As a result, a run was started on the bank by the depositors. I was called to Fort Worth along with the Banking Commissioner and two other examiners. We did everything we knew to stem the tide and to obtain funds for Guaranty Bank to remain open, but no other bank in Fort Worth would even consider taking over any of the automobile loans. I stoutly maintained that the bank was solvent and that the loans were good, although no one else agreed with me.

The bank was closed and its affairs placed in the hands of the Banking Commissioner for liquidation. At one time the Banking Commissioner offered to recommend a contribution of $500,000 from the Guaranty Fund if a party would organize a new bank, purchase the assets and assume the deposit liabilities of the Guaranty Bank. This was refused. I finally told the Commissioner, after the bank had been closed for some thirty days, that I would recommend placing a crew of liquidating employees in the bank to just see what could be done. The Commissioner agreed. We started active liquidation of the bank, and within ninety days sufficient funds were collected to pay the depositors in full without loss to the Guaranty Fund; and in another ninety days or so, sufficient assets liquidated to pay the stockholders about ninety cents on the dollar on their stock. To me, this was one of the tragic closings of a good bank.[28]

According to the statistics compiled by Clark Warburton (statistics that are considered more fully below), heavy withdrawals were a primary cause of suspension in 135 cases and a contributing cause in another 39 cases.[29] Unfortunately, it is not known how many of the cases of "heavy withdrawals" were actually "runs" in the traditional sense. In the oil towns of Stephens and Eastland counties, for example, withdrawals usually occurred gradually over a period of several months as the boom subsided. And in some instances this slow attrition of deposits was culminated by a

Table 14

Causes of State Bank Failures in Texas, 1921-1930

Cause	Failures* Primary cause	Contributing cause
Defalcation	33	24
Incompetent management	135	39
Insufficient diversification	0	26
Agricultural or industrial disaster	1	123
Decline in real estate values	0	16
Heavy withdrawals	135	39
Failure of affiliated institution or correspondent	11	0
Other causes	10	70

*Total failures in the sample studied: 188.
Source: "Material Prepared for the Information of the Federal Reserve Committee on Branch, Group, and Chain Banking" (Washington, D.C.: Federal Reserve Board, 1930), mimeographed.

full-fledged run by depositors. In any event, it is probable that the existence of the Depositors Guaranty Law, until several years before its repeal, reduced the likelihood of "runs" on banks.

Statistical Evidence

Official banking records for individual banks that failed before 1934 were destroyed many years ago. This accounts in large part for the attention accorded in this work to the statistical studies of state bank failures during the twenties prepared by Findley Weaver and later by Clark Warburton. The Weaver study, dating from 1926, was made in an attempt to obtain more accurate information on the importance of different causes of bank failures from 1920 to 1925. The sample selected by Weaver included 66.6 percent of the failures from 1920 to 1925. The sources of the information were reported to be persons "in a position to know all the facts regarding the failures on which they reported," and it was asserted that "the data were carefully given." In the absence of primary information, Weaver's tabulation, which is presented in table 11, is considered to be a valuable source of data. The study compiled by Clark Warburton in 1955 (covering the period from 1921 to 1930) is probably more reliable, since it is based on an official report prepared by the Texas banking commissioner in 1930 for the Federal Reserve Committee on Branch, Group, and Chain Banking. The statistical evidence, which is presented in table 14, enumerates the causes of failure for 188 state banks that failed in Texas between 1921 and 1930.

These data underscore the significance of incompetent and dishonest management in causing bank failures during the 1920s. Incompetent management was listed as a "primary cause" in 71.8 percent of the failures and a "contributing cause" in 20.7 percent. Defalcation or dishonesty on the part of management was cited as a primary cause in 17.5 percent of the failures and a contributing cause in 12.8 percent. In 64.4 percent of the failures, economic conditions were found to be a contributing cause.

The only major inconsistency between the studies by Weaver and Warburton concerns the importance of "heavy withdrawals" as a cause of failure. (In part the differences in results may be attributed to the choice of different time periods.) Weaver lists only one failure caused by heavy withdrawals, whereas according to Warburton's table heavy withdrawals were a cause of a substantial majority of state bank failures (a primary cause of 71.8 percent of the failures comprising the sample for 1921 to 1930 analyzed by Warburton and a contributing cause of 20.7 percent of those failures). A possible reason for the discrepancy could be that Weaver included under "heavy withdrawals" only banks that failed because of "runs," while the banking commissioner in 1930 probably considered any major attrition of deposits, regardless of its rapidity, as a cause of failure and included it under "heavy withdrawals."

Voluntary Liquidations

From September 1, 1920, through December 31, 1929, 369 state banks voluntarily surrendered their charters. Of these banks,

56 dissolved their operations, 131 were nationalized, 180 either merged with or sold out to another bank, and 2 banks never opened their doors, although they had received charters (see table 4).

During the years of severe economic stress in the 1920s and 1930s many of the banks that were classified as "voluntary liquidations" in Texas actually surrendered their charters under duress from the Department of Banking. A financially troubled bank was officially classified as a failure and turned over to the Liquidation Division of the department only if it was beyond all redemption or an arrangement with another bank could not be worked out. The ideal solution was to reorganize the bank with new capital and, in most cases, new management. If this was not possible, the next alternative was to arrange for another bank to buy, assume, or merge with the failed bank. The exact number of "voluntary liquidations" that took place under these circumstances cannot be determined from existing records. However, according to some who were employed by the department during the periods of greatest economic strain, most of the banks that entered "voluntary liquidation," except for those that were nationalized, did so because of financial difficulty. The factors that caused the actual failures from 1920 to 1933 also accounted for most of the "voluntary liquidations" that took place.

The large number of conversions from state to national charters during the 1920s occurred mainly because of the heavy Guaranty Fund assessments on state banks, which in turn arose from the high current level of state bank failures. Indeed, since membership in either the Guaranty Fund or the Bond Security System was compulsory for state banks, and the law before 1925 prohibited switching from one plan to the other, the only way that a Guaranty Fund bank could escape the burden of assessment was to surrender its charter. The Depositors Guaranty Law was amended to permit conversion from one plan to the other in 1925 and finally repealed some two years later. After 1925 the number of state bank conversions to national charters dropped off substantially. The increase in voluntary liquidations of state banks in Texas in the last two years of the 1920s can be directly attributed to Commissioner Shaw's "clean-up campaign," which began on September 1, 1927, and lasted throughout his tenure of office. Most of the banks liquidated, according to Commissioner Shaw, were in financial difficulty and had been for years.

Efforts of the Department of Banking to Avert Bank Failures

Many involuntary liquidations of state banks were prevented during the twenties by the policies and practices of the state Department of Banking with respect to the institutions that became insolvent (experienced impairment of their capital stock accounts). The goals of the department in handling troubled banks have been the same throughout the duration of the state banking system—namely, to provide uninterrupted service to the public, to avoid devastating losses, and to protect the public image of the banks of Texas.

The courses of action for dealing with insolvent banks were basically the same in the 1920s as those available to the Banking Department today. First, the bank in difficulty can be kept open and the business continued, but under the supervision of the department. Assessment of the stockholders may become necessary to overcome the impairment of the capital stock account. During the 1920s and well into the 1930s the assessment of each stockholder in such instances was usually the maximum permitted by law—100 percent of his capital stock holdings—but the proportion of aggregate assessments collected was typically quite small. A second possible course of action is for the insolvent bank to be reorganized, with additional capital and the same or new management, depending upon the Banking Department's evaluation of the existing management. Many reorganizations in the 1920s were hastily arranged and entailed a minimal change in the bank name to avoid loss, or further loss, of depositor confidence; these were called "overnight reorganizations." If a reorganization is not practicable, the next most desirable solution is to merge the troubled bank with or sell it to a second institution. If this, too, does not prove to be feasible, then the Banking Department has no choice but to liquidate the bank. In the following sections these various courses of action are developed more fully and are illustrated with cases that are drawn mainly from the experiences of the 1920s.

Keeping Insolvent Banks Open

A course often followed before and during the 1920s was to keep the problem bank open and continue the business, even though it was well known that the institution was insolvent or at least in trouble. This was the procedure followed in the case of the West Texas Bank and Trust Company in San Antonio before it was finally closed on April 3, 1916. The commissioner had allowed the bank to stay open, despite severe financial problems, in the hope that under his supervision efforts to better its affairs would be successful. This strategy enabled the bank to improve its position significantly, and had it not been for "unlooked-for events" the West Texas Bank and Trust Company probably would have survived.

Another case in which the department was aware of insolvency but delayed the closing of the bank was that of the First State Bank of Eastland. This bank was insolvent in 1921, but strenuous efforts were made to delay its closing because the commissioner did not want to have to withdraw funds from the Guaranty Fund. The bank was finally closed on January 19, 1924.

Although the West Texas Bank and Trust Company and the First State Bank of Eastland were the only insolvent banks known to have been kept open by the department, the practice was apparently followed extensively. This is evident from a statement made by Commissioner Charles O. Austin in 1925:

To the best of my knowledge and belief at the present time all of the banks about which the department has had any serious concern have closed and are now in the process of liquidation. Most of these failures were banks known to this department to be absolutely insolvent for a long time, but which appear to have been kept open with the hope that they might work out their own salvation. Bank failures do not develop overnight, but are usually the result of conditions well known and fully recognized for a long time before the crisis develops. None of the failures which have occurred so far this year should have been any surprise to any person having access to the bank examiner's reports, and most of them should have been no surprise to the public at large, for the reason that the banks have been notoriously insolvent and generally discussed in the communities where they existed for many months prior to their closing.[30]

It was hoped that in every instance in which an insolvent bank was deliberately kept open, failure might be avoided. Also, the longer a bank could be kept open, the less the loss might be in the event of failure. One reason for this was the average borrower's attitude toward a failed bank—he was more inclined to make an effort to continue loan payments to a bank that was open and operating as usual than he was to a bank that had failed. This was due to his desire to protect his credit rating and secure additional loans in the future. Furthermore, the regular bank officers were normally more effective in making collections than was a liquidating agent, who was usually a stranger to most of the debtors. It was estimated by J. M. Faulkner, banking commissioner from September 13, 1947, to June 30, 1970, A. J. Lewis, and other former department officials that during the 1920s the ultimate loss in liquidation was usually at least one-third more than that indicated at the time the bank was closed.[31]

Stockholder Assessments

If it was judged that the bank would not be able to work out its own problems and that it was insolvent, then there was no alternative except for the commissioner to take charge of the bank. Upon doing this, the commissioner immediately assessed the stockholders in an amount necessary to restore the capital of the institution. However, since attempts to collect the assessments were usually unsuccessful, the amount of the assessment in almost every instance was the maximum allowed under the law—an amount equal to 100 percent of the capital stock.

According to Findley Weaver, it was estimated by department officials that in the early 1920s not over 15 percent of aggregate assessments was collected.[32] The reason given for this poor experience was that the principal stockholders were often officers of the bank, who in an attempt to save their business and reputation, had already depleted their personal resources prior to the bank's failure. Also, the stockholders and officers were often debtors of the bank themselves. In most instances, they could hardly liquidate their debt, much less meet an assessment.

"Overnight Reorganizations"

When the commissioner was forced to take charge of a defunct institution, the preferred action if its capital could not be restored through stockholder assessments was to raise new capital through the sale of additional shares and reorganize the bank. The procedure involved in reorganization was as follows. First, new capital was raised, from the same stockholders and/or new stockholders, and a charter for the new bank was secured from the State Banking Board. Then, after obtaining permission from the district judge, the new bank would purchase the assets and assume the liabilities of the defunct institution.

In many cases the reorganization was what was commonly referred to as an "overnight reorganization." That is, the previously described process was consummated between the time the defunct bank regularly closed its doors and the time it was scheduled to reopen on the next business day. The reorganization was undertaken with the hope that only those individuals directly involved would have knowledge of it. For this to take place, the name of the bank was changed only slightly; for example, from the First State Bank, Dallas, to the First State Bank of Dallas.

The number of "overnight reorganizations" that took place is undetermined; reportedly there were many. W. A. Sandlin, a former state bank examiner who personally supervised many "overnight reorganizations" during the 1920s, provided the authors with the following statement concerning his activities:

One case I recall distinctly was a bank in Somerville that was out of money and in trouble. On Sunday afternoon in Brenham, we organized a new bank to take place of the bank in trouble, and I returned to Austin Sunday night, obtained a charter from the State Banking Board for the new bank on early Monday morning and returned to Brenham on Monday afternoon and proceeded to the small bank in Somerville to meet with the interested stockholders. The old bank was closed by order of the board of directors and its affairs placed in the hands of the Commissioner. The sale had to be approved by the district judge. He was holding court in Caldwell, Texas, so we proceeded there, and fortunately, found the judge holding court at 11:30 that night. We explained the situation to him and obtained his approval of the sale.[33]

Maintaining secrecy was extremely important in dealing with troubled banks to prevent a loss of confidence in the bank and consequent runs by depositors. During the days of greatest stress in the 1920s and 1930s, even the news that the bank examiners were in town was enough to cause a run. Because of the tenuous position of a financially troubled bank, even a small run usually meant disaster.

An illustration of an instance in which a withdrawal as small as five dollars might have led to at least temporary closure of a bank was provided by Sandlin, who stated:

Another time during Commissioner Austin's administration, a bank at Kress, Texas—which is near Plainview—was desperately calling for help for it was out of money and the cashier had disappeared. A reception committee was waiting for me at the depot upon my arrival at Kress. The bank had a capital of $20,000 and we decided during the night we would attempt to organize a new bank with a like capital and take over the old bank. I advised the directors to simply tell the people the truth—it was either organize a new bank and get some new money or else the bank would have to close. The directors left the meeting about daybreak for their homes and to scour the country for new stockholders. I remained at the bank and what little sleep I got was perched up in a chair in the director's room. The only employee of the bank was a young man of sixteen or eighteen years of age who had no banking experience of any consequence. Along in the afternoon while waiting for the directors to report, the young man came back to where I was waiting in the director's room and reported he had less than $5 cash on hand and, of course, the bank had no balances with any correspondent bank. The young man asked what he should do if someone came in and wanted to cash a check. I told him the weather was bad and perhaps no one would come in needing cash, but if they did, we would try to handle the situation. In about thirty minutes he returned trembling like the proverbial leaf and said a customer was up front and wanted to cash a check for $15. I asked the young man to find out what the customer wanted to do with the money, and he reported the customer wanted to drive over to Tulia to pay his taxes. I told the young man he could save the customer that twenty-mile drive by simply writing the tax collector a letter and enclosing the man's check for the amount of taxes—that if the bank could not be reorganized, the man would be in the same position that he was at the present time—that is, the bank did not have the money to pay the check. The bank was reorganized. With the completed charter application some directors went with me to Austin where a new bank charter was granted by the Banking Board. I returned to Kress, opened the new bank, closed the old one, perfected the sale of the old to the new, and was on my way to another assignment. There was no misapplication of funds. The bank was over-loaned, out of money and could not find any more. The pressure was too great for the cashier and he just left without leaving a forwarding address.[34]

Activities of the Liquidation Division during the Guaranty Fund Years

If none of the less drastic courses of action was feasible, the bank was turned over to the Liquidation Division for dissolution. Each defunct bank was placed in the hands of a special agent, who was responsible for carrying out the liquidation. This involved taking charge of and selling the assets of the bank, then turning the proceeds over to the State Banking Board. These proceeds were paid into the Guaranty Fund in order to offset the withdrawal that had been made to pay off the unsecured, non-interest-bearing depositors. Each special agent was required to submit a report to the commissioner on the fifteenth and the last days of each month; the report included a list of all collections made and a report on the status of notes still being collected.

For supervisory purposes the state was divided into three districts, with a liquidating examiner in charge of each. The liquidating examiners were responsible for making periodic examinations of the banks being liquidated and for determining whether the special agents were conducting the liquidations as they should. The examination of a failed bank was conducted in collaboration with a committee of neighboring or local state bankers selected for that purpose by the liquidating examiner. The primary purpose of the examination was to appraise the assets of the bank and report the results of the appraisal to the commissioner.

Most of the assets in the hands of the Liquidation Division consisted of notes, individual stockholders' assessments, and real estate. Every effort was made to collect the notes in cash or else, when possible, to obtain more collateral. When a debtor did not show good faith and made no effort to pay, the debt was placed in the hands of attorneys for collection. With regard to stockholders' assessments, basically the same procedure was followed. Every effort was made to collect the assessment or to obtain a satisfactory note for the amount; if this was not possible, the matter was referred to attorneys in order to initiate judgment proceedings. In those cases where it was a foregone conclusion that a judgment would be uncollectible, no judgment was sought, of course. Real estate was disposed of on a best-effort basis.

Funds were also recovered by the Liquidation Division from surety companies on bonds of state bank officers. Considering the large number of defalcations in banks that failed, the total amount of the claims was probably substantial.

Another source from which funds were recovered was the Internal Revenue Service. From 1917 to 1921 many of the state banks that later failed had incurred large profits; as a consequence, they had paid a significant sum in income taxes. The fact that they subsequently failed was prima facie evidence of the fact that the taxes were erroneously paid. In order to recover these taxes, the department hired a firm of income-tax accountants to determine the appropriate amount of the overpayment. In May 1923 it was reported that claims totaling $40,000 had already been filed with the federal government and that at least another $100,000 would be recovered from that source.[35]

Legal and Institutional Changes in Later Years

Although the policies followed by the state Department of Banking pertaining to insolvent or impaired banks in the 1920s were basically the same as those followed in the 1930s and in the years since then, legal and institutional changes have altered procedures somewhat. Among the most notable of these changes were the repeal of the Depositors Guaranty Law on February 11, 1927, and the repeal of double liability for state bank stockholders on August 23, 1937. Perhaps the change having the greatest effect on the department was the implementation of federal deposit insurance on January 1, 1934. Because of the wide acceptance of federal deposit insurance by the state banks and of the establishment by the Federal Deposit Insurance Corporation of its own Liquidation Division, the Department of Banking abolished its Liquidation Division. Since 1949 all defunct state banks have been liquidated by the Federal Deposit Insurance Corporation.

New State Banking Laws Enacted during the Twenties

Most of the banking reforms suggested but not achieved during the 1910-1919 period were again sought in the 1920s; in addition, a substantial amount of legislation pertaining to the Depositors Guaranty Law was introduced, particularly in the thirty-ninth and fortieth legislatures. As a result, a voluminous amount of banking legislation was considered during the 1920-1929 era.

The most notable legislative accomplishments, aside from those pertaining to the Depositors Guaranty Law, were the following: the passage of a law prohibiting the future organization of private banks and bringing those already existing under the supervision of the Department of Banking; the approval of an amendment to the State Bank Law raising the minimum capital requirement for a state bank from $10,000 to $17,500; and the enactment of a statute creating a separate department of banking.

The legislation adopted by the Thirty-eighth Legislature with regard to private banks resolved the private bank controversy in Texas once and for all. The measure enacted, Senate Bill No. 52, not only prohibited the subsequent formation of private banks but also allowed only those that had been in operation for two years before the passage of the law to continue in business.[36] Within thirty days those private banks that were permitted to stay in business were required to file statements of financial condition showing that their businesses were solvent. In addition, private banks were required to file annual statements of financial condition and to publish such statements in a local newspaper. The emergency clause of the bill stated that the measures taken were necessary because the depositors of private banks were not adequately protected.

In the nineteenth century private banks had provided a vital service to the people of Texas. During the days of the Republic of Texas and until the first national bank was established in 1865, the private banks were virtually the only banking institutions in the state. After the passage of the National Bank Act of 1863 and until the inauguration of the state banking system in 1905, they continued to flourish. However, with the reduction of the minimum capital requirement for national banks to $25,000 in 1900 and the rapid growth of the state banking system beginning in 1905, the private banks were no longer essential to the economy. Moreover, in time it became generally recognized that their continued existence without supervision or regulation of any kind was not in the public interest. Consequently, serious attempts for their control began shortly after the passage of the Texas State Bank Law in 1905; had it not been for the strong political influence of a few of the private bankers, they undoubtedly would have been regulated long before they were.

Another important revision in Texas banking law passed by the Thirty-eighth Legislature increased the minimum capital stock required to organize a state bank. The house bill that was introduced would have raised the minimum from $10,000 to $25,000 and allowed banks already organized with less than $25,000 to continue to operate.[37] Had the bill passed, the minimum requirement for new state banks would have been the same as that for national banks. The feeling of many lawmakers that this was unduly restrictive was reflected in the introduction of Senate Bill No. 110, which was enacted into law as a compromise; it raised the minimum capital requirement to $17,500.[38]

During the second called session of the Thirty-eighth Legislature a bill establishing a separate department of banking was introduced and passed by both the senate and the house. It provided for the appointment by the governor of a commissioner of banking for a two-year term with an annual salary of $6,000. The commissioner was required to be a citizen of the state with at least five years of banking experience in a position not lower than that of cashier. His duties were to be the same as those previously performed by the commissioner of the Department of Insurance and Banking with regard to banking. The new statute authorized the commissioner to appoint not more than one bank examiner for every forty banks, so that each bank could be examined at least three times per year.[39]

The enactment of Senate Bill No. 82 ended a long struggle on the part of the state bankers to create a separate department of banking. Practically every commissioner of insurance and banking since the inception of the state banking system had suggested that the supervision of insurance and of banking be separated. However, it was not until the 1920s that the volume and complexity of regulatory business to be conducted became such that it could not be handled efficiently in one office. Shortly before the law was passed that created a separate department of banking, Commissioner Chapman reported that there were about 1,000 banks, 528 fire and life insurance companies, and nearly 100 building, loan and investment companies under his supervision.[40]

When the state banking system was created in 1905, its supervision was assigned to the Department of Agriculture, Insurance, Statistics, and History as an economy measure. Shortly thereafter a separate department of agriculture was formed and the Department of Insurance and Banking was created. Even in these early years, before the state banking system had experienced great growth, the arrangement had basic weaknesses. Principal among these was placement of the supervision of two unrelated types of institutions, each operating under separate and distinct laws, in the hands of one individual. It would have been unusual indeed to have found a commissioner who was well versed on both subjects. The burden of the job was such that it could not be successfully carried by any individual for any considerable period. This, according to Commissioner Chapman, was the principal cause of the rapid turnover in the office of commissioner, which was, needless to say, very detrimental to the administration of the law.[41] Another shortcoming from the outset was the failure of the legislature to provide sufficient funds for the proper management of the department and remuneration of its employees. If the legislature had initially taken the necessary measures to assure the effective administration of the State Bank Law, perhaps some of the difficulties encountered by the state banking system during the 1920s and 1930s could have been avoided.

Notes

1. Milton Friedman and Anna Jacobson Schwartz, *A Monetary History of the United States, 1867-1960* (Princeton: Princeton University Press, 1963), p. 220.
2. Paul Studenski and Herman Krooss, *Financial History of the United States* (New York: McGraw-Hill, 1952), p. 303.
3. Southwestern Bell Telephone Company, *Economic Survey of Texas*, 1928, p. 112.
4. *The Texas Almanac and State Industrial Guide, 1928* (Dallas: A. H. Belo, 1928), p. 199.
5. A. J. Lewis, written statement of May 19, 1969.
6. J. L. Chapman, "A Message from the Department," address before the Texas Bankers Association's annual convention, Dallas, May 15, 1923, *Texas Bankers Record* 7 (June 1923): 70-71.
7. Studenski and Krooss, pp. 334-335.
8. R. L. Thornton, "The Guaranty Fund System," *Texas Bankers Record* 14 (September 1925): 9-10.
9. *Texas Bankers Journal*, March 1912, p. 15.
10. M. L. Riddle, "Changes that Ought to be Made in the Banking Law," read before the Panhandle Bankers Association, September 1912, in *Texas Bankers Record* 2 (October 1912): 8.
11. J. L. Chapman, "Separating Department of Insurance and Banking," *Texas Bankers Record* 12 (November 1922): 10.
12. *Forty-seventh Annual Report of the Commissioner of Insurance and Banking for the Year Ending August 31, 1922, Pertaining to Banking* (Austin: Von Boeckmann-Jones, 1922), p. 8.

13. Banking Department of Texas, official records.
14. Findley Weaver, "State Banking in Texas" (M.A. thesis, University of Texas, 1926), pp. 96-97.
15. Noel Hollingsworth, "The Oil Town Bank," address before the Texas Bankers Association's annual convention, Houston, May 19, 1925, in *Texas Bankers Record* 14 (June 1925): 16-19.
16. C. B. Sullivan, written statement of June 1969.
17. Ibid.
18. *United States Department of Agriculture Yearbook, 1921* (Washington, D.C.: Government Printing Office, 1922), pp. 323-407.
19. *Texas Bankers Record* 15 (February 1926): 29.
20. W. L. Peterson, "Liquidating State Banks," address before the state bank section of the Texas Bankers Association's annual convention, Dallas, May 16, 1923, in *Texas Bankers Record* 12 (June 1923): 49.
21. James Shaw, reported in *Journal of the American Bankers Association* 21 (July 1928): 64.
22. Clark Warburton, "Deposit Guaranty in Texas" (unpublished monograph dated June 1958 and presented to J. M. Falkner, banking commissioner), p. 46.
23. J. L. Chapman, address before the state bank section at the Texas Bankers Association's annual convention, Dallas, May 16, 1923, in *Texas Bankers Record* 13 (June 1923): 53-55.
24. Proceedings of the meeting of the state bank section at the Texas Bankers Association's annual convention, Dallas, May 16, 1923, in *Texas Bankers Record* 12 (June 1923): 57.
25. J. L. Chapman, "Economic Conditions," address before Texas Bankers Association's annual convention, Austin, May 20, 1924, in *Texas Bankers Record* 8 (June 1924): 29-32.
26. Commissioner Charles O. Austin to the state bankers, *Southwestern Bankers Journal*, April 1925, p. 36.
27. Carlson, *Monetary and Banking History*, p. 62.
28. W. A. Sandlin, written statement of June 1969.
29. Warburton, p. 46.
30. Austin, p. 11.
31. From a conference held in Austin, Texas, on August 28, 1969, attended by A. J. Lewis, C. B. Sullivan, W. A. Sandlin,

John M. Falkner, William Z. Gossett, Maurice Burns, Lawrence L. Crum, and Joseph M. Grant.
32. Weaver, p. 72.
33. W. A. Sandlin, written statement of June 1969.
34. Ibid.
35. Peterson, "Liquidating State Banks," pp. 118-119.
36. *General Laws of Texas, Thirty-eighth Legislature, Regular Session, 1923* (Austin: A. C. Baldwin and Sons, 1923), p. 421.
37. *House Journal, Texas, Thirty-eighth Legislature, Regular Session, 1923* (Austin: Von Boeckmann-Jones, 1923), p. 389.
38. *General Laws of Texas, Thirty-eighth Legislature, Regular Session, 1923*, p. 93.
39. *General Laws of Texas, Thirty-eighth Legislature, First, Second, and Third Called Sessions, 1923* (Austin: A. C. Baldwin and Sons, 1923), p. 107.
40. J. L. Chapman, "Separating Department of Insurance and Banking," *Texas Bankers Record* 7 (November 1922): 9-10.
41. Ibid., p. 9.

9

Repeal of the Depositors Guaranty Law

Favorable Experience before the 1920-1921 Recession

As noted in chapter 6, the Depositors Guaranty Law, which created the Depositors Guaranty Fund and the Bond Security System, was signed into law by Governor Thomas M. Campbell on May 12, 1909, and became effective on January 1 of the following year. When Governor Campbell sent his farewell message to the legislature on January 11, 1911, the law had only been in effect one year, and it had never been tested by a bank failure. Nevertheless, Governor Campbell proclaimed that the legislature had enacted a law giving "absolute security and protection to noninterest-bearing deposits in state banks." It was Governor Campbell's belief that through the more rigorous supervision and more frequent examination of state and national banks that had followed the passage of the law, the stockholders of all banks had been accorded an added protection to their investment; greater stability and safety in banking had been provided; loss to depositors in state banks had been rendered impossible; and loss to depositors in national banks doing business in Texas had been made improbable.[1]

Governor Campbell's remarks may have been premature, but at the time it would have been difficult to anticipate the events and conditions that ultimately caused the collapse of the Guaranty Fund in the 1920s. Before the recession of 1920-1921 the Depositors Guaranty Law was an unqualified success, and there was no hint of the difficulties that were to follow.

Table 15

Special Assessments, Withdrawals, and Losses of the Texas Depositors Guaranty Fund
1910-1927

Year ended August 31*	Special assessments levied	Recoveries from failed banks repaid to participating banks	Banks closed			
			Withdrawals from fund	Recoveries	Net losses	Number of banks
Total	$17,090,883	$4,184,246	$17,978,492	$6,332,768	$11,645,724	138
1912	133,314	55,808	133,348	77,920	55,428	3
1913	0	22,112	658	0	658	1
1914	61,234	0	61,234	61,234	0	1
1915	17,710	28,436	79,249	64,091	15,158	4
1916	200,000	17,495	362,961	86,334	276,627	5
1917	61,539	13,206	0	0	0	0
1918	0	601	0	0	0	0
1919	0	27,433	123,607	123,607	0	2
1920	0	30,770	115,316	104,867	10,449	2
1921	3,991,453	52,104	4,025,113	863,817	3,161,296	21
1922	4,179,380	222,777	4,207,247	1,229,249	2,977,998	31
1923	1,244,680	1,184,407	1,948,389	750,547	1,197,842	11
1924	2,416,448	1,265,938	1,743,686	524,212	1,219,474	11
1925	3,772,317	0	3,744,070	2,040,210	1,703,860	26
1926	875,639	1,263,159	858,157	352,909	505,248	11
1927	137,169	0	575,458	53,770	521,688	9

*No failure occurred and consequently no special assessment was made in the fiscal years ending in 1910 and 1911.
Source: Clark Warburton, "Deposit Guaranty in Texas," unpublished monograph available from Banking Department of Texas, June 1958.

In approximately eleven years, from the time the Depositors Guaranty Law became effective until August 31, 1920, eighteen Guaranty Fund banks required liquidation by the commissioner of insurance and banking. Of the $876,358 withdrawn to pay the protected depositors of these banks, there was a net loss of $358,320. Prorated over the ten-year period, the cost was about .001 percent per annum of the average capital of the Guaranty Fund banks and .0002 percent of deposits.[2] It is thus not surprising that throughout the period before the 1920-1921 recession the Guaranty Fund was praised.

The Beginning of the End of the Guaranty Fund

Unfortunately, the favorable conditions that prevailed in the first ten years of the Guaranty Fund came to an abrupt end with the beginning of the 1920-1921 recession. The recession induced a veritable avalanche of Guaranty Fund bank failures. Beginning with the collapse of the First State Bank, Tomball, on November 9, 1920, fifty-two Guaranty Fund banks failed in the next two years. Fifty of the banks that failed were in such condition that special assessments were required of the Guaranty Fund banks in an aggregate amount of $8,170,833. No depositor of a Guaranty Fund bank lost a cent, however.

During the latter part of 1921 and in 1922 a series of departures from the state banking system began. In the 1921 fiscal year only one state bank converted to a national charter. But from September 1, 1921, until December 31, 1923, an additional thirty-two state banks joined the national system (see table 4, page 40). This does not seem like a particularly large number; considering, however, that only forty-eight conversions had occurred in the previous sixteen years, including the fall of 1914, when the Federal Reserve began operation, the number of conversions during the period between 1921 and 1923 was alarming. The concern of the commissioner and the Texas Bankers Association was evidenced in an article (appearing in the February 1922 edition of the *Texas Bankers Record*) that urged state banks to remain in the state banking system.[3]

Agitation for Repeal of the Guaranty Fund Law

By the time of the Texas Bankers Association annual convention in May 1923, which was held in Dallas, the Guaranty Fund banks had already been assessed $9,168,000 since November 1, 1920, and would soon be assessed another $750,000 to pay the depositors of Guaranty Fund banks closed since January 1, 1923.[4] With these heavy assessments and the unpleasant experiences of the past several years fresh in their memories, bankers allowed the undercurrent of opposition to the Guaranty Fund that had been slowly building up to surface. However, there was no way to abolish the Guaranty Fund before the next session of the legislature in 1925, and consequently most of the rhetoric was concerned with mitigating problems in the interim.[5]

During 1923 and 1924 the business climate in Texas improved significantly, as did the condition of the state banks. In the 1923 fiscal year only eleven state banks that were Guaranty Fund members failed, whereas thirty-one failed in the previous year. Assessments were reduced from $4,179,380 to $1,244,680. In fiscal 1924 there were also eleven failures of Guaranty Fund banks, which resulted in assessments of $2,416,488 (see table 15). Although this experience was less favorable than that enjoyed before the 1920-1921 recession, it was a welcome relief from that of the previous two years. As a result, in the 1924 calendar year only three state banks left the system to become national banks. Moreover, open opposition to the Guaranty Fund seemed to subside. At the 1924 Texas Bankers Association Convention, held in Austin, very little was said against the Guaranty Fund, and the outlook for the future seemed favorable.

The Bankers Association elected as its president for the coming year R. L. Thornton, president of the Mercantile Bank and Trust Company of Dallas and a recognized opponent of the Guaranty Fund. After being in office for only three months Thornton, with the full cooperation of the editor of the official organ of the association, the *Texas Bankers Record*, embarked upon an assault on the Guaranty Fund that ultimately led to its demise. Thornton set forth his position on the Guaranty Fund in an article written for the September 1924 issue of the publication.

After expounding the arguments against the fund, the article concluded with the following passage:

The Guaranty Fund Law, after a fair trial, in my humble opinion, has failed and the experiment has cost the solvent banks an assessment exceeding 10 million dollars. Isn't that time enough for experimenting and isn't the cost enough to pay, and why shouldn't Texas follow at least the lead of Oklahoma again and repeal it, or so modify it that a bank can pay the bill and not live the life of a cripple.

It is my judgment that if the Guaranty Fund Law is repealed by the next Legislature that within three months after its repeal there is not a banker in Texas that would hear anything about it and that the Texas state banking system soon would rank with the best and largest in the nation and would grow strong and virile as our great state develops.

My conclusions are that the Guaranty Fund System of securing deposits is economically unsound, unworkable, and unfair.

The opinions given above are not fancies of an idle moment. I have given this matter much mature thought and study. This problem, I believe, is of pressing importance at this time, not only to both state and national banks in our state, but also to the people at large in Texas. I will go further and say the very foundation of our future prosperity and development as a commonwealth is at stake because it can be no stronger than its financial system. What are we going to do about it?[6]

The publication of Thornton's article stimulated a torrent of correspondence from state and national bankers. Of the several hundred letters received by Thornton and the editor of the *Texas Bankers Record*, not one disagreed with Thornton's reasoning or conclusion. Moreover, most of the letters advocated complete repeal of the Depositors Guaranty Law and urged Thornton to organize the state bankers and work toward that goal.

The stand taken by Thornton was a bold one, indeed, since very little opposition to the Guaranty Fund had been openly acknowledged previously. The response, however, overwhelmingly proved that there was a strong undercurrent of discontent and that there was grass-roots support for the repeal of the fund.

Between the time when Thornton's article appeared, in September 1924, and the opening of the Thirty-ninth Session of the Texas legislature, on January 13, 1925, the *Texas Bankers Record* devoted its pages largely to the Guaranty Fund question.

Articles, letters, and speeches by prominent state bankers, as well as editorials—all urging repeal of the Guaranty Fund—appeared in the magazine.

Arguments against the Guaranty Fund

The strongest arguments presented against the Guaranty Fund were that it encouraged the organization of too many banks and contributed to loose and illicit banking practices. Another criticism was that the Guaranty Fund made it virtually impossible to convict a dishonest state banker or even to have an indictment brought against one. The reason for this problem, it was pointed out, was that under state laws the indictment and trial had to be procured and held in the defendant's own county, before his friends. If a banker knew that his depositors would suffer as a result of his deeds and would therefore demand his indictment, trial, and conviction, he would be more reluctant to commit unlawful acts.[7]

One of the basic faults found with the concept of deposit protection was that it was not based upon sound principles of insurance. Under the Guaranty Fund every good and solvent bank automatically assumed the risk and guaranteed the "business, integrity, and honesty" of bank managers they had never seen or heard of.[8]

One virtue commonly attributed to the Guaranty Fund was embodied in the slogan "No noninterest-bearing and unsecured depositor has ever lost a single dollar deposited in a Guaranty Fund Bank in Texas." This was the platform upon which all advocates of the law stood. Thornton admitted that the claim was true, but he pointed out that as of September 1923 over $10 million had been assessed against the good and solvent banks and paid to the depositors of defunct institutions.

The essential question was whether the state as a whole had benefited from the operation of the fund. Thornton contended that it had not and that what had been one man's or community's gain had been the loss of others. He reasoned that assessments levied against solvent banks to pay depositors of insolvent banks were essentially taxes over which the solvent banks had no control.

The solvent banks were thus unfairly penalized, whereas the depositors of the insolvent banks benefited even though they may have been negligent in not investigating the bank's condition and the integrity of management before the failure. The net effect of the Depositors Guaranty Fund on the state as a whole was neutral, since the amount assessed was equal to the amount paid depositors—it merely represented a transfer of funds from one community to another.[9]

Another question to which the bankers opposed to the Guaranty Fund addressed themselves was whether the fund had produced the benefits it was supposed to produce. In the first place, had the Guaranty Fund stabilized the banking business and rendered panics impossible, as its proponents proclaimed it would when the law was enacted? According to Z. D. Bonner, a former banker and deputy banking commissioner, experience demonstrated that it had not.[10] In his opinion it was the Federal Reserve Act that had reduced the probability of a currency panic, mainly by providing an elastic supply of credit and greater mobility of funds. Although Bonner's assertion about the Federal Reserve Act is correct, there was evidence that the Guaranty Fund had contributed to a reduction of the threat of runs, even though it had not entirely eliminated them.

One of the main arguments in favor of the Guaranty Fund system was that it would attract and hold deposits. It is true that during the first eleven years the state banking system enjoyed significant growth in the number of banking offices and in total resources, but that was before the cost of the Guaranty Fund in the form of assessments became apparent.[11] From 1920 to the end of 1926 the state banking system experienced a decline while national banks in Texas increased in number and resources. On December 29, 1920, 1,031 state banks reported resources of $391.1 million; by December 31, 1926, the number of banks reporting had declined to 782, with total resources of $290.5 million. During the same period, the number of national banks increased from 556 to 656, and resources from $789.2 million to $1,020.1 million. These figures, of course, reflect the many conversions from state to national charters that took place during 1922, 1923, and 1925. Nevertheless, there was sufficient evidence

Table 16

**Texas National and State Bank Deposits on
Selected Call Dates, 1920-1928**

	National banks*		State banks		
Date	Banks	Deposits ($000)	Banks	Deposits ($000)	Deposits as percentage of total
December 29, 1920	556	789,246	1,031	391,127	33.4
December 31, 1926	656	1,020,113	782	290,554	22.1
December 31, 1928	632	1,230,469	713	334,870	21.4

Sources: *Annual Report of the Comptroller of the Currency* (Washington, D.C.: Government Printing Office, 1920, 1926, 1928); official records of the Banking Department of Texas.

to cast doubt upon the claim that the Guaranty Fund attracted and held deposits.

Bonner also asserted that the experience of the state banks after converting to the national system demonstrated beyond dispute that the public did not demand the Guaranty Fund.[12] It was his opinion that these banks after nationalizing had not lost deposits but, in most cases, had gained deposits. This contention was verified by the results of an investigation conducted by and printed in the *Texas Bankers Record* in December 1924.[13] All banks that had converted in the previous four years were polled. At press time, twenty-three of the thirty-three banks to which questionnaires were sent had responded. The deposits of the banks in aggregate had increased from $33.3 million at the time of conversion to $50.7 million on the date of the poll. The aggregate deposit figures for these banks, which were only about one-fifth of the total number that converted during the 1920-1926 period, accounted for a significant percentage of the $100 million decrease in state bank deposits and the $240 million increase in national bank deposits in this period.

Another way of judging the impact of the state bank conversions on aggregate deposits of Texas state banks on the one hand and national banks on the other is to compare the contribution of each system to total Texas commercial bank deposits before the conversion movement began with the contribution after it was over. Again, factors other than conversions influenced the changes in deposits. At the beginning of the 1920-1921 recession, before the conversion movement began, the state banks accounted for about 33.4 percent of Texas commercial bank deposits. By December 31, 1926, the state banks accounted for only 22.1 percent of deposits. Moreover, after the Guaranty Fund was repealed in February 1927 there was no evidence that the trend was reversed; that is, those banks that had left the state system showed no inclination to return.

Another argument that had been advanced in favor of the Guaranty Fund was that it would produce a "more rigid application of the law, more stringent examinations, and a greater condition of solvency." Bonner felt that this claim had been repudiated by the many failures of the previous few years.[14]

Finally, it was alleged in the beginning by proponents of the Guaranty Fund that the fund would enable its members to make more money and thus be stronger institutions. The heavy assessment, of course, had made this impossible. However, Bonner asserted that had it not been for the Guaranty Fund and the assessment levied under it, a state bank would have been able to make more money than a comparable national bank.[15]

Perhaps the most convincing argument advanced against the continuance of the Guaranty Fund was that the heavy assessments would eventually drive the healthy banks, and especially the large city banks, out of the state banking system and as a result the system would ultimately collapse.

When the Guaranty Fund was originally established, the maximum annual assessment allowed under the law of 2 percent of the average daily deposits was thought to be very reasonable and an amount that would work no undue hardship on any bank. But under the law any portion of the 2 percent not assessed in one year could be carried over into the next year. Also, an assessment of only 2 percent of deposits amounted to anywhere from 10 to 24 percent of capital for the average bank, whose deposits were from five to twelve times its capital.[16] Bonner's bank, before converting to the national system, paid out in thirteen months an amount equal to 35 percent of its capital stock of $54,000; it had received back only 20 percent of that amount in the form of liquidating dividends and expected to receive no more than 35 percent of the total.[17] Wharton State Bank and Trust Company of Wharton, which was still in the state system, had paid out an amount equivalent to 40 percent of its capital stock and presumably had received back little more than Bonner's bank.[18] These assessments, however, were not reflected in a reduction in the capital, surplus, or undivided profits of many of the banks owing to the common practice of carrying the entire assessment as an asset instead of charging off the greatest portion of it.[19] Such a practice obviously could not have continued indefinitely.

Many of the bankers who responded to Thornton's article in the *Texas Bankers Record* suggested that under the Guaranty Fund the state banking system would never amount to much and that their only salvation was to go into the national system. Apparently the only reason the state banks were converting was because of the Guaranty Fund; the bankers believed that the state system otherwise offered many advantages not offered by the national system.

The temptation to convert was particularly great for the large city banks, which individually and in aggregate shouldered a disproportionate share of the burden of assessments because the large city banks generally had greater deposit-to-capital ratios than did the smaller banks. As a matter of fact, Bonner asserted in his article for the November 1924 issue of the *Record* that no large reserve city bank remained in the state banking system. The reason for this was not that national laws were more attractive but simply that the assessments under the Guaranty Fund on a large city bank were "more than the traffic would bear."[20]

The consensus was that the state banking system could not survive unless the Guaranty Fund was repealed. It was believed that all of the strong state banks that had not converted to a national charter would eventually do so and that the continued heavy assessments would ultimately bring about the collapse of those banks remaining under the Guaranty Fund.

Response of the Thirty-ninth Legislature

In response to the urgent demands of the state bankers, the Thirty-ninth Legislature changed the law protecting bank depositors. Legislation was passed during the regular session that allowed state banks to change from the Guaranty Fund plan to the Bond Security plan for protection of bank deposits.[21] Banks choosing to exercise the option under the new provision were required to protect deposits by depositing with the state banking commissioner "a bond, policy of insurance or bonds of the United States, or municipal or district bonds approved by the Attorney General's Department, or other guaranty of indemnity" equal to their capital stock. The law was thus changed in two respects. The original law required the bond to be equal to capital plus the amount by which deposits exceeded six times the capital stock and to be a "bond, policy of insurance, or other guarantee or indemnity."

Almost immediately after these changes in the Depositors Guaranty Law were passed the question arose as to whether the municipal or government bonds presented to the commissioner could be a part of the bank's assets. The matter was settled by the Supreme Court of Texas, which issued a mandamus on February 3, 1926, requiring the commissioner to accept bonds that were assets of the bank as protection for depositors.

Shifts to the Bond Security Plan and the National Banking System

As a result of the revisions in the law, state banks rushed to change from the Guaranty Fund to the Bond Security System. The Department of Banking reported that between the date on which the amendment to the law became effective, February 7, 1925, and May 15, 1925, approximately three hundred banks had changed to the Bond Security System. Commissioner Austin, in issuing this report, expressed the belief that the rush to change plans was over.[22]

The *Texas Bankers Record* also disclosed in May 1925 that approximately thirty state banks had taken out national charters in the preceding two or three months. Moreover, reports from the

Federal Reserve Bank and the chief examiner's office of the eleventh district indicated that "several score more" had applied for national charters.

The movement in the early part of 1925 to convert to the Bond Security System and the national banking system was induced primarily by the unusual number of state bank failures. The slowdown in bank failures that occurred in 1923 and 1924, along with the improvement in business conditions, had given the state bankers reason for optimism. Their hopes, however, were shattered by the landslide of suspensions in 1925. In 1924 only twenty-three failures had occurred. An equal number occurred in the first four months of 1925, and by the end of the year forty-seven state banks had failed (see table 4). The large number of failures undoubtedly accounted for the abundance of conversions to the Bond Security System, but it does not explain why so many banks were obtaining national charters: under the revised law it was possible for a bank to escape from the heavy assessments of the Guaranty Fund and still remain in the state banking system.

The primary reasons for the large number of state bank conversions to the national banking system during 1925 were disappointment that the Guaranty Fund had not been repealed and dissatisfaction with the alternative to the Guaranty Fund, the Bond Security System.

The Bond Security System was considered objectionable in a number of respects. Both methods of supplying the bond—through a surety company and a personal bond with the department—had disadvantages. The posting of a personal bond, in addition to the double liability for the amount of their stock, was unpalatable to many bank directors and stockholders. On the other hand, the rates proposed by the surety companies had been "outrageously high," and in some instances the surety companies also demanded personal indemnity from the directors or stockholders of the bank. With regard to the rates, Commissioner Charles O. Austin quoted what he considered to be a very reasonable premium of a maximum of 2 percent on the capital and a minimum of 1.5 percent.[23]

Thus either alternative had drawbacks; one required a cash premium of not less than 1.5 percent of capital per annum, and the other involved the assumption of a contingent liability by stockholders or directors. Even the ruling of the Supreme Court of Texas allowing the commissioner to accept government and municipal bonds that were part of the bank's assets in satisfaction of the bond probably did not help most of the banks, since it is likely that they did not have the required amount of securities that were not already pledged.

The only alternative for those banks opposed to the Bond Security plan, but wishing to escape from the burden of the Guaranty Fund, was to obtain a national charter. According to the *Record*, before 1925 bankers had apparently been reticent to take this action due to the common belief that a bank operated under the Guaranty Fund would suffer "a material reduction in deposits" if it converted to a national charter. However, such fears were allayed with the publication, in December 1924, of the survey conducted by the *Texas Bankers Record* that showed the contrary was true.[24] As a result, when the high rate of bank failures resumed in 1925, and all hopes for repeal of the Guaranty Fund appeared to vanish, many banks chose to obtain national charters instead of joining the Bond Security System. During 1925 alone, 80 state banks converted to the national banking system. Between September 1, 1920, when the Guaranty Fund's difficulties began, and February 1927, when the law was finally repealed, a total of 127 banks had left the state banking system to become national banks (see table 4).

Failure of the Thirty-ninth Legislature to Repeal the Guaranty Fund

Had the Thirty-ninth Legislature repealed the Guaranty Fund, most of the banks that converted to national charters during 1925 and 1926 would not have left the state banking system.

One reason the Thirty-ninth Legislature did not repeal the Depositors Guaranty Law must have been that the campaign against the Guaranty Fund was initiated in September 1924, only four months before the legislature was scheduled to convene. As a result the state bankers had little time to organize, prepare legislation, rally public support for repeal of the law, and convince the legislators that such was desirable.

A second and perhaps more important reason that the movement fell short of its goal was the lack of support from the commissioner of banking. The explanation for this lack of support may have been that Commissioner Chapman was not yet convinced that the Depositors Guaranty Law should be repealed. More probably, though, the explanation lies in the fact that the office of commissioner was in transition during these critical months. Commissioner Chapman's term expired as of January 19, 1925, less than one week after the legislature convened. Undoubtedly his last months in office were hectic, as he endeavored to clean up unfinished business and make the transition as smooth as possible. Moreover, the new commissioner, Charles O. Austin, who assumed office on January 20, would have had little time to influence the legislature at that late date.

Repeal of the Depositors Guaranty Law

The amendment to the Depositors Guaranty Law that allowed state banks to change from the Guaranty Fund plan to the Bond Security plan caused the ultimate collapse of the Guaranty Fund. From the date the amendment was signed into law, the Guaranty Fund banks began changing to the bond system at an average of one a day—as fast as they could make proper bond and satisfy the banking commissioner.[25]

In January 1926 Commissioner Austin, in an interview with the editor of the *Texas Bankers Record*, expressed the opinion that the Guaranty Fund plan for protecting depositors would become inoperative "within the next year or so" because of the notable exodus to the Bond Security plan.[26] At that time, 484 banks were using the Bond Security System, while 358 banks remained in the Guaranty Fund. In discussing the changes, Austin said that his main concern was to prevent the weak banks from being left in the Guaranty Fund system because of their inability to make the bond. To prevent this, the commissioner reported that more than 50 banks had been reorganized and rendered stable and that the work was continuing.

In May 1926 Commissioner Austin reported that only 180 banks remained in the Guaranty Fund, and it was anticipated that within the next twelve months most of those would transfer to the Bond Security plan. But, he pointed out, the Department of Banking would not allow unsound banks to leave the Guaranty Fund and thereby expose depositors to inadequate protection in case of failure.[27]

The September 1926 edition of the *Texas Bankers Record* announced that the Department of Banking would recommend the repeal of the Depositors Guaranty Law to the Fortieth Legislature, which would convene in January 1927. The article also reported that as of August 1, 1926, only 127 banks, with capital of $4.0 million and deposits of $17.0 million were left in the Guaranty Fund.[28]

Table 17

Banks Participating in the Guaranty Fund and
Bond Security System in Texas
January 1, 1925, through February 2, 1927

Date	Guaranty Fund	Bond Security System
January 1, 1925	900	33
January 1926	358	484
June 1926	160	654
August 1, 1926	127	679
December 1, 1926	75	800
February 2, 1927	27	739

Source: *Texas Bankers Record*, various issues, 1925-1927.

The banks that remained in the Guaranty Fund during 1926 were under a heavy burden of assessment. By August 1 the 2 percent maximum assessment allowed had already been levied, collected, and paid out. Assessments during 1926 alone had amounted to about $340,000, or 8.5 percent of the capital of the 127 banks left in the system. At this time further assessments could not be levied. If an additional bank or banks failed and such failures necessitated payments to noninterest-bearing, unsecured depositors in excess of the amount that the remaining Guaranty Fund banks had as their interest in the fund, the Guaranty Fund would be depleted.

The next Guaranty Fund bank to fail was the Commercial State Bank of Longview, which closed its doors on September 29, 1926. On that date 109 banks remained in the Guaranty Fund, with an aggregate interest therein of approximately $344,000. According to James Shaw, commissioner of banking from September 1, 1927, until July 12, 1933, $44,000 of this amount was encumbered because of the liability of these banks for assessments not levied and adjustments to be made. The remainder, approximately $300,000, was applicable to the payment of depositors of the Longview bank and to subsequent failures—of which there were eight before the law was repealed on February 11, 1927.[29]

With the Texas Bankers Association, the state Department of Banking, and the state bankers overwhelmingly in favor of repeal of the Guaranty Fund, the Legislative Committee of the Texas Bankers Association began in the fall of 1926 to work toward this end. The committee chairman, Paul D. Page, a former state senator and president of the Citizens State Bank of Bastrop, drafted a bill that was referred to the banking commissioner, his legal department, and prominent state bankers for their consideration. It was then carefully redrawn and sent to the legislature, where it was introduced in the house and the senate.[30]

The senate bill was passed without a dissenting vote. Even Thomas B. Love, who had authored the Depositors Guaranty Law, voted for its repeal. He explained his position by stating that in his opinion the Depositors Guaranty Law, as originally adopted, had been sound but that the amendment adopted by the Thirty-ninth Legislature had destroyed it. When the bill reached the house, it was passed with only nine dissenting votes and promptly sent to Governor Dan Moody for his signature. On February 11, 1927, Governor Moody signed the bill that repealed both the Depositors Guaranty Fund and the Bond Security System.[31]

Review of the Depositors Guaranty Law

With the repeal of the Depositors Guaranty Law, the Texas experiment with deposit insurance was over. It had met the same fate as had the experiment in the seven other states that had adopted some form of deposit protection after the Panic of 1907.

From the time that the Guaranty Fund went into effect on January 1, 1910, until its repeal on February 11, 1927, approximately $18 million had been paid to the noninterest-bearing, unsecured depositors of 138 defunct banks. These payments had necessitated special assessments amounting to nearly $17.1 million and had resulted in a net loss of about $11.6 million to the Guaranty Fund.

As a system of bank deposit protection, the Guaranty Fund was an unqualified success as long as most of the state banks were participants. The authors of the Depositors Guaranty Law had wisely prohibited changes from one deposit insurance plan to the other, but there was no way to prevent member banks from leaving the Guaranty Fund by converting to the national banking system. And, of course, it was not anticipated that state bank failures would ever be so numerous or assessments so heavy that the actual survival of the state banking system would be threatened by exodus to the national banking system. But by the fall of 1924 such an eventuality not only appeared possible but probable. As a result, the state bankers and the Texas Bankers Association urged that the Depositors Guaranty Law be repealed.

The Thirty-ninth Legislature, which convened in January 1925, attempted to offer relief to the Guaranty Fund banks by allowing them to change to the Bond Security System. A flight from the Guaranty Fund to the Bond Security System began and did not subside until September 1926, when only the small and weaker banks were left in the fund. To that time, not a single noninterest-bearing, unsecured depositor of a Guaranty Fund bank had lost money due to the failure of a bank. However, on September 29, 1926, the Commercial State Bank of Longview failed, and as a consequence the Guaranty Fund was rendered insolvent. On February 11, 1927, the Depositors Guaranty Law was repealed.

W. A. Sandlin, state bank examiner during the 1920s, made the following comment with respect to the failure of the Guaranty Fund:

In my opinion the weakness in the Guaranty Fund was primarily in not having a limit on the amount of deposits covered and no provision was made for the creation of a reserve fund. All noninterest-bearing, unsecured deposits, regardless of amount, were protected under the Guaranty Fund. When so many banks left the Guaranty Fund to become bond banks, converted to national banks, or merged with other banks, naturally, the total deposit base of existing banks under the Guaranty Fund declined, increasing the assessments.[32]

Charles O. Austin had recommended in 1922 that a limit be placed upon the deposits of one individual covered by the fund. If Austin's recommendations had been adopted by the Thirty-eighth Legislature in 1923, it is possible that the Guaranty Fund might have survived—at least until the Great Depression. If it had survived, however, undoubtedly more banks would have converted to the national banking system and the continuation of the dual banking system in Texas might have been threatened.

In a speech before the Texas Bankers Association in May 1926 Commissioner Austin reported that since the enactment of the Depositors Guaranty Law in 1909 only two Bond Security banks had failed.[33] One of them was reorganized, and the depositors paid in full. The other had failed only a few weeks before Austin's speech, but he stated that its depositors would also be paid in full and that it was likely that the casualty company would sustain very little loss, if any.

In spite of the successful record of the Bond Security System indicated by Commissioner Austin, the plan was generally considered to be objectionable by state bankers. As previously noted, its principal disadvantages were the high premium rates applied when a bond was obtained through a surety company and the personal liability incurred when a personal bond was posted. As a result, there was no effort to retain the Bond Security System when the Depositors Guaranty Law was repealed.

The Depositors Guaranty Law caused a substantial number of banks to convert to the national banking system. During the last five years of the law 126 state banks obtained national charters, an average of about 25 per year; before that time the average was 3 conversions per year.

One of the results of the conversions from the state banking system to the national banking system was a net decrease in the aggregate deposits of the state banks and a net increase in the aggregate deposits of the national banks. Of course, the changes in the deposit totals experienced by both systems were influenced by factors other than conversions—the state banking system totals being particularly affected by the many failures of state banks.

The existence of the Guaranty Fund in the 1920s resulted in a severe setback for the Texas state banking system, as evidenced by the loss of the 128 banks that converted from the state to the national banking system and the substantial loss in deposits that resulted. The banks that converted to national charters included some of the largest and strongest institutions in the state banking system. Among them were the following:

State bank	Converted to
Mercantile Bank and Trust Company	Mercantile National Bank, Dallas
Guaranty Bank and Trust Company	Republic National Bank, Dallas
First State Bank	State National Bank, Corpus Christi
Security State Bank and Trust Company	Lubbock National Bank, Lubbock
The Lubbock State Bank	First National Bank, Lubbock

The damage sustained by the state banking system as a result of the conversions was not only severe but also long lasting. Only recently has the state banking system regained the position it held before the conversion movement began, as measured by its percentage of aggregate deposits.

Although the Guaranty Fund law was repealed on February 11, 1927, the liquidation of the fund required another four years. In July 1931 Governor Sterling signed a bill authorizing the payment of $1.7 million to the Guaranty Fund banks.[34]

Notes

1. *House Journal, Texas, Thirty-second Legislature, Regular Session, 1911* (Austin: Austin Printing Company, 1911), p. 34.
2. The amount of the withdrawals, assessments, and losses and the cost as a percentage of deposits were obtained from Ed Hall, "The Workings of the Guaranty Fund," address before the First District Bankers of Houston, February 14, 1922, in *Texas Bankers Record* 11 (March 1922): 33.
3. "Banks Should Not Convert Now, Says Commissioner Hall," *Texas Bankers Record* 9 (February 1922): 25.
4. Peterson, "Liquidating State Banks," p. 48.
5. R. L. Thornton, address before the state bank section at the Texas Bankers Association's annual convention, Dallas, May 16, 1923, in *Texas Bankers Record* 12 (June 1923): 56.
6. R. L. Thornton, "Some Thoughts on the Guaranty Fund System of Securing Deposits," *Texas Bankers Record* 14 (September 1924): 9-11.
7. Joe E. Lawther, "Do You Find the Guaranty Fund Assessments to Your Liking?" *Texas Bankers Record* 14 (December 1924): 9.
8. Thornton, "Thoughts on the Guaranty Fund System," p. 9.
9. W. C. Page, "The Guaranty Fund Law in Texas," address before the Guaranty Fund Bankers, reported in *Texas Bankers Record* 14 (October 1924): 15.
10. Z. D. Bonner, "How About an Absolute Repeal of the Guaranty Law," *Texas Bankers Record* 14 (November 1924): 10.
11. Ibid.
12. Ibid.

13. "Does Conversion Decrease Deposits?" *Texas Bankers Record* 14 (December 1924): 11-12.
14. Bonner, "How About an Absolute Repeal," pp. 10-11.
15. Ibid., p. 11.
16. Thornton, "Thoughts on the Guaranty Fund System," p. 10.
17. Bonner, "How About an Absolute Repeal," pp. 10-11.
18. B. C. Roberts, "Answer This—What Shall We Do With the Guaranty Fund?" *Texas Bankers Record* 14 (November 1924): 13.
19. Bonner, "How About an Absolute Repeal," p. 11.
20. Ibid., p. 10.
21. *General Laws of Texas, Thirty-ninth Legislature, Regular Session, 1925* (Austin: A. C. Baldwin and Sons, 1925), p. 26.
22. *Texas Bankers Record* 14 (May 1925): 32.
23. Charles O. Austin, *Texas Bankers Record* 14 (April 1925): 9-11.
24. "Does Conversion Decrease Deposits?"
25. "Commissioner Austin Says Guaranty Fund Plan Will Become Inoperative," *Texas Bankers Record* 15 (January 1926): 9.
26. Ibid.
27. Charles O. Austin, "Our State Banking System," address before the Texas Bankers Association's annual convention, Galveston, May 25, 1926, *Texas Bankers Record* 15 (June 1926): 37.
28. *Texas Bankers Record* 16 (September 1926): 33.
29. James Shaw, "The Aftermath of the Guaranty Fund," *Texas Bankers Record* 17 (June 1928): 61-63.
30. Paul Page, "The Guaranty Fund is Dead," *Texas Bankers Record* 16 (April 1927): 14-15.
31. Ibid.
32. W. A. Sandlin, written statement of June 1969.
33. Austin, "Our State Banking System," p. 37.
34. *Texas Bankers Record* 20 (July 1931): 33.

10

The Depression and Its Aftermath 1930-1939

Continued Decline of the State Banking System

The decline of the state banking system that began during the 1920-1921 recession and lasted throughout most of the twenties entered its second and final phase with the onslaught of the Great Depression. In 1929 the banking climate in Texas improved significantly; the number of state bank failures was lower than in any other year since before the 1920-1921 recession. But beginning in 1930 the state banking system came under severe pressure, which did not abate until the middle of 1933.

During the period between 1930 and 1939 the number of state banks in Texas declined from 699 to 395, or by 304; 391 state banks were liquidated—268 voluntarily and 123 involuntarily—and 90 new charters were granted, mostly to reorganized banks, although three of these were not open by the end of the period. The total reduction in the numbers from the peak of 1,031 banks on December 31, 1920, to December 31, 1939, was a startling 636 banks.

The decrease in the number of banks in operation during the thirties was naturally accompanied by a decline in total state bank capital and resources. While the call of December 31, 1929, was answered by 699 banks with capital, surplus, and undivided profits of $52.4 million and resources of $332.5 million, exactly ten years later only 395 banks answered the call, with aggregate capital accounts of $33.1 million and total resources of $241.8 million. In other words, the number of banks had decreased by 43.5 percent; capital, surplus, and undivided profits by nearly 37 percent; and resources by more than 27 percent.

The Economic Setting

Economic Conditions in the United States

According to the National Bureau of Economic Research, the Great Depression began with a cyclical peak in August 1929 and reached a trough in March 1933. The economic contraction that occurred during this period was and still is the most severe in the history of the United States. Production, employment, income, and prices all fell precipitously. In addition, approximately one third of the nation's commercial banks, holding nearly one tenth of total bank deposits, suspended operations because of financial difficulties.

Economic conditions in the 1920s in the United States were generally mixed. The industrial sector of the economy enjoyed relative prosperity after the 1920-1921 recession, and at the beginning of 1929 the outlook was favorable. The agricultural sector of the economy during the same period was not so prosperous. This was particularly true in the South and Southwest, where cotton and cattle predominated. From 1921 through the middle of 1927 cattle prices were very depressed, and they did not reach prerecession levels until the middle of 1929. It is by now an all too familiar theme that cotton farmers generally suffered from overproduction, drought, pestilence, and wildly gyrating prices throughout most of the twenties.

There is a general misconception that the Great Depression was preceded by a period of severe inflation. Nothing could be further from the truth. By 1923 wholesale prices had recovered only one sixth of their 1920-1921 decline. During the industrial recession of 1924 they declined slightly, then rose again in 1925 before beginning a protracted downturn that left them roughly equivalent in 1929 to their 1921 level. If anything, the 1920s was a period of deflation of prices rather than inflation. Much of the misconception about prices in general probably stems from the tremendous increase in the prices of common stocks—which began in 1924 and ended with the market crash in October 1929. The events that led up to the crash of 1929 and the crash itself deserve special attention because of their significance to the Depression.

The Speculative Fever of the 1920s

The bull stock market of the 1920s got under way in mid-1924. At that time the *New York Times* average of twenty-five industrial stocks was 106. By the end of the year the index was 134, and by the end of 1925 it was 181. In 1926 the market suffered a brief setback in the early part of the year and again in October, but it finished the year on a strong note.

The year 1927 stands out in stock market history, for it was during that year that the spectacular market upsurge of the latter 1920s began in earnest. At the start of the year the *New York Times* average was 176, but by the end of the year it had advanced 69 points to 245.

Another event of major significance that occurred in 1927—one that most authorities regard as instrumental in bringing on the ultimate worldwide economic contraction—was the return of Great Britain to the gold standard at the pre-World War I exchange rate of $4.86 per English pound sterling. This move greatly overvalued the pound: as a result Great Britain's exports decreased and her imports increased, causing an outflow of gold to the United States. The Federal Reserve responded by reducing the rediscount rate from 4 to 3.5 percent and by purchasing substantial quantities of government securities. The latter move provided the banks and people selling the government securities with funds that either were invested directly in common stocks or became available to help finance the purchase of stocks by others.

Speculative fever began to grip the country in 1928. This was evidenced by the nearly twofold increase in brokers' loans—loans collateralized by securities purchased on margin. The rush to buy stocks on margin drove the interest rate on brokers' loans from about 5 percent at the beginning of 1928 to 12 percent by year-end. These high rates and the alleged safety of the loans attracted an avalanche of funds into Wall Street. As a result the *New York Times* industrial stock index advanced 86 points, to 331, during the year.

By 1928 Federal Reserve System officials faced a dilemma. On the one hand, they felt a responsibility to curb speculation in an attempt to avert a runaway boom in the stock market. On the other hand, they were sensitive to general economic conditions.

They did not want to put a pinch on legitimate business or take the chance of initiating a business decline in the United States; neither did they wish to endanger the gold standard in Europe. In retrospect, though, it appears that concern for the dangers of overspeculation in the stock market took precedence. In the first half of 1928 the discount rate was raised in half-point increments from 3.5 percent to 5 percent, and heavy sales of government securities were initiated in an effort to diminish the supply of funds going into the market.

These tactics only discouraged speculation temporarily. As bank reserves were absorbed by Federal Reserve open-market operations, the member banks replenished them by rediscounting. Moreover, in an effort to finance ordinary nonspeculative commerce the Board continued to buy acceptances, which, of course, provided the commercial banks with reserves to lend more money in the stock market.

The boom went on. In January the *New York Times* industrial index advanced 30 points. There was no appreciable gain in February, however. The news that the Federal Reserve Board was meeting daily in Washington reached Wall Street in March. A few months later, during the summer of 1929, the averages climbed from 339 to 449. The volume was consistently heavy, and the stock market dominated the news.

In September 1929 the great bull market came to an end. The immediate cause is often attributed to a September 5 speech by economist Roger Babson in which he predicted that a crash was inevitable, that the market averages would probably drop 60 to 80 points, and that there would be a business depression.

The Stock Market Crash of 1929 and Its Aftermath

Thursday, October 24, 1929, is generally recognized as the first day of the stock market collapse of 1929. On the previous day the *New York Times* industrial average had fallen from 415 to 384, wiping out all of its gain since the previous June. On Thursday morning, from the opening bell, volume was large and prices plummeted. The ticker tape fell behind, prices fell, and by eleven o'clock the market had degenerated into a wild scramble to sell. Panic, disorder, fright, and confusion characterized the morning hours. By noon, however, the panic was over. At twelve o'clock reporters had learned that the heads of the nation's largest banks were meeting at the offices of J. P. Morgan. Word spread quickly, and the speculation that the banks would pool their resources to support the market stemmed the tide. However, the worst was yet to come.

On Friday and Saturday volume was heavy, and the market and prices were relatively steady. The meeting of the bankers, the announcement of their intentions to avert a panic, and their overt actions on Thursday afternoon had stabilized the market. However, on Monday, October 28, the market resumed its decline. The *New York Times* average fell 49 points during the day, and there was no recovery.

Tuesday, October 29, 1929, was the most disastrous day in the history of the New York stock market. The volume was 16,410,030 shares, considerably more than the record 12,894,650 shares traded on the previous Thursday. The ticker tape at the close was running two and one-half hours late. And the *New York Times* index was off 43 points for the day.

From the panic of October 1929, the stock market declined almost continuously through June of 1932. The *New York Times* index had reached 224 by November 13, 1929—a decline of 50 percent from the previous summer. From January through March 1930, there was substantial recovery, but thereafter the market declined until, on July 8, 1932, the *New York Times* industrial stock index reached 58, 87 percent below its high of 449 recorded in the summer of 1929.

Causes and Consequences of the Crash of 1929

The opinions about the cause of the stock market crash of 1929 are quite varied. Perhaps the most widely accepted view is that the crash was merely a reflection of the depression that had begun during the summer of 1929. However, in the opinion of Professor John Kenneth Galbraith, a depression, serious or otherwise, could not have been foreseen at the time the crash occurred.

It is his belief that the speculation that preceded the crash was the basic cause. In his opinion:

> The collapse in the stock market in the autumn of 1929 was implicit in the speculation that went before. The only question concerning that speculation was how long it would last. Sometime, sooner or later, confidence in the short-run reality of increasing common stock values would weaken. When this happened, some people would sell, and this would destroy the reality of increasing values. Holding for an increase would now become meaningless; the new reality would be falling prices. There would be a rush, pellmell, to unload. This was the way past speculative orgies had ended. It was the way the end came in 1929. It is the way speculation will end in the future.[1]

Regardless of the cause or causes of the stock market crash of 1929, there is little doubt that one of its consequences was to deepen the contraction of business that had begun in the preceding summer. It changed the atmosphere in which people were doing business and replaced optimistic expectations for the future with uncertainty. Accordingly, the willingness of consumers and businesses to spend was reduced, additional unemployment resulted, and the recession was intensified.

The Deflation of the Economy

Although prosperity had begun to fade in mid-1929, the decline seemed moderate, and it was generally believed that if a recession were to occur, it would probably not be any worse than those of 1924 and 1927. Then the stock market fell precipitously, and optimism was replaced by doubt and anxiety. Yet there were still no signs of panic in the money market or of large-scale liquidation of assets in commercial banking. By early 1930, though, it was abundantly clear that a depression of more than usual severity was under way.

The deflation that had begun in 1929 showed a marked acceleration. From the cyclical peak in August 1929 to the stock market crash in October, production, personal income, and wholesale prices had declined at annual rates of 20.0 percent, 7.5 percent, and 5.0 percent, respectively. But during the months immediately after the crash the annual rates of decline accelerated to 27.0 percent, 13.5 percent, and 17.0 percent, respectively. In other words, during 1930 what had appeared to have been a mild recession in the fall of 1929 developed into a protracted and intense depression—the most severe on record in the history of the United States.

During 1930 industrial production declined 17.2 percent; personal income, 10.4 percent; wholesale prices, 9.3 percent; housing starts, 32.5 percent; and farm income, 20.0 percent. In 1930 unemployment increased to 8.7 percent of the labor force

Table 18

Selected U.S. Economic Indicators, 1929-1942

Year	Wholesale prices[a]	Personal income[b]	Industrial production[c]	Unemployment[d]	Housing starts[e]	Farm income[f]
1929	95.3	85.8	58	3.2	509.0	11,312
1930	86.4	76.9	48	8.7	330.0	9,055
1931	73.0	65.7	39	15.9	254.0	6,381
1932	64.8	50.1	30	23.6	134.0	4,748
1933	65.9	47.2	36	24.9	93.0	5,463
1934	74.9	53.6	39	21.7	126.0	6,803
1935	80.0	60.2	46	20.1	221.0	7,693
1936	80.8	68.5	55	16.9	319.0	7,669
1937	86.3	73.9	60	14.3	336.0	9,200
1938	78.6	68.6	46	19.0	406.0	8,169
1939	77.1	72.9	57	17.2	515.0	8,635
1940	78.6	78.7	66	14.6	602.6	9,105
1941	87.3	96.3	88	9.9	706.1	11,655
1942	98.8	123.5	110	4.7	356.0	16,215

[a]Wholesale price index of the Department of Labor (1926=100).
[b]Billions of dollars (current prices).
[c]Federal Reserve Board index (1947-1949=100).
[d]Percentage of the civilian labor force unemployed.
[e]Thousands of units.
[f]Millions of dollars (current prices).
Source: U.S. Department of Commerce, *Historical Statistics of the United States—Colonial Times to 1957* (Washington, D.C.: Government Printing Office, 1958).

from 3.2 percent the year before, thereby reaching the highest annual rate since the recession of 1920-1921. Moreover, the failure rate per 10,000 business concerns rose from 104 in 1929 to 122 in 1930, and bank suspensions increased from 659 to 1,350.

The prevailing pessimism deepened and prolonged the depression. The unwillingness of business, investors, and consumers to spend created lower incomes and lower demand. The outlook worsened and people became more despondent. Businesses laid off additional employees; the unhappy sequence of lower incomes and lower demand repeated itself. In short, there was a chain reaction of responses, each of which tended to exacerbate the depression.

Table 19

Commercial Bank Failures in the United States
1929-1939

Year	Commercial bank failures	Number of banks as of June 30	Failure rate
1929	659	25,330	2.60
1930	1,350	24,079	5.61
1931	2,293	22,071	10.39
1932	1,453	19,163	7.58
1933	2,428*	14,624	17.29
1934	57	15,894	0.04
1935	34	16,053	0.02
1936	44	15,803	0.03
1937	59	15,580	0.04
1938	55	15,341	0.04
1939	42	15,146	0.03

*Includes all banks closed during the banking holiday and not reopened by December 31, 1936.

Sources: Milton Friedman and Anna Jacobson Schwartz, *A Monetary History of the United States, 1867-1960* (Princeton: Princeton University Press, 1963), p. 426; *Statistical Abstract of the United States: 1940* (Washington, D.C.: Government Printing Office, 1941), p. 266.

This process continued through 1931 and 1932 and finally ended during 1933, when recovery began.

Over the duration of the Great Depression, from 1929 through 1933, total spending in the economy declined persistently from $104 billion to $56 billion. Business firms cut back production and laid off employees until, in 1932 and 1933, about one worker out of four was unemployed; the total drop in production was 48.3 percent from 1929 to the low point reached in 1932. Personal income during the period declined $38.6 billion, or by 45 percent. On the farms the situation was even more severe, since aggregate farm income declined 58 percent, from $11.3 billion in 1929 to $4.7 billion in 1932. However, perhaps no industry suffered more than residential construction. For several years before the beginning of the depression housing starts had been declining—from a high of 937,000 units in 1925 to 753,000 units in 1928. In the following year 509,000 units were built. At the nadir of the depression in 1933 only 93,000 units were constructed—a reduction of more than 80 percent from 1929.

By 1933 the number of manufacturing establishments had declined to 139,325 (from 206,663 in 1929); the failure rate of business concerns had reached 154 in 10,000, the highest on record before or since; and 9,106 commercial banks with deposits of $6,859 million had suspended operations either temporarily or permanently.

Commercial Bank Failures

During the depression, there was, of course, a sharp rise in commercial bank failures in the United States. As in the 1920s, failures were much more numerous among nonmember banks, small banks, and banks in agricultural communities. Nonmembers of the Federal Reserve System accounted for 80 percent of total failures but only 57 percent of the deposits of the banks that failed; 85 percent of all failures involved banks located in the nation's five agricultural sections. As a matter of fact, it was not until December 1930 that a large city bank failed. At that time the Bank of the United States in New York City was closed.

The bank failures during the depression occurred in clusters, rather than being concentrated in the panic phase of the cycle as in previous recessions. The first banking crisis began in October 1930; the second banking crisis in March 1931; the third banking crisis in October 1931; and the final and most severe banking crisis, commonly referred to as "the banking panic of 1933," began in January 1933 and ended with the nationwide banking holiday in March 1933.[2] The worst years for bank closings were 1931 and 1933.

Although the bank failures for the most part were triggered by the events of the 1930s, poor loans and investments made in the twenties had weakened the banks and made them sensitive to any economic reversal. And the deflation of the economy in the fall of 1929 and in 1930 was, by any standard, rapid and severe. As unemployment increased and income and prices decreased, bank borrowers found themselves unable to liquidate debt. Moreover, a severe depreciation in bank investment portfolios occurred as bond prices fell sharply during the initial phase of the downturn; this further weakened bank assets. In short, commercial bank liquidity was severely impaired.

Awareness of the increasing financial difficulties of the banks caused a general uneasiness among depositors and ultimately a stampede for liquidity. This was unfortunate because, in order to meet the demands for currency, banks were forced to dump securities in large amounts at substantial discounts, which further weakened the bond markets. As portfolio values declined and liquidity was further impaired, it became impossible for many banks to meet withdrawal demands of depositors, and they had no alternative but to suspend payments. Other banks were forced to close by bank examiners, who became increasingly critical as the deterioration of assets continued. Another condition that caused failures was the nature of the reserve system—a system in which each bank kept its liquidity reserves principally in other commercial banks; when one bank failed, the reserves of the other banks deposited with the defunct bank were frozen. Depositors, being aware of the situation, would panic and initiate runs on the banks still open. Thus one failure led to another.

The failures during the first banking crisis, which began in October 1930, were basically caused by a scramble for liquidity. It started in the agricultural states of the Midwest, spread across the country, and culminated with the failure of the Bank of the United States in New York. In November and December of that year more than 600 banks across the nation failed.

In 1931 the financial panic intensified. Depositors and banks, with the experience of the first banking crisis still lingering, were bound to react more vigorously to any new wave of failures. Moreover, a worsening of the financial situation abroad amplified the panic. The foreign situation did not seem to play such a significant role in the banking crisis of March 1931—which again resulted from a quest for liquidity. However, the crisis in the fall of 1931 was definitely influenced by Britain's departure from the gold standard in September, the subsequent flight from the dollar and dollar assets, and the higher interest rates that followed. In October alone, 522 banks failed. During the six months from August through January 1932, some 1,860 banks with over $1.4 billion in deposits closed.

The Role of the Federal Reserve

It might be asked at this point why the Federal Reserve, which had been created to prevent a crisis such as the one under way, had not been effective in halting the decline. At the time of the stock market crash the Federal Reserve did begin to take action. On November 1, 1929, the discount rate was lowered from 6 to 5 percent, and the New York Bank purchased $160 million in government securities on the open market. Shortly thereafter, further reductions in the discount rates were initiated; the rate reached 2.5 percent in June 1930 and 1.5 percent in November of that year. Additional purchases of government securities totaling $300 million were also undertaken by October. These actions, however, did not succeed in expanding the use of credit, since there was a pervasive desire for liquidity in the economy. Commercial bank loans declined, and currency in circulation increased steadily to satisfy domestic hoarding. Moreover, attempts to relieve the liquidity problem of individual commercial banks through the rediscount system were thwarted by a dearth of eligible paper in bank loan portfolios. As business declined, so did the amount of paper eligible for rediscount and the volume of Federal Reserve rediscounts. The decrease in eligible paper also hampered efforts to put more currency into circulation, since eligible paper was necessary as backing for Federal Reserve notes.

In the fall of 1931, at the time Great Britain left the gold standard, the Federal Reserve was confronted again with a policy dilemma. Low interest rates were needed to fight the depression at home, but higher interest rates seemed necessary to prevent withdrawals of gold from the United States. A sharp increase in gold exports and the decrease in the reserve ratio that followed Britain's departure from gold compelled the Federal Reserve to increase the discount rate to 3.5 percent in October. This increase and the unstable international situation intensified the banking crisis during the fall of 1931. However, in the months following the Federal Reserve action there was a net import of gold; and, as a result, the reserve ratio increased. In February 1932 the Federal Reserve returned to an easy-money policy, facilitated by the passage late that month of the Glass-Steagall Act, which permitted the Federal Reserve to count government securities—as well as eligible paper rediscounted for member banks and gold—as collateral for Federal Reserve notes.

The Reconstruction Finance Corporation

In January 1932 Congress took another helpful step by creating the Reconstruction Finance Corporation (R.F.C.). It was authorized to make "fully and adequately secured" loans to banks and insurance companies, temporary loans to railroads, and, by the Emergency Relief and Construction Act of 1932, loans to states and to farmers. The capital, $500 million, was subscribed by the United States, and the R.F.C. was authorized to borrow $1.5 billion through the issuance of debentures; its borrowing limit was soon increased to $3.3 billion. In March 1933 the R.F.C. was authorized to supplement bank capital (and liquid assets) by purchasing a special issue of preferred stock for cash.

The R.F.C. undoubtedly saved many banks. Up to March 1933 it had extended loans of $2.2 billion, approximately one third of which were to banks. Most of the banks receiving help were located in small communities. For example, of the first 5,000 banks receiving aid, 70 percent were located in towns of less than 5,000 population.

In the course of providing its benefits the R.F.C. also contributed to problems in banking. One of the most serious was that funds lent by the R.F.C. were often used to pay off favored depositors before a bank closed. This, of course, left other depositors in a very unfavorable position, since the R.F.C. had usually taken the best of the bank's loans as collateral for its credit extension.

Another shortcoming of the R.F.C. operation was a provision that required the corporation to report to the president of the United States and to Congress the names of borrowers, the amounts of the loans, and the rates of interest charged. The clerk of the House interpreted this to mean that the information was to be disclosed to the public. Thus the public was informed of every bank that was in financial difficulty; this, in many instances, led to increased demands for currency by depositors. For some institutions the demands were of sufficient magnitude to constitute a run and cause suspension.

The foregoing, in the opinion of most authorities, directly led to an intensification of financial panic conditions in 1932. There were, of course, other factors involved. President Hoover charged that the responsibility for the increased tempo of the panic was caused by the failure of Congress to balance the budget and by the exclusion by the Democratic platform of support for the gold standard, as well as by the publication of information on R.F.C. loans.[3] In any event, public confidence in banks had not been restored and suspensions continued.

Bank failures increased substantially in the late spring and early summer of 1932. Throughout the summer the desire for liquidity continued to increase, more banks failed, the demand for currency intensified, and finally the crisis developed into a full-fledged panic. On October 31, 1932, Nevada proclaimed a twelve-day banking holiday. On February 4, 1933, Louisiana closed its banks for the day. Confidence waned. On February 14 the Michigan banking system closed its doors. The panic gained momentum daily. During the last week of February and the first few days of March $400 million in gold was withdrawn from the Federal Reserve banks and more state governors declared bank holidays. President Hoover suggested federal insurance of bank deposits to the Federal Reserve Board. The Board, in turn, recommended that the president proclaim a general bank holiday. On March 4 Governor Lehman closed the New York banks because of heavy and continuous withdrawals. By this time almost all of the commercial banks in the country were closed.

The Banking Holiday of March 1933

Virtually the first act of President Roosevelt after his inauguration on March 4 was to proclaim a nationwide banking holiday from March 6 to March 9. At the same time the president ordered the suspension of currency redemption in gold in the United States and the cessation of gold shipments abroad.

On March 9 Congress, meeting in special session, passed the Emergency Banking Act, Title I of which approved and confirmed the action taken on March 6 and gave the president powers over currency and banking. Title II of the act provided for the reopening and operation of certain national banks with impaired assets under the supervision of a "conservator" appointed by the comptroller of the currency. The issuance of nonassessable preferred stock by national banks, to be subscribed by the R.F.C. or the general public, was provided for in the emergency banking legislation. The R.F.C. was also authorized to buy similar issues from state banks. Another feature of the act provided for emergency issues of Federal Reserve Bank notes secured by U.S. government obligations, eligible paper, and bankers' acceptances. Federal Reserve banks were also authorized for one year to make special loans to member banks "in exceptional and exigent circumstances," secured by satisfactory assets at 1 percent above the rediscount rate; this authority was subsequently extended for two more years. By the authority vested in him by the Emergency Banking Act, President Roosevelt officially took the United States off the gold standard on March 19, 1933.

When the banking holiday terminated on March 9, the president extended it. On the following day member banks were directed to make application to the Federal Reserve Bank of their district for a license to reopen, and state authorities were authorized to reopen their sound nonmember banks. Licensed member and nonmember banks were authorized to reopen on an unrestricted basis on March 13 in the twelve Federal Reserve Bank cities; on March 14 in some 250 other cities with clearinghouses; and on March 15 elsewhere.

At the end of 1932, approximately two months before the holiday, there were 17,796 commercial banks doing business in the United States. In the following two and one-half months, or by the termination of the banking holiday on March 15, 1933, 396 of these banks had failed and another 51 had either merged or been liquidated voluntarily. Of the 17,349 banks still in existence, only 11,919 were licensed to open and do business—the other 5,430 banks remained closed. By the end of the year 14,459 banks had reopened for business; 2,890 of their sister institutions were still closed. In the next two years an additional 758 banks received licenses to reopen and the other 2,132 presumably were either liquidated or merged. Total deposits of the more than 5,000 unlicensed banks on March 15, 1933, were slightly over $4 billion. Although three fifths of these banks ultimately resumed business, they held only three eighths of the aggregate deposits of the group.

The R.F.C. played a major role in the reconstruction of the banking system. In 1932 and 1933 it purchased from more than 6,000 banks a total of $1.3 billion in capital stock—a sum equal to about one third of total bank capital in 1933. It lent $187 million to banks that remained open and over $900 million to banks that were closed. During the two years the R.F.C. provided financial assistance to 8,589 banks amounting to more than $2 billion.

The New Deal Recovery

While the commercial banks of the country were closed, President Roosevelt set about the task of restoring confidence. On March 12 he delivered the first of his renowned "fireside chats." The president's address was a psychological masterpiece; on the following day, when the banks began to reopen, there were no runs. On the contrary, money flowed back into the banking system. Confidence in the banks had been restored and the recovery of the economy began.

Unfortunately the process of recovery was a slow and tedious one, even though credit was made abundantly available. Beginning in March 1933 the Federal Reserve reduced the discount rate in several successive steps, culminating with the 1 percent rate (established in the summer of 1937) that prevailed through 1941. From March through October 1933 the Federal Reserve injected funds into the banking system by purchasing government securities totaling $600 million. At the same time reserves were further augmented by large gold inflows from Europe. Excess reserves of the member commercial banks rose from $379 million in April 1933 to $3 billion in July 1936.

The easy-money policy of the Federal Reserve was interrupted only once after recovery began, in the summer of 1936, when it appeared that the excess reserves in the banking system might induce dangerous inflation. Steps were taken at that time to tighten the money market. However, in the spring of the following year a sharp business recession began and the Federal Reserve Board returned to an easy-money policy. By October 1937 excess reserves exceeded $1 billion. Thereafter, excess reserves increased steadily until they reached nearly $7 billion in October 1940.

Despite the almost unlimited availability of funds and rock-bottom interest rates, consumer spending was at a very low level. As a consequence businesses hesitated to increase capital expenditures, hesitation that in turn prevented personal incomes and thus consumer expenditures from rising materially. It soon became apparent that the only way to increase personal income was through massive government spending and tax reductions. Such action, however, called for large budgetary deficits, which were deplored by the early Roosevelt administration as they had been by Hoover's administration. Between 1933 and 1936 the administration attempted to balance the budget, offsetting higher expenditures with higher taxes. The increased taxes, of course, tended to hold down the rise of consumer incomes and expenditures and retard the recovery of the economy. The balanced-budget concept was not abandoned until the business recession of 1937 forced a change in the administration's fiscal thinking.

The increased government expenditures during and after 1933 did help to push the country in the right direction. But it was not until 1939 and 1940 that the economy recovered to the predepression levels of the 1920s.

The New Deal programs included an extensive revision and reconstruction of the financial system. The first step was the passage of the Banking Act of June 16, 1933, an act "designed to strengthen the commercial banks, weaken the connection between speculation and banking, and give added powers to the Federal Reserve System."[4] Perhaps its most important provision established the Federal Deposit Insurance Corporation, which did much to restore trust in the banking system. The next step was the passage of the Banking Act of 1935, which greatly broadened the powers of the Board of Governors of the Federal Reserve System over member bank reserve requirements, open-market operations, and rediscount rates. It also eliminated the double liability on all national bank stock.

Economic Conditions in Texas

Effects of the Stock Market Crash

Texas endured relatively well the dramatic decline of the stock market in October 1929. Certainly some persons who had invested primarily in stocks sustained significant financial damage. Most of the citizens, however, were either farmers (59 percent of the population was rural) and hence had the majority of their assets tied up in their farms or they were in the lower-income and middle-income categories and had little to invest in securities. Moreover, Texas banks apparently had not lent heavily to their customers to finance positions in common stocks. Only two state banks failed in the fall of 1929 after the stock market crash, and the evidence strongly suggests that these failures resulted from the adverse cotton conditions.

Deflation and Recovery of the Texas Economy

Although the impact in Texas of the stock market decline was slight, the deflation of the economy that followed it was pronounced. Naturally, since Texas was basically agrarian, the most significant aspect of the deflation was the decrease in agricultural prices. The occurrence in 1930 of the most serious drought in the history of the United States to that time compounded the difficulties by reducing the cotton crop and the yields of other crops in Texas.

Agriculture was not the only Texas industry to experience a major setback during the early phases of the Great Depression. The value of manufactured products declined from $1,450.2 million to $845.2 million from 1929 to 1930. Even the production of oil decreased for a brief period, from 296 million barrels in 1929 to 290 million in 1930, the first year-to-year reduction to occur since 1910.

From 1929 to the low point reached in 1932, prices received by Texas farmers for cotton declined 62.2 percent; for all crops, the price decline was 65.5 percent during that time span. Beef cattle prices dropped 58.9 percent. Over the same period, lumber production fell more than 70 percent. The number of manufacturing establishments in Texas declined from 5,198 in 1929 to 4,326 at the trough of the depression in 1933, or by 16.8 percent. The number of wage earners in manufacturing establishments fell by almost one third, and their aggregate wages by more than half.

Following the national banking holiday spawned by the depression (March 6-15, 1933), business confidence was gradually restored and economic conditions began to improve. Between 1934 and 1939 cotton acreage continued to be reduced, as it had been since the onslaught of the depression, and the production of other crops increased. Land values resumed an upward trend and the demand for farms improved steadily. Proration exerted a stabilizing influence on petroleum production beginning in the early 1930s and the price of crude oil slowly rose from a low of five cents a barrel in 1931 to over one dollar a barrel by 1937. Petroleum output remained at relatively high levels through 1935 then increased sharply because of the discovery of a number of new fields. Among the related benefits, increased production of natural gas stimulated the development of manufacturing industries in the state. As restoration of economic values began to occur in the midthirties, banks were able to convert some of their frozen assets to cash.

The recession of 1937-1938 passed practically unnoticed in Texas. According to J. E. Woods, chairman of Farmers State Bank, Temple, and president of the Texas Bankers Association, the recession was "more threatened than real."[5] This he attributed to excellent yields from the soil, favorable livestock conditions, and continued development of oil, gas, sulphur, and other natural resources. Speaking on the same program as Mr. Woods, Banking Commissioner Zeta Gossett remarked that the state banks were in the best financial condition in their history. Earnings, liquidity, and capital ratios were all very favorable.[6]

Relative Severity of the Depression in Texas

The impact of the Great Depression, while indisputably substantial in Texas, was not as severe as in many other states. The agricultural sector of the Texas economy did not suffer as markedly during the depression of the 1930s as it had during the 1920s. This is partially owing to the fact that the farmers of Texas had lived with adversity during most of the twenties and had learned to cope with it.

It is true that the prices of cotton, other crops, and cattle declined to lower levels in the early 1930s than during either the 1920-1921 recession or, in the case of cotton, the period after the overproduction of 1926 (see table 8, page 124). However, the rate of decline in prices in the 1930s was slower than that experienced during the 1920-1921 recession. For example, the index of average prices received by Texas farmers for all crops declined 56.2 percent during the first year of the 1920-1921 recession, whereas the same index declined only 25.5 percent during the first year of the Great Depression. The decline in the index of livestock and livestock products for the same years was 33.7 percent and 19.2 percent. The significance of the more gradual deflation during the depression of the 1930s was that it permitted an easier and more orderly adjustment to the changing economic environment. Consequently, even though prices were low and the total value of crops was less, the profit margin did not narrow as much because of the lower cost of production.

Another reason that the agricultural sector did not suffer as severely was that the depression forced the farmer to reduce his total acreage devoted to cotton, a development that, in turn, led to greater diversification and self-sufficiency. Beginning in 1931 the domination of cotton in the Texas economy began to diminish (see table 10). In the four years 1931 through 1934 the number of acres of cotton harvested in Texas declined substantially each year. The total reduction over the period was approximately six million acres, which represents a decline of 37.4 percent from the 1930 level.

The large decrease in the acreage devoted to cotton reflected the recognition by Texas farmers, at last, that cotton acreage had to be reduced to balance supply with demand. The bankers, the Texas Cotton Association, the state and federal governments, and the agricultural authorities had for years urged the farmers to diversify and reduce cotton acreage. Probably the first time that the farmer had doubts about cotton was when the overproduction of 1926 caused prices to drop to their lowest levels since 1914—a calamity that left the farmer indebted and weakened for years to come. The cotton farmer was generally troubled through 1929 either by overproduction and depressed prices or by poor crops caused by drought, disease, and insect infestation. The short crop of 1930 and the collapse in prices at the onset of the depression must have been the final and convincing blow to many farmers, as evidenced by the 8.6 percent reduction from 1930 to 1931 in cotton acreage harvested.

Evidence of declining demand beginning in 1929 also induced farmers to reduce cotton acreage. Approximately 90 percent of the Texas cotton production in the late twenties was exported from the state, and the largest part of that production went to foreign markets. The decline in foreign demand that began in 1929 was caused by a number of factors: efforts by foreign countries to improve their trade balance with the United States by reducing imports; the passage in June 1930 of the Hawley-Smoot Tariff Act, which raised the tariff to such heights that foreign countries could no longer finance cotton purchases with revenues from exports to the United States; increased competition from foreign producers, especially India and China; and, particularly after 1929, the effects of the depression, which appreciably reduced the demand for cotton at home as well. Burris C. Jackson, president of the Texas Cotton Association, estimated in May 1938 that the demand for cotton had declined by 50 percent since 1929.[7]

An additional reason for the reduction in cotton acreage in Texas in the thirties was action taken by both the state and federal governments to achieve such a reduction. On September 22, 1931, the Texas legislature passed a law that restricted the amount of acreage planted in cotton or other soil-exhausting plants. Although it is probable the law was flagrantly violated because of lax enforcement, presumably it did help to bring about the reduction in cotton acreage in 1932 and 1933.

Efforts by the federal government to reduce cotton acreage began with the passage in 1932 of the Agricultural Adjustment Act, which had a profound impact upon agriculture in the South. In 1934 and 1935 alone, about fourteen million acres, or approximately one third of the total acres in cotton, were shifted to the production of other crops. In Texas, according to the 1936 edition of the *Texas Almanac*, the result of the federal program was a drastic cutting of acreage and production. The increased price that resulted, "plus government rentals and benefit payments brought a measure of prosperity to the farming industry of Texas that it had not known since the beginning of the Depression."[8]

By 1935 slightly less than 50 percent of the citizens of Texas were estimated to be primarily dependent upon cotton; this figure represents a substantial reduction from the estimate of 70 percent for 1930.[9] In 1940 the cotton acreage was lower than in any year since 1905 and about one half the peak of 1924-1926. It was estimated that probably less than 40 percent of the population in 1940 was dependent upon cotton.[10] Furthermore, the number of tenant farmers and sharecroppers had decreased by nearly 40 percent since 1930; most of these people had been drawn into manufacturing and other industries. The *Texas Almanac* called this radical shift in population "the most momentous development of any census decennium since that of 1860-1870, which witnessed the freeing of the slaves."[11]

Naturally, as farm acreage was diverted from cotton the diversification of Texas agriculture greatly increased. Of the land diverted during the thirties—about eight million acres—approximately one half went out of cultivation as cotton land and was converted to range land again.

In the opinion of W. B. Lee, chairman of the Agricultural Committee of the Texas Bankers Association in 1933, if the one-crop system had prevailed after 1930, Texas farmers would have been bankrupt by the end of the depression.[12] Instead, one of the primary sources of the strength of Texas during the depression was its vast agricultural resources. Because Texas was producing staple crops, there was a continued demand for its products, albeit at greatly reduced prices. Consequently, most of the population remained at work even during the hardest times and thus received some income. This situation is a sharp contrast to that in the heavily industrialized states; they produced mainly durable manufactured goods, the demand for which was sharply reduced by the depression. The Michigan economy, for example, suffered severely because of the large cutback in automobile production (from 4,455,178 units in 1929 to 1,103,577 units in 1932). Coincidentally, banking difficulties were more serious in Michigan than anywhere else in the country. According to Jesse H. Jones, president of the R.F.C. during the depression and author of *Fifty Billion Dollars*,

In no other large city was the drama of the banking crisis so prolonged or so tense as in Detroit. The closing of all banks in the motor capital on February 14, 1933, by proclamation of the governor, was the principal prelude to the collapse during the next three weeks of the nation's entire financial system.[13]

Another significant factor ameliorating instability in the Texas economy during the depression was the continued growth of the state's oil and other mineral industries. From 1920 to 1930 the production of oil increased threefold, to approximately 296.5 million barrels per year. While the combined effects of overproduction between 1930 and 1933 and the deepening of the Great Depression lowered the price of oil to such an extent that the value of total production in Texas fell during the early thirties, the continued upsurge in the oil industry's physical output nevertheless helped to cushion the drop in employment and other economic variables wrought by the general business downturn.

According to official statistics, the average value of Texas oil production for 1930 to 1933 was $238.6 million, only slightly less than the average yearly value of $242.6 million during the twenties. However, data regarding the value of oil production before 1935 are of limited utility since they are based on posted prices, and prior to the passage by the U.S. Congress of the

Table 20

Texas Oil Production and Value, Selected Years, 1910-1940

Year	Official production* (barrels)	Value[†] (dollars)
1910	8,899,266	6,605,755
1920	96,868,000	313,781,000
1929	296,876,000	322,520,000
1930	290,457,000	288,410,000
1931	309,460,916	170,315,000
1932	311,069,000	270,650,000
1933	402,609,000	225,000,000
1934	374,811,191	374,000,000
1935	391,097,000	371,664,170
1936	427,280,000	438,000,000
1937	510,318,000	594,500,000
1938	475,850,000	539,150,000
1939	483,528,000	478,330,000
1940	493,126,000	488,194,740

*Does not include oil produced in violation of state control of production, which began in 1931; before passage of the "Connally Hot Oil Act" by the U.S. Congress in 1935, a considerable amount of such "hot oil" was sold into interstate commerce and was a major factor in depressing oil prices.

[†]Based on official posted prices.

Source: *The Texas Almanac and State Industrial Guide, 1941-1942* (Dallas: A. H. Belo, 1940), p. 229.

"Connally Hot Oil Act" in 1935, overproduction generally caused much oil to sell at substantially less than the posted prices. Nonetheless, the continued increase in oil production in Texas during the early 1930s contributed significantly to the stability of the state's overall economy.

In addition to the production of crude oil, rapid development of other mineral industries occurred during the 1930s. From 1930 to 1940 the value of production of minerals other than crude oil increased from $95 million to $223 million. About three quarters of the 1940 total was accounted for by natural gas and gasoline production. The remaining $50 million to $60 million was contributed by sulphur, lignite, salt, stone, silver, gypsum, sand, and gravel. During the last few years of the thirties the diversity of minerals produced increased rapidly. The discovery and development of natural gas resources in Texas during the 1920s and 1930s had a profound impact upon Texas industrialization during the thirties. With great fuel supplies available, industry developed rapidly. According to the 1940 census, the physical volume of manufactured goods increased by 50 percent during the decade. The most notable steps toward the industrialization of the state were taken by the chemical industry. In 1934 the Southern Alkali Company completed the first major chemical plant in Texas at Corpus Christi. This was followed by the completion of the Dow Chemical Company plant at Freeport. Great strides were also made in oil well drilling and supply manufacturing, paper manufacturing, and food processing. One outgrowth of the reduction of cotton acreage and the increase in grain sorghum and corn acreage was the continued expansion of the cattle-feeding and meat-packing industries.

That conditions in Texas were more favorable than in many other states during the Great Depression and its aftermath can be attributed to the greater strength of the agricultural sector of the economy, continued demand for agricultural and petroleum products, and industrialization that followed the discovery and development of the state's natural gas resources. By the end of the 1930s, the economy of Texas had achieved a level of performance that, in terms of physical output, surpassed that of 1929, the best predepression year, and in other respects showed substantial progress toward recovering the prosperity that had existed in the late twenties.

State Bank Liquidations in the Thirties

During the 1930-1939 period there were 391 state bank liquidations in Texas, of which 265, or about two thirds, were concentrated in the four depression years, 1930 to 1933. The voluntary liquidation and failure situation in the Texas state banking system during the depression years was far superior to that for the commercial banking system of the entire United States. Unfortunately, the overall liquidation rate (for both voluntary and involuntary liquidations) for the entire country could be computed only for 1931, which was the worst year for Texas state banks during the depression. Even so, the liquidation rate was lower in Texas in that year than in the country as a whole—13.30 percent versus 13.79 percent. While a comparison of the overall liquidation rate for Texas with that for the United States for every year between 1930 and 1933 was not possible because data are unavailable, the information obtainable did permit the computation of failure rates, which are presented in table 9 (page 128). The data reveal that in each year the rate for Texas was substantially below that for the entire country; the average rate over the four years was 4.30 percent for Texas, 10.72 percent for the United States as a whole. While the Texas state banking system represented 2.98 percent of the total banks in the country, it accounted for only 1.35 percent of all failures for 1930 to 1933 and 0.80 percent of all restricted banks at the close of the banking holiday. The more favorable experience in Texas is attributed to the relatively strong position of the state banks at the onset of the Great Depression and the comparatively favorable condition of the Texas economy.

The strength of the state banks at the beginning of the depression is related to Commissioner James Shaw's "cleanup campaign." From late 1920 through 1926 the agricultural sector of the Texas economy had been depressed; as a result, many weak state banks had failed, merged, or liquidated voluntarily. In September 1927 Commissioner Shaw came into office and began the restoration of the state banking system. In late 1927 and during 1928 and 1929, every bank in the state was subjected to rigid examination, $15 million in doubtful and bad assets was charged off, and $11 million in new capital was paid in. A sizable number of voluntary liquidations ensued from the more vigorous regulatory measures. The stringent examinations and policies resulted in the adoption of more conservative banking practices by most of the other state banks, particularly with regard to lending. Furthermore, many, if not most, of the dishonest bankers and a considerable proportion of the truly incompetent ones had been ferreted out and expelled from the state banking system during the previous fifteen years. Thus at the beginning of the Great Depression most of the state banks in Texas were stronger financially and better managed and more closely supervised than at any time since the establishment of the system.

From 1934 until the end of the decade 126 state banks were liquidated. Naturally, both the liquidation rate and the failure rate for this period were greatly reduced from those of the earlier, more difficult thirties. In fact, compared with either the 1930-1933 period or the 1920s, the 1934-1939 period can be considered extremely favorable. Reasons for the improvement included a better economic climate than in some of the preceding years; the large amount of funds lent to the state banks by the Reconstruction Finance Corporation, funds that helped to restore them to solvency; renewed confidence in the banking system owing to the establishment of the Federal Deposit Insurance Corporation; and stricter supervision imposed upon the banks by the Banking Department and the F.D.I.C. Most of the banks that did liquidate were small institutions located in areas where there was insufficient business to permit profitable operation. These banks were, of course, seriously weakened by the depression and their earnings were adversely affected by the extremely low interest rates and the limited demand for loans that prevailed in subsequent years.

Bank Failures

From January 31, 1930, until December 31, 1939, 123 state banks in Texas failed, and 103 of these failures—or about 26 per year—occurred during the depression years of 1930 to 1933.

The failure experience was less severe than during the 1920s, though, when an average of 31 closures were ordered by the Banking Department each year. From the beginning of 1934 through 1939, there were only 21 state bank failures in Texas, or slightly over 3 per year, a negligible figure compared with the showing of the previous fourteen years.

The causes of failures of state banks in Texas during the thirties can be resolved into multiple levels of influence. Many of the unfavorable conditions that debilitated the state banking system during the 1920s still existed at the beginning of the 1930s. There were too many banks in existence; some banks were undercapitalized; supervision, albeit much improved, was in a state of transition; and the economy of the state still lacked sufficient diversification. Adverse economic conditions also were a contributing element in bank failures in the thirties. Previously, adverse economic conditions had in most cases not actually caused bank failures but instead had acted as catalysts upon and had brought to prominence individual weaknesses in the banks that were the immediate causes of failure. However, in 1931 when panic conditions stemming from the depression and news of depression effects elsewhere erupted in Texas, runs were initiated on numerous state banks and many strong as well as weak banks were forced to close. Thus in the 1930s adverse economic conditions both directly and indirectly caused state bank failures. The immediate cause of failure in most instances, however, continued to be deficient management, manifested in loose and unsound banking practices. In some instances, dishonesty was also a factor, although its incidence was much reduced from the previous decade.

Too Many Banks—Insufficient Capital

While the problems of the 1920s had caused well over 200 state banks to pass from existence (the state bank count fell from 948 at the beginning of the 1920s to 699 ten years later), Texas was still overbanked in the early 1930s. In a May 1930 speech to the Texas Bankers Association convention, Banking Commissioner James Shaw acknowledged that [in the past] many charters were granted and little attention was given to the question of whether the community actually needed the banking facilities that were being provided. There are banks in communities in Texas today that do not have sufficient volume of business to even pay the overhead expenses, and others that are barely hanging on.[14]

Two years later, in his address before the convention of the same organization, Commissioner Shaw expressed similar views in reflections upon the state bank failures that had occurred during the interim. He said:

The main trouble was that most of the banks that failed should never have been chartered. There were too many banks, and the weak ones were carried down in the whirlpool of overexpansion that was so rampant during the halcyon days following the world war, and consequent inflated prices and values all down the line.[15]

In that speech Commissioner Shaw called for an amendment to raise the minimum capital requirement for state banks from $17,500 to not less than $25,000. The purpose of the low minimum capital requirement, which was originally $10,000 and was raised to $17,500 in 1923, was to permit the capitalization of banks in small communities that would have otherwise been without a bank. By 1930 most small communities had one or more banks, and the continuation of low minimum capital requirements now contributed to the persistence of overbanking in many parts of the state. Very low minimum capital requirements also rendered banks susceptible to insolvency as a result of a few large losses on loans.

Inefficient and Law Supervision during the 1920s

While the supervision of state banks became increasingly more effective throughout the 1920s (and particularly during Commissioner Shaw's tenure—beginning September 1, 1927), the system still suffered from the deficiencies of the past. The deficiencies stemmed basically from inadequate appropriations by the state legislature, deficiencies that caused a serious turnover in the office of the banking commissioner, in the examining force, and in the clerical staff of the Banking Department and thus hampered the operation of the department. In retrospect, however, it appears that one of the prime deficiencies was in the leadership itself. Certainly the commissioners during the 1920s were generally capable, honest, and dedicated men. But it must be remembered that the times were difficult and the pressures of the job were immense. From the end of 1920 through 1926 banks failed in rapid succession, and scores of others experienced financial difficulty. The commissioners serving during this era believed that every effort should be made to keep troubled banks from closing—even though they may have been insolvent or seriously impaired: the practice of "nursing along" sick banks was initiated. This practice came to full bloom under the administration of J. L. Chapman and was perpetuated during Charles O. Austin's term of office. Had it been continued by James Shaw, in all probability there would have been many more state bank failures in Texas during the Great Depression than there were.

Lack of Diversity in the Texas Economy

The condition that had caused the most severe problems for the bankers and for Texas in general in the 1920s—the lack of diversification of the economy—had changed very little by the beginning of the Great Depression. In 1930, as in 1925, Texas was basically an agrarian society, and approximately 70 percent of the population still depended primarily upon cotton for a living. Even though the dependence on agriculture and particularly cotton diminished significantly during the 1930s, conditions at the beginning of the depression left the banking system extremely vulnerable to adversities in the agricultural sector of the economy.

Consequently, state bank failures were concentrated in small rural cities and towns: about 40 percent of the 103 failures between 1930 and 1933 were in towns with population of less than 1,000 and 80 percent occurred in towns whose population was less than 5,000. Furthermore, the majority of the failures occurred in the areas of the state most heavily dependent upon agriculture. These were the counties of the fertile blackland belt; Haskell, Knox, Taylor, and Callahan counties in the lower plains of

North Texas; DeWitt, Karnes, Bee, Refugio, and San Patricio counties in the Gulf Coast plains; and Hidalgo and Cameron counties in the lower Rio Grande valley. In the aftermath of the depression, from 1934 to 1939, state bank failures in Texas declined markedly in number, but those that did occur continued to be confined mainly to small rural communities that were almost entirely dependent upon agriculture.

Adverse Economic Conditions and Financial Panics

In September 1931 the banking climate in Texas changed abruptly. Since the latter 1920s Texas had suffered relatively few bank failures compared with the numbers in other states. Only thirty state banks had closed their doors, an average of about fifteen per year, since the stock market crash in October 1929, and it is believed that many of these would have survived had it not been for the very poor cotton crops of 1929 and 1930. In February 1931 Commissioner Shaw asserted that the state banks of Texas were "as sound as any banks in the United States."[16] Two months later he made the following prediction for the near-term future:

It is indeed gratifying that at a time when many banks are failing in other states . . . such is not the case in Texas. In my opinion, after a careful survey of the situation, there will be few bank failures in our state during the year 1931.[17]

Unfortunately, as the international financial framework collapsed in September 1931 the banking panic in the United States greatly intensified and, for the first time since the beginning of the depression, runs on Texas banks began.

The banking panic in Texas in the fall of 1931 began with the closing of the City Central Bank and Trust Company in San Antonio on September 28, 1931.[18] The City Central Bank, which held correspondent balances for many banking institutions throughout Texas, experienced difficulties for a considerable time before its closing. The bank had originated from an amalgamation and consolidation of six banks over the previous two years; most of these banks had been absorbed and consolidated because of their own financial problems, which the City Central Bank inherited.

The City Central Bank failure has been attributed to two fundamental internal problems—lack of leadership and coordination in the bank's management and depreciation of assets, particularly real estate. According to A. J. Lewis, former office counsel of the state Banking Department, one of the bank's greatest problems was the failure to develop an effective management team. The bank was dominated by its president, who was not considered to be a seasoned banker. Basically a real estate man, he had brought a large portfolio of real estate loans with his bank, Central Trust Company, into the consolidated organization that became the City Central Bank and Trust Company. Furthermore, there was much discontent among the other senior officers of the bank. As a result, gossip and rumors spread throughout San Antonio, and the reputation of the bank was damaged. The bank was prone to failure because of the depressed value of its stock and bond portfolio, real estate owned by the bank, collateral repossessed on bad debts, and other assets. As with all other banks at this time, its collections on notes were slow and its liquidity poor.

Concerted attempts were made to save the bank because some realized that if the bank closed, many others that had funds on deposit with the City Central Bank would follow. But all efforts were to no avail. Having assets of about $16 million and deposits of $12.5 million, it was the largest bank in Texas to fail during the depression.

Several days after the City Central Bank's doors were closed the Commonwealth Bank and Trust Company of San Antonio suspended payment of deposits and a run on the Frost National Bank developed. The panic quickly spread to various other parts of the state. From the middle of September 1931 through February 1932 forty-seven state banks in Texas failed, twenty-five of the failures occurring in October and November. According to the *Texas Bankers Record*, in nine out of ten of the suspensions during September and October the bank was closed by the directors after heavy withdrawals or rumor of withdrawals.

The November issue of the *Record* carried the following editorial by W. A. Philpott, entitled "An Eruption of Fear":

For two months past, the high nervous tension which has characterized the public mind in these United States has erupted in the form of frenzied runs on banks and the loss of public confidence. The hysteria has touched Texas with its withering hand. Spots of our great state have been scorched and left bare of banks. Thriving communities have suffered the first bank failures in their histories. Solvent as well as weak banks have succumbed. High class, conscientious bankers as well as mediocre plow hands have seen institutions of a life-time's building topple about their defeated heads. Strong bankers as well as spineless 'fraidcats' have thrown up their hands! Many good banks and many sound bankers have passed from the stage.

Fear and uncertainty in the heart, distrust and loss of confidence, coupled with human inclination toward self-preservation, always wreaks with havoc [sic]. Bankers have feared to leave their desks, they have piled up actual money in their vaults to stem runs, they have trembled in their very breath at gossip and rumor.[19]

Several incidents in Texas banking history in which runs were averted testify to the ingenuity of the bankers and the lack of sophistication of many of the depositors. One incident involves a bank in Jacksonville that ran out of money in 1914. Currency was on its way from Dallas by train, but people in the bank lobby were growing impatient and demanding their money. To avert a crisis the president gathered all of the bank's money sacks, went to the local hardware shop, bought all of the washers in the store, and put them in the sacks. He then loaded the sacks into his car, drove up to the front of the bank, and loaded his cargo in full view of the panicked depositors. The sight of this "currency" restored the people's confidence and the run was ended.[20]

Another case involves a bank in South Texas that was the object of a run in 1928. At the height of the ordeal $100,000 in currency—a small part of what might have been needed—arrived from San Antonio by airplane and was immediately rushed to the bank. The enterprising pilot then devised a scheme to divert the attention of the depositors. He began stunt flying and later offered to take passengers for free rides. The citizens of the community, having seen the money delivered and never having ridden in an airplane, could not pass up the opportunity. The mob was thus removed from the bank to the local airfield.[21]

A third example of a bank defeating a run occurred in Agua Dulce in the early thirties. The bank manager merely told the depositors that a shipment of currency was on its way but that he was not sure when it would arrive. He then offered the depositors the bank's own cashier's check in lieu of cash. Depositors were paid for three days in this manner and the bank was saved.[22]

Because of the wild rumors against banks and bankers— which in many cases precipitated runs on thoroughly solvent institutions and forced their suspension—some banks restricted withdrawals by depositors. One outstanding instance of this involved seventeen banks in the lower Rio Grande valley during the thirties. Joining together and adopting restrictions to prevent unwarranted withdrawals, the banks issued a circular to notify depositors that they could withdraw no more than fifty dollars per week.[23] The restrictions were adopted by these banks on the same day that the State Bank and Trust Company of Mission closed its doors, October 23, 1931. Not another bank failed in the area until May 16, 1932, when the Farmers State Bank of San Benito, which had not participated in the plan of valley banks to restrict withdrawals, closed.

Between February and September of 1932 the banking crisis in Texas subsided, there having been only three state bank failures during that interval. In September the banking crisis in the United States intensified; some states—including Texas—were forced to declare banking holidays in the next several months and finally, on March 6, 1933, President Roosevelt proclaimed a nationwide banking holiday as previously indicated.

Financial panic elsewhere in the United States in the fall of 1932 apparently had little impact upon Texas banking; only nine state banks in Texas failed during those months. Even in the first two months of 1933, when panic in other parts of the country was reaching the point of hysteria, there were only three state bank suspensions in Texas. But by March 1, 1933, the effects of bank failures in many other states and of declaration of banking moratoriums in some of them were beginning to be felt in the bank reserve cities in Texas. Fortunately, March 2 was a state holiday, Texas Independence Day, and all banks were closed. Every city banker in Texas sat in conference that day "watching out-of-state developments and tabulating moratoriums in other states, which were coming thick and fast."[24] Officials of the Federal Reserve Bank of Dallas met with the bankers and Governor Miriam A. Ferguson, wife of the former governor and banker James E. Ferguson, was advised of the seriousness of the situation.

Texas was the twenty-second state in the country to declare a banking holiday. At 4:30 p.m. on March 2, 1933, Governor Ferguson issued a proclamation declaring a holiday for all Texas banks from March 3 through March 7. In the next two days emergency legislation was enacted to give the commissioner of banking authority to reopen the banks "when and as he saw fit, with proper restrictions and regulations." The action of the legislature was, of course, subsequently obviated by President Roosevelt's declaration of the nationwide banking holiday on March 6.

On March 11 President Roosevelt announced that, beginning two days later, the sound banks in the country would reopen and that there would be plenty of new money to meet all demands. On Sunday night, March 12, the president made his famous "fireside" speech. The banks in the twelve Federal Reserve cities reopened on Monday, March 13. All Dallas banks, except one small state bank, reopened on an unrestricted basis. They functioned normally despite a huge backlog of work, and there was no evidence of tension or uneasiness. When the banking holiday was officially over on March 15, all but ninety of the state and national banks in Texas had received licenses to reopen. While Texas had about 6 percent of the commercial banks of the United States, it had only 1.6 percent of the unlicensed banks on March 15. By April 5, twenty days after the holiday, only twenty-six of the original ninety not permitted to reopen were still closed. It was anticipated that most of these would be reorganized or reopened by a conservator so that the ultimate loss would be small.

By the middle of May 1933 just twenty-one banks, with deposits of $3.5 million, were restricted. Only twelve of these were still restricted in mid-1934; the others presumably had either been allowed to operate on an unrestricted basis or had been liquidated. Of the twelve, restriction was lifted on ten, one bank was liquidated, and one small institution was still restricted in March 1935.

During the panics spawned by the Great Depression, bank depositors did not discriminate between strong and weak institutions, and numerous sound, well-managed banks in Texas, as in other states, were wrecked by depositor runs. In these instances the runs were often touched off by false rumors about the banks.

But in substantially more cases during these hectic times, depositors no doubt were justified in demanding their funds, as the subject banks were on the verge of collapse because of improvidence on the part of management or because of dishonesty.

Incompetent Management and Dishonesty

During the thirties, as in the past, the ultimate responsibility for the majority of bank failures belonged to management, unfavorable economic conditions notwithstanding. In April 1931 Commissioner Shaw commented in a speech given at a Texas Bankers Association meeting,

My experience in the last four years has shown me that the principal cause of failures in banks is incompetence of officers and directors, and that is a very weak excuse to offer to the public; it's an indictment of our system.[25]

On a similar occasion one year later the commissioner spoke specifically about the way in which management leads a bank into difficulty:

[experience reveals] that most of the failures of banks come from large lines of credit. Another thing—officers and directors of banks should be most careful in borrowing from their institutions. It is my observation that, almost invariably, where officers and directors are continuous borrowers from their banks, they become unfitted to operate the institution as they should and the bank is very apt to get into serious trouble.[26]

Empirical Evidence

Examination reports from a sample of twenty-eight banks that failed from 1933 through 1939 confirm that management deficiencies were the principal cause of failures. For twelve of the banks incompetent or weak management was cited as the principal factor that caused the crisis at hand. Usually the management deficiency manifested itself in the form of overextended loans, lenient credit policies, undue concentrations of loans, and lax collection procedures. Defalcation or misappropriation of bank funds was the primary cause of failure in three of the institutions.

Shortages were attributed to the president of the bank in two of these instances; in the other, failure was caused by illegal loans to an officer of the bank. In the remaining thirteen banks it is likely that weak management contributed substantially to the difficulties that led to failure, though the examination reports are not explicit in this regard. The possible exception is the four of the thirteen whose problems were attributed to insufficient business. However, in three of these, losses on loans were reported to be very high. This normally indicates management deficiencies.

In twenty-four of the twenty-eight banks, there were undue concentrations of loans—in some instances to one category of borrower, such as farmers or directors; in other instances in one type of loan, such as real estate credit; and in still other instances, to one or two individuals or companies. Thirteen of the banks had an inordinate proportion of loans to farmers in the bank portfolios, loans secured mainly by crops, horses, mules, and other livestock or real estate. Seven banks were cited for an excessive amount of credit extended to stockholders, officers, and directors and to their relatives; in most of these instances the concentration was of sufficient magnitude to be considered a contributing cause of failure. Irregularities were discovered in three of the seven banks; these consisted of loans to the officers and their relatives in excess of the banks' legal limit. As for the remaining four banks among the twenty-four in the sample that had undue concentrations of loans, two made real estate loans almost exclusively, one had a loan to an oil company in excess of its legal limit, and the other had a legal-limit loan to an automobile dealer in addition to a large portfolio of automobile installment loans generated by that dealer.

The absence of examination reports for defunct state banks prior to 1933, the partial absence of those for 1933, and the inadequacy of some of the existing reports for 1933 and thereafter complicated the authors' analysis of state bank failures during the 1930s. However, it is believed that the general conclusions drawn from the available reports are valid. They are corroborated by written statements and testimony obtained from reliable individuals who were directly involved in the events of the era, from speeches and journal articles from the period, and from official records (other than examination reports) of the Banking Department.

Voluntary Liquidations

Of the 268 state banks that voluntarily surrendered their charters during the thirties, 109 dissolved their business, eighteen were nationalized, and 141 were either merged with, assumed by, or sold to another bank. It bears reiteration that most of the banks classified as "voluntary liquidations" were actually financially distressed and closed under some degree of duress from the Department of Banking. A majority of the voluntary liquidations—162 of them—occurred during the immediate tenure of the Great Depression, 1930-1933. The limited number of voluntary liquidations characterized above as banks that were nationalized occurred mainly during 1933 and 1934. To qualify for Federal Deposit Insurance Corporation coverage, which became effective on January 1, 1934, state banks were required to submit to examination by the F.D.I.C.; presumably, those state banks that converted in 1933 and 1934 chose to join the national banking system rather than be subjected to dual examinations—that is, by both state and national authorities.

Table 21

State Bank Voluntary Liquidations in Texas, 1930-1939

Year	Business dissolved	Nationalized	Sold, assumed, or merged	Total
1930	7	1	23	31
1931	10	0	27	37
1932	15	1	30	46
1933	25	3	20	48
1934	16	9	11	36
1935	13	0	6	19
1936	7	1	9	17
1937	8	3	5	16
1938	4	0	1	5
1939	4	0	9	13
Total	109	18	141	268

Source: Compiled from official records of Banking Department of Texas.

Role of the R.F.C. and the F.D.I.C. in Rehabilitation

The relatively favorable experience of the Texas state banks, and for that matter all banks in the United States, following the banking holiday was due largely to the Reconstruction Finance Corporation, which played a major role in restoring the banks to a sound and solvent condition, and to the Federal Deposit Insurance Corporation, which helped to renew and maintain confidence in the banking system.

Establishment of the F.D.I.C.

While the banks of the United States were struggling for survival during 1932 and early 1933, Congress was frantically debating various measures aimed at shoring up the system's remnants. The ultimate result of these debates was the passage on June 16 of the Banking Act of 1933 (Glass-Steagall Act), which provided, among other reforms and measures, for the Federal Deposit Insurance Corporation. Under the new law, which became effective January 1, 1934, all members of the Federal Reserve System were required to have their deposits insured by the F.D.I.C. Nonmember banks were eligible for insurance with the approval of the corporation. Coverage was initially limited to $2,500 per depositor, but on July 1, 1934, coverage was raised to $5,000. Premiums were calculated as a percentage of each member's deposits.

Texas Opposition to the F.D.I.C.

Texas state bankers, with few exceptions, were opposed to federal legislation providing for bank deposit insurance. In April 1932, when deposit insurance bills were "flooding" Congress, the *Texas Bankers Record* termed attempts at such legislation as "radical." At the annual convention of the Texas Bankers Association in May 1932 Commissioner Shaw, in referring to the bills before Congress, described the deposit insurance system as "that pernicious system whereby the incompetent and unscrupulous banker is placed on equal footing with the one who has built up a good name and sound institution."[27] In the January 1933 issue of the *Texas Bankers Record* the editor, W. A. Philpott, commented on the sentiment of Texas bankers toward deposit insurance as follows:

We of Texas know what a nightmare and mockery and basically unsound thing this guaranteeing of deposits is. We have had about 18 years experience and the good and solvent banks in our state were taxed $25,000,000 to pay for the mistakes and mismanagement and crookedness of people who should never have attempted banking. All Texas bankers have long since agreed that such a scheme will not work—that it encourages more and poorer banks and more and poorer bank managers. There is no necessity for arguments to be expended against the principle of guarantee of bank deposits with bankers of Texas. No sales talk is necessary against the proposed law.[28]

A poll of 1,000 Texas banks (national as well as state institutions), conducted in 1933 by the vice-president of a national bank in Galveston, provides evidence that a majority of Texas bankers were opposed to deposit insurance. Of the 628 responses received, 617 were in opposition to the new law in "varying degrees of intensity."[29] In light of the state's experience with the Guaranty Fund, the opposition to the F.D.I.C. evidenced by the poll is relatively easy to comprehend. On the other hand, it seems likely that many of the opinions formed were based more upon emotional considerations than upon fundamental analysis of the law. The same observation applies to the opposition in the many other states where a majority of the bankers disapproved of the F.D.I.C.

The Texas Alternative to F.D.I.C.

In view of the opposition in Texas to the federal deposit insurance program, Governor Miriam A. Ferguson called a special session of the state legislature in September 1933 to provide an alternative system for Texas state banks and trust companies. The legislature passed a bill creating the Bank Deposit Insurance Company, and the bill was signed into law on October 11. The measure became effective on January 1, 1934, the same day that the F.D.I.C. began operations. If a state bank did not wish to join the new state deposit insurance system, it was to notify the commissioner of banking in writing.

The Bank Deposit Insurance Company's capital was to be subscribed for in an amount equal to 5 percent of each member bank's capital, three fourths of which could be maintained in a demand deposit account on the bank's own books in the name of the insurance corporation and one fourth of which was to be remitted to the corporation. A surplus fund was to be created by monthly assessment of each member on all interest-bearing loans at a rate of .75 percent per annum until January 1, 1937, at .50 percent per annum from January 1, 1937, until January 1, 1940, and at .25 percent per annum thereafter; and on all obligations of political subdivisions of Texas owned by the member at a rate of .50 percent per annum until January 1, 1940, and at .25 percent per annum thereafter. When the surplus of the corporation exceeded $25 million, the directors of the corporation could suspend assessments and when it fell below $24 million the assessments would start again. Unsecured deposits of member banks were insured up to $2,500 from January 1, 1934, to July 1, 1934. After July 1, deposits were insured as follows: 100 percent of amounts not exceeding $10,000, 75 percent of amounts exceeding $10,000 but not exceeding $50,000, and 50 percent of amounts exceeding $50,000.

Implementation of the R.F.C. and the F.D.I.C. in Texas

After the banking holiday the Reconstruction Finance Corporation, with its newly acquired authority to purchase preferred stock of national and state banks, began the resuscitation of the banking system. Needless to say, at first the work was slow, because of a lack of organization and a lack of personnel.

In the fall of 1933 W. A. Sandlin, who had been with the R.F.C. in Washington since early 1933, was "lent" by the comptroller of the currency to the F.D.I.C. for the purpose of supervising the examination and insurance of all nonmember state banks in Texas. In the meantime Dan Lydick, president of Union Bank and Trust Company in Fort Worth, had been elected president of the Bank Deposit Insurance Company and had immediately commenced to screen applications for membership in the state deposit insurance system. At the outset Sandlin warned Lydick that the Bank Deposit Insurance Company was not going to be a success because there were too many state banks that would be unacceptable for membership and that consequently these and other state banks would find it necessary to join the F.D.I.C. The screening process continued; shortly thereafter Lydick received applications from two banks whose capital had been depleted. He went to the F.D.I.C. office, admitted to Sandlin that he probably was right, and asked his advice.

It was decided at that time—Saturday, December 10, 1933—that Lydick should call a meeting of the state bankers and explain that the Bank Deposit Insurance Company was an unworkable concept. The rest of the day was spent sending telegrams to all of the state banks to announce a meeting in Austin the following Monday. At the same time Sandlin telephoned Jesse Jones, president of the R.F.C., in Washington to apprise him of the new developments. In order to cope with the situation, Jones agreed to send seventy-five additional examiners to Texas. He also appointed Sandlin chairman of a special committee, whose members included Guy Heath of the Department of Banking and Linnie Snyder of the American National Bank in Austin, for the purpose of authorizing and approving R.F.C. loans to any state bank that in their judgment needed the money in order to obtain F.D.I.C. insurance. These loans were actually purchases of capital debentures. (Texas law prohibited the issuance of preferred stock by state banks.) The debentures bore interest of 4 percent per annum and had a twenty-year maturity. The principal could be retired out of earnings at the option of the issuing bank. Most banks capitalized the debt, as it was retired by paying stock dividends for a like amount.

The meeting on December 12 was attended by more than four hundred state bankers. Lydick stated that he personally was abandoning the idea of the Bank Deposit Insurance Company and that his bank was applying for F.D.I.C. insurance and a $150,000 loan from the R.F.C. Commissioner of Banking E. C. Brand, who had succeeded James Shaw on July 12, 1933, also addressed the meeting and urged all of the bankers to file their applications for

F.D.I.C. insurance. He assured the bankers that the F.D.I.C. had sufficient men to examine every bank and have them all insured by January 1, 1934, when the law became effective. He called attention to the fact that the R.F.C. stood ready to buy debentures of state banks and implored the bankers to take advantage of these loans. At the end of the meeting, more than three hundred of the bankers indicated their intention of applying for F.D.I.C. insurance.

Because of Sandlin's dual capacity as head of the F.D.I.C. in Texas and final authority for R.F.C. loans, examinations for F.D.I.C. insurance and R.F.C. loans were made concurrently. If an examination for the F.D.I.C. revealed that a bank was unsound or insolvent, a loan from the R.F.C. was arranged in order to place the bank in sound condition and qualify it for federal insurance. An outgrowth of this procedure was that banks were induced to join the F.D.I.C. in order to obtain R.F.C. loans. Most state banks were painfully in need of funds, and the quickest and perhaps the only way to obtain an R.F.C. loan at the time was to request an examination for federal deposit insurance—the reason being that all of the examiners for R.F.C. loans were busy trying to qualify banks for membership in the F.D.I.C. by the January 1, 1934, deadline. The operation of the Bank Deposit Insurance Company of Texas was thus placed in further jeopardy since most of the state banks were signing up for F.D.I.C. insurance in order to obtain an R.F.C. loan.

One of the remarkable feats in Texas banking history was achieved by Sandlin, his clerical and supervisory staff, and one hundred bank examiners. Their task was to complete examinations of all applicant banks in Texas in time for them to participate in the new federal deposit insurance plan when it became effective at the beginning of 1934. In order to accomplish this the Austin office was kept open twenty-four hours a day, and the examiners were kept on the road continuously, being routed from one bank to the next. From December 13 to December 31, 1933, 225 state banks were examined and approved for F.D.I.C. membership. Every bank that had applied had been examined and the report was mailed to Washington by December 31.[30]

In the beginning 815 banks in Texas were insured under F.D.I.C. Of these, 351 were state and 464 were national banks. Another 138 state banks and 46 private banks, which were ineligible, remained outside of the F.D.I.C. By March 1935, 383, or 82.5 percent, of the state banks, with 87 percent of the deposits, were insured either by the F.D.I.C. or under the state plan. At that time Department of Banking officials felt that deposit insurance had attracted a considerable amount of hoarded funds back into the banks.[31]

Only seventeen banks ever became members of the Bank Deposit Insurance Company—all on January 1, 1934. The company was finally dissolved under the provisions of a bill passed by the Forty-fifth Legislature in the spring of 1937. The reasons given for the action were that the company had failed to function satisfactorily and F.D.I.C. coverage was available as an alternative.[32]

From the national banking holiday until midyear 1939, the Reconstruction Finance Corporation disbursed loans to 256 state banks in Texas, amounting to $7.75 million, of which $4.8 million was outstanding at the end of the period. Most of this credit, of course, was extended during the depression and shortly thereafter—loans of $7.4 million were made to 245 Texas state banks between the time of the national banking holiday and the end of 1934. In March 1935 it was estimated that the sale of capital debentures to the R.F.C. had augmented the capital structures of state banks in Texas by 34 percent.[33] (R.F.C. loans to national banks in Texas from the banking holiday through mid-1939 were made to 147 banks and aggregated $23.6 million, of which $12.2 million was outstanding at the close of the period.)

State Bank Legislation Enacted during the Thirties

Most of the banking legislation passed during the 1930-1939 period in Texas was to enable state banks to take advantage of the R.F.C. and the F.D.I.C. and to reconcile state law with federal law. The Forty-second Legislature enacted two measures aimed at curbing loans to state bank directors, officers, and employees (such loans were a source of trouble in numerous banks during the twenties and in 1930). One bill made it illegal for any director, officer, or employee to borrow trust funds of a bank[34] and the other prohibited any bank director from borrowing an amount in excess of 10 percent of the bank's capital and surplus without the prior permission of the board of directors.[35] The Forty-second Legislature also changed the banking laws to enable state banks to borrow funds from the Reconstruction Finance Corporation. One bill was passed to allow banks to pledge their securities and other assets as collateral for indebtedness to the R.F.C.[36] The other change excluded R.F.C. loans from the restrictions imposed on state bank indebtedness, thereby permitting banks to borrow in unlimited amounts from the corporation.[37]

The most important banking bills enacted by the Forty-third Legislature ratified the action taken by Governor Ferguson in proclaiming the state banking holiday on March 2, 1933, and created the Bank Deposit Insurance Company. Three other significant banking bills were passed during that legislative session. One authorized the commissioner as liquidator of a state bank to borrow money from the R.F.C. against a subordinated claim on the bank's assets as security for the loan. The subordinated lien, of course, enabled the bank to make payments to its depositors before paying the R.F.C. in the event that liquidation became necessary.[38] The second bill permitted state banks to invest in obligations issued by federal agencies.[39] And the third allowed a bank's board of directors to suspend operations for thirty days, with the commissioner's consent, in order to work out a plan of reorganization. The commissioner could extend the period of suspension to ninety days. If it became apparent that the bank could not be reorganized, he could then take charge of and liquidate it.[40]

The most important legislation passed by the Forty-fourth Legislature (1935-1936) was requested by the Federal Deposit Insurance Corporation to enable state banks to take advantage of its benefits. In accordance with the F.D.I.C. request Governor James V. Allred asked the legislature on April 3, 1935, to pass the following bills:

One of these bills authorizes the Federal Deposit Insurance Corporation to be appointed receiver of closed state banks; it provides that the Federal Deposit Insurance Corporation shall be subrogated to the rights of depositors to whom it makes payments; makes available to the Federal Deposit Insurance Corporation reports made by state banking examiners and authorizes the statutory receiver or the Banking Commissioner to borrow money where the same is necessary to conserve the assets of closed banks in the process of liquidation.

The second bill authorized state banks to issue capital notes and debentures, subject to the approval of the Banking Commissioner, and redefines the term "capital" as used in state statutes relating to solvency as including such capital notes and debentures outstanding; and among other provisions of the Act, provision is made for payment of capital notes and debentures so issued.

The third Act exempts banks from furnishing security for public deposits to the extent that the same are insured by the Federal Deposit Insurance Corporation.[41]

The bills ultimately enacted into law had essentially the same provisions as those requested by Governor Allred.

The most important matter concerning banking taken up by the Forty-fifth Legislature was the double-liability question. Agitation for repeal of the double-liability feature of state bank stock was promoted by federal legislation—the Banking Act of 1935, which eliminated double-liability for national bank stockholders, effective July 1, 1937. On that date, unless the state provision had been eliminated, national bank stock would have become a far more attractive investment than state bank stock.

In order to eliminate the double-liability feature, it was first necessary to submit the question to the legislature and then to the people, since it was a constitutional provision. During the regular session of the Forty-fifth Legislature, Joint Resolution No. 9 was passed to allow the people of Texas to decide by referendum whether or not the Texas constitution should be amended to delete the double-liability clause from the Texas State Bank Law of 1905.[42] The resolution set the constitutional amendment election for August 23, 1937. As a result of an extensive advertising campaign by the state bankers and the recommendation of the governor, the people voted to repeal double liability for state bank stockholders.

Another problem dealt with by the same legislature was to reconcile Texas law with the provision of the Banking Act of 1935 that prohibited the payment of interest on demand deposits of the United States, any state, or its subdivisions. The Texas law, which required that deposits of public funds draw interest, was thus repealed.⁴³ Finally, liquidation of the Bank Deposit Insurance Company was provided for by the Forty-fifth Legislature.

Few banking bills were considered by the Forty-sixth Legislature. One that was introduced but did not receive serious consideration would have permitted countywide branch banking in Texas.⁴⁴

Notes

1. John Kenneth Galbraith, *The Great Crash, 1929* (Boston: Houghton Mifflin Company, 1955).
2. Milton Friedman and Anna Jacobson Schwartz, *A Monetary History of the United States, 1867-1960* (Princeton: Princeton University Press, 1963), pp. 299-332.
3. Paul Studenski and Herman Krooss, *Financial History of the United States* (New York: McGraw-Hill, 1952), p. 379.
4. Studenski and Krooss, *Financial History of the United States*, pp. 389-400.
5. J. E. Woods, "Annual Address of the President," address before the Texas Bankers Association's annual convention, Fort Worth, May 17, 1938, *Texas Bankers Record* 27 (June 1938): 8.
6. Zeta Gossett, address before the Texas Bankers Association's annual convention, Fort Worth, May 17, 1938, *Texas Bankers Record* 27 (June 1938): 28.
7. Burris C. Jackson, "The Real Cotton Problem," *Texas Bankers Record* 27 (June 1938): 57.
8. *Texas Almanac and State Industrial Guide, 1936*, p. 237.
9. Ibid.
10. *Texas Almanac and State Industrial Guide, 1941-1942*, p. 204.
11. Ibid.
12. W. B. Lee, "The Inseparable Twins—Safe Banking and Safe Farming," address before the Texas Bankers Association's annual convention, San Angelo, May 15, 1933, *Texas Bankers Record* 22 (June 1933): 41.
13. Jesse H. Jones, *Fifty Billion Dollars* (New York: McMillan Company, 1951), p. 20.

14. James Shaw, "The Trouble with Banking," address before the Texas Bankers Association's annual convention, Fort Worth, May 14, 1930, *Texas Bankers Record* 19 (June 1930): 26.
15. James Shaw, "An Address by the Commissioner," address before the Texas Bankers Association's annual convention, Austin, May 10, 1932, *Texas Bankers Record* 21 (June 1932): 24.
16. *Texas Bankers Record* 20 (February 1931): 45.
17. Shaw, "Scenting Trouble before it Arrives," p. 16.
18. Conference with selected bank regulatory officials and retired officials arranged by the authors and held in Austin, Texas, August 28, 1969.
19. Philpott, editorial in the *Texas Bankers Record* 21 (November 1931): 3.
20. Conference held in Austin, Texas, August 28, 1969.
21. *Texas Bankers Record* 17 (June 1928): 37.
22. Conference held in Austin, Texas, August 28, 1969.
23. *Texas Bankers Record* 21 (November 1931): iii.
24. "Banking Holiday," *Texas Bankers Record* 22 (March 1933): 6.
25. James Shaw, "The Commissioner Speaks Up," address before the Texas Bankers Association, San Angelo, May 13, 1931, *Texas Bankers Record* (June 1931), p. 46.
26. Shaw, "An Address by the Commissioner," p. 25.
27. James Shaw, "An Address by the Commissioner," address before the Texas Bankers Association's annual convention, Austin, May 10, 1932, *Texas Bankers Record* 21 (June 1932): 24.
28. "Guaranteeing Bank Deposits," *Texas Bankers Record* 22 (January 1933): 25.
29. *Texas Bankers Record* 23 (September 1933): 29.
30. The source for this section is a letter written by W. A. Sandlin on September 3, 1969, to A. J. Lewis.
31. R. F. Siddons, "Time for Banks to Lend," address before the San Antonio and Lampasas group meetings, Texas Bankers Association, March 1935, *Texas Bankers Record* 24 (March 1935): 27.

32. *General and Special Laws, Texas Forty-fifth Legislature, Regular Session, 1937* (Austin: A. C. Baldwin and Sons, 1937), p. 370.
33. Siddons, "Time for Banks to Lend," p. 29.
34. *General Laws of Texas Forty-second Legislature, Regular Session, 1931*, p. 16.
35. Ibid., p. 318.
36. *General and Special Laws, Texas, Forty-second Legislature, Third Called Session, 1932* (n.p., n.d.), p. 2.
37. Ibid., p. 4
38. *General Laws of Texas, Forty-third Legislature, Regular Session, 1933*, p. 197.
39. Ibid., p. 406.
40. *General and Special Laws, Forty-third Legislature, First Called Session, 1933* (n.p., n.d.), p. 191.
41. *House Journal, Texas, Forty-fourth Legislature, Regular Session, 1935* (Austin: Von Boeckmann-Jones, 1935), p. 1010.
42. *General and Special Laws, Texas Forty-fifth Legislature, Regular Session, 1937* (Austin: A. C. Baldwin and Sons, 1937), p. 1495.
43. Ibid., p. 319.
44. *Senate Journal, Texas Forty-sixth Legislature, Regular Session, 1939* (Austin: Von Boeckmann-Jones, 1939), p. 48.

II
Unprecedented Growth of the State Banking System, 1940-1970

The State Banking System during World War II

During World War II the state banks of Texas enjoyed exceptional prosperity. Nothing else could have been expected to result from the economic conditions that were induced by war spending. Even before December 1941, when the United States became directly involved in the war, the economy had benefited from increased foreign demand for American goods. Then, in the summer of 1940, the United States began to spend huge sums of money on defense: total defense spending for 1941 through 1945 was $281.4 billion, almost seven eighths of all federal government expenditures and $222.7 billion more than the total spent during the New Deal era of 1933-1940. Naturally the economic impact of the massive federal expenditures and of budget deficits of $190.5 billion in aggregate for 1941 to 1945 was profound. From 1940 through 1945 the gross national product increased from $100.6 billion to $213.6 billion, or by 113 percent; the index of industrial production rose 63.6 percent; and unemployment declined to an average of 1.66 percent between 1943 and 1945, the lowest percentage on record for any sustained period.

The Texas economy, like that of the entire United States, experienced significant gains during the war; all segments of the economy prospered. For example, from 1940 to 1945 Texas farm cash income rose from $589.1 million to $1,189.3 million, or by 101.9 percent. Over the same period prices received by Texas farmers for all crops increased 119.7 percent; for all livestock and livestock products, 74.6 percent. The production of crude oil increased from 493.2 million barrels in 1940 to 754.7 million barrels in 1945, while the aggregate value of all mineral products rose from $945.2 million to $1,425.0 million. The most significant gains, however, were recorded in manufacturing. From 1940 to 1944 the number of wage earners more than doubled, their wages increased nearly fourfold, and the value of manufactured products rose an astounding 333.3 percent to $6.5 billion.

Favorable Experience of the State Banks

During the prosperous war years the state banking system enjoyed relative stability in the number of banks in operation but exceptional growth in total resources. The number of state banks operating in Texas increased from 395 to 409 from the beginning of 1940 through 1945. Forty-seven new charters were granted and thirty-one banks were liquidated—thirty voluntarily and one involuntarily. Of the thirty voluntary liquidations, sixteen involved banks that dissolved their business; three banks were nationalized; nine were merged with, sold to, or assumed by other banks; and two were granted charters but never opened (see table 4 page 49).

From December 31, 1939, to December 31, 1945, total state bank resources increased from $241,883,328 to $998,354,543, or by 312.7 percent, and capital accounts increased from $33,110,394 to $44,739,871, or by 35.1 percent. Of the increase in total resources, 48.1 percent, or $364,157,254, was used to increase holdings of U.S. government obligations; 13.7 percent, or $103,548,154, was used to make loans; and 36.1 percent, or $273,328,573, was used to augment cash and reserves. These changes were a direct result of the significant role played by the banking system in financing war expenditures. This was facilitated by the monetary authorities, who followed an easy money policy, enabling the commercial banks to purchase vast quantities of securities issued by the federal government between 1942 and 1945.

The favorable experience of the state banking system during the 1940-1945 period was particularly evident in the virtual absence of bank failures. There was only one failure, the Guaranty Bond State Bank, North Zulch, which closed on January 1, 1940. The last examination report that could be found for this bank, dated July 11, 1938, indicated that the bank's troubles actually began several years earlier. The failure of the bank was apparently due to the general economic difficulties of the thirties, insufficient business (the population of North Zulch was only 400 and the total deposits of the bank only $125,000), and incompetent management.

During the war the percentage of total Texas bank deposits held by state banks increased from 12.5 percent in 1939 to 16.2 percent in 1945.

Activities of State Banks During World War II

The contribution of Texas state banks to the war effort was similar to that of most banks throughout the country. Nevertheless, because of the critical importance of the wartime activities of the commercial banks, this history would not be complete without the devotion of some attention to the highlights of such activities among Texas state-chartered banks.

Perhaps the most significant contribution of the banks was their immediate role in federal financing. The state banks in Texas purchased huge amounts of government securities for their own portfolios. From December 31, 1939, to December 31, 1945, state bank holdings of U.S. government securities increased by 792.5 percent, from $45,945,836 to $410,103,090, the latter amount being nearly twice as much as total state bank resources six years earlier. On December 31, 1945, U.S. government securities accounted for 41.1 percent of aggregate state bank assets, compared with 19.0 percent for governments and municipals at the close of 1939. Much of the proceeds from the sale of government securities to the Texas banks was rechanneled into the Texas economy through government loans to industry. Thus the importance of the state banks in financing the war economy in Texas was far greater than the increase in direct bank loans to business would indicate.

Most of the state banks took all of the government-guaranteed, war-related financing that was available to them, and banks made war financing loans almost to the exclusion of other, more lucrative types of loans, even though by doing so the banks' profits were reduced.

Table 22
Texas Banks and Bank Resources and Deposits, 1905-1969

	State banks			National banks		
Date	Banks	Total resources ($000)	Deposits ($000)	Banks	Total resources ($000)	Deposits ($000)
September 30, 1905	29	4,341	2,213	440	189,484	101,285
October 31, 1906	136	19,322	13,585	483	221,574	116,331
December 3, 1907	309	34,734	20,478	521	261,724	141,803
November 27, 1908	340	40,981	27,014	535	243,240	115,843
December 31, 1909	515	72,947	51,472	523	273,473	139,024
November 10, 1910	621	88,103	59,766	519	293,245	145,249
December 5, 1911	688	98,814	63,708	513	313,685	156,083
November 26, 1912	744	138,856	101,258	515	352,796	179,736
October 21, 1913	832	151,620	101,081	517	359,732	183,623
December 31, 1914	849	129,053	73,965	533	377,516	216,953
December 31, 1915	831	149,773	101,483	534	418,094	273,509
December 27, 1916	836	206,396	160,416	530	567,809	430,302
December 31, 1917	874	268,382	215,906	539	679,316	531,066
December 31, 1918	884	259,881	191,500	543	631,978	431,612
December 31, 1919	948	405,130	336,018	552	965,855	777,942
December 29, 1920	1,031	391,127	280,429	556	780,246	564,135
December 31, 1921	1,004	334,907	237,848	551	691,087	501,493
December 29, 1922	970	338,693	262,478	557	823,254	634,408

Table 22 (continued)

		State banks			National banks	
Date	Banks	Total resources ($000)	Deposits ($000)	Banks	Total resources ($000)	Deposits ($000)
September 14, 1923	950	376,775	306,372	569	860,173	648,954
December 31, 1924	933	391,040	322,392	572	999,981	820,676
December 31, 1925	834	336,966	268,586	656	1,020,124	832,425
December 31, 1926	782	290,554	228,741	656	1,020,113	820,778
December 31, 1927	748	328,574	267,559	643	1,134,595	938,129
December 31, 1928	713	334,870	276,875	632	1,230,469	1,017,168
December 31, 1929	699	332,534	264,013	609	1,124,369	897,538
December 31, 1930	655	299,012	231,909	560	1,028,420	826,723
December 31, 1931	594	235,681	172,806	508	865,910	677,307
December 31, 1932	540	208,142	148,070	483	822,857	625,586
December 30, 1933	489	185,476	132,389	445	900,810	733,810
December 31, 1934	460	197,969	148,333	456	1,063,453	892,264
December 31, 1935	442	205,729	162,926	454	1,145,488	1,009,172
June 30, 1936	426	228,877	169,652	456	1,192,845	1,054,284
December 31, 1937	415	217,355	177,514	453	1,343,076	1,194,463
September 28, 1938	406	217,944	170,286	449	1,359,719	1,206,882
December 31, 1939	395	241,883*	201,620	445	1,565,108	1,409,821
December 31, 1940	393	227,866	179,027	446	1,695,662	1,534,702
December 31, 1941	391	312,861	269,505	444	1,975,022	1,805,773
December 31, 1942	391	417,058	353,109	439	2,696,768	2,525,299

Table 22 (continued)

Date	State banks			National banks		
	Banks	Total resources ($000)	Deposits ($000)	Banks	Total resources ($000)	Deposits ($000)
December 31, 1943	391	574,463	536,327	439	3,281,853	3,099,964
December 31, 1944	398	780,910	738,779	436	4,092,473	3,891,999
December 31, 1945	409	998,355	952,258	434	5,166,434	4,934,773
December 31, 1946	418	1,019,369	964,938	434	4,883,558	4,609,538
December 31, 1947	436	1,149,887	1,087,347	437	5,334,309	5,039,963
December 31, 1948	444	1,208,884	1,137,259	437	5,507,823	5,191,334
December 31, 1949	446	1,283,139	1,203,244	440	5,797,407	5,454,118
December 31, 1950	449	1,427,680	1,338,540	442	6,467,275	6,076,006
December 31, 1951	453	1,571,823	1,473,569	443	6,951,836	6,501,307
December 31, 1952	457	1,742,270	1,631,757	444	7,388,030	6,882,623
December 31, 1953	460	1,813,034	1,696,297	443	7,751,667	7,211,162
December 31, 1954	465	1,981,483	1,851,724	441	8,295,686	7,698,690
December 31, 1955	472	2,087,066	1,941,706	446	8,640,239	7,983,681
December 31, 1956	480	2,231,497	2,067,927	452	8,986,456	8,241,159
December 31, 1957	486	2,349,935	2,169,898	457	8,975,321	8,170,271
December 31, 1958	499	2,662,270	2,449,474	458	9,887,737	9,049,580
December 31, 1959	511	2,813,006	2,581,404	466	10,011,949	9,033,495
December 31, 1960	532	2,997,609	2,735,726	468	10,520,690	9,560,668
December 30, 1961	538	3,297,588	3,009,499	473	11,466,767	10,426,812
December 28, 1962	551	3,646,404	3,307,714	486	12,070,803	10,712,253

Table 22 (continued)

	State banks			National banks		
Date	Banks	Total resources ($000)	Deposits ($000)	Banks	Total resources ($000)	Deposits ($000)
December 20, 1963	570	4,021,033	3,637,559	519	12,682,674	11,193,194
December 31, 1964	581	4,495,074	4,099,543	539	14,015,957	12,539,142
December 31, 1965	585	4,966,947	4,530,675	545	14,944,319	13,315,367
December 31, 1966	591	5,332,385	4,859,906	546	15,647,346	13,864,727
December 31, 1967	597	6,112,900	5,574,735	542	17,201,752	15,253,496
December 31, 1968	609	7,107,310	6,489,357	535	19,395,045	16,963,003
December 31, 1969	637	7,931,966	7,069,822	529	19,937,396	16,687,720

Source: *Texas Almanac and State Industrial Guide, 1974-1975* (Dallas: A. H. Belo, 1973), p. 429.
*These figures have been changed by the authors to conform to Banking Department of Texas official records.

Another important contribution of the banking system was the sale of war bonds. The banks of Texas, state and national, assumed the dominant role in the sale of war bonds in the state. The experience of the Gonzales State Bank was probably typical of that of many rural state banks. The Gonzales State Bank was the only bank in Gonzales, a rural town of 6,000 people and the county seat of Gonzales County. The president of the bank, V. S. Marett, served as county chairman of the Gonzales County War Bond Committee. Through his work and that of other bank employees, the Gonzales State Bank accounted for over 50 percent of all "government defense securities" sold in the county. Such an effort necessitated the hiring of additional employees during special drives and the establishment of special facilities to promote and expedite the sale of the securities. Marett estimated that the sales cost his bank approximately $2,500 per year in donations and expenses.[1]

In addition to handling and promoting the sale of war bonds in their communities, the banks encouraged their own employees to allocate part of their monthly salary to the purchase of bonds and inaugurated automatic payroll deductions for that purpose.

An invaluable contribution of the state banks to the war effort—one which in some cases resulted in financial loss—was handling ration coupons. The Office of Price Administration directed the operation, with the banks acting as an "agency" of the O.P.A. On Wednesday, January 27, 1943, the banks began handling ration coupons for sugar, coffee, and gasoline. While the O.P.A. was supposed to pay the cost of handling ration accounts, there is evidence that the compensation fell far short of covering the expense. For example, the State Bank of DeKalb calculated that the monthly cost per account was $1.98, which left the bank with a loss of $1.7183 after the O.P.A. allotment of $0.2617 per account.[2]

While the war heightened economic activity and brought general prosperity, it also caused dislocations in the normal order of business. One of the first problems that the state banks in Texas, like banks everywhere, had to face was that of personnel shortages created by the military draft. Most young men, including bank officers and clerical staff, were called into military service.

The banks met this shortage by replacing the men with women. For the first time in Texas women came into what had been regarded for the most part as a male domain. It was estimated that by October 1942 the percentage of women employees in Texas banks had risen from about 10 to 15 percent before the war to 50 percent.[3] As the war consumed more and more manpower the percentage of women working in state banks steadily increased. Moreover, many of the women stayed in their jobs after the war, which encouraged other women to seek careers in banking.

During the war the state banks, most of which were located in rural areas, became greatly concerned about competition from federal government lending agencies in the field of agricultural credit. When the government announced in 1943 that the Regional Agricultural Credit Corporation would be revived, the Texas bankers organized in opposition.

In spite of the extensive efforts of Banking Commissioner John Q. McAdams, who had been a country banker for twenty-five years before becoming commissioner on September 15, 1941, and those of bankers all over the country, the R.A.C.C. was revived, and it continued, along with other government lending agencies, to compete for agricultural loans throughout the duration of the war.[4] The competition hurt some of the smaller country banks, but these agencies served a vital need by supplying credit to marginal borrowers at low rates of interest.

The Texas state banks contributed significantly to the war effort. Texas bankers were in favor of high taxes and low profits to help fight inflation and to finance the war. They handled a huge volume of paperwork and other such activity that flowed through the banks—all of which resulted in higher expenses. They purchased large amounts of low-yielding federal government securities and made war-related loans in preference to other, higher-yielding investments. All of this was done in order to contribute to the war effort and to help cope with the economic problems associated with wartime activities.

The Texas Banking Code of 1943

Although state bankers in Texas were preoccupied with the war effort during the 1940-1945 period, in the early 1940s an effort was undertaken to rewrite the Texas State Bank Law. Since the passage of the legislation in 1905 that had created the state banking system there had been no major revision of the law. From time to time the original law had been amended and some sections repealed, but the consensus in the early 1940s was that the existing statute was "indistinct, obscure, ambiguous, and in many sections unworkable."[5] The numerous amendments had created repetition and overlapping, and much of the statute had become obsolete.

In order to rectify the situation, Commissioner John Q. McAdams initiated a movement to recodify the Texas State Bank Law shortly after he assumed office in September 1941. Under the direction of Commissioner McAdams, Deputy Commissioner H. A. Jamison, attorney Joe T. Goodwin, and the entire personnel of the commissioner's office labored for over a year in preparing the code. Their work was supervised by the State Bank Committee of the Texas Bankers Association, which was chaired by Clarence M. Malone of Houston.

Although the law of 1905 provided the basic foundation for the new code, the best laws of other states were studied and some of the features of those laws were incorporated into the revision as well. The Texas Banking Code of 1943 was one of the first bills introduced in the Forty-eighth Legislature when it convened on January 12, 1943. House Bill No. 79 was approved on March 31, 1943, and enacted into law by Governor Coke Stevenson on April 1, 1943. It became effective on August 10, 1943.

The new code eliminated ambiguity, conflicts, repetition, and outmoded, meaningless provisions relating to the old Depositors Guaranty Law. Perhaps the most important change, though, was the creation of the Finance Commission.[6] The Finance Commission was charged with the responsibility of appointing the banking commissioner and given responsibility for surveillance of the Banking Department's receipts and expenditures. It was also given the right to promulgate general rules and regulations to protect the rights of bank depositors and stockholders. The new law provided that the commission would be composed of nine members: four bank executives, two savings and loan executives and three individuals selected on the basis of recognized business ability. A banking section and a savings and loan section were designated and each was charged with carrying out the provisions of the law as they pertained to their respective industries. It was provided that members of the commission are to be appointed by the governor, subject to senate confirmation, for a term of six years each, with the term of one third of the members of each section expiring every two years.

Except for the creation of the Finance Commission, the new code did not differ in substance from the law of 1905, but it did achieve much needed clarification and modernization. Upon signing the legislation, Governor Stevenson commented: "I think this is possibly the most constructive bill that has passed the Texas Legislature in the past 25 years."[7]

Postwar Development of the State Banking System

(Note: The principal research for this work was completed in 1970, which serves as the terminal date for this section.)

Extraordinary Growth of the System

One of the most significant developments in the history of the Texas state banking system has been the phenomenal growth that it has experienced since World War II. From January 1, 1946, to December 31, 1969, the number of state banks operating in Texas increased from 409 to 630, or by 54.0 percent; total state bank resources rose from $998,354,543 to $7,906,054,136, or by 691.9 percent (see table 22); and capital accounts increased from $44,739,871 to $601,042,339, or by 1,243.4 percent.

The rapid growth of the state banking system over the last quarter century has been a by-product of the extraordinary development of the Texas economy during the same period. The increase in the population from 6.4 million in 1940 to 11.2 million in 1970 and the uninterrupted migration of Texans from rural to urban centers necessitated a large increase in banking facilities in the larger cities and suburbs. Moreover, as a result of the vast growth in the population and the continued development of the economy, the money income of the state greatly expanded. For example, from 1945 to 1968 farm income rose from $1.2 billion to $3.0 billion, and the wages of those employed in manufacturing increased from $555.4 million to $2,065.2 million. This income contributed significantly to the tremendous growth of state and national bank deposits, resources, and capital. However, judging from the increase in the state banks' share of aggregate resources of Texas banks from 16.2 percent in 1945 to 28.4 percent in 1969, the state banking system experienced significantly greater growth than its national bank counterpart.

Changes in the Structure of the System

During the period beginning January 1, 1946, and ending December 31, 1969, there were 291 charters for new banks granted and sixty-one liquidations—forty-three voluntary and eighteen involuntary. The postwar demand for state bank charters is partially explained by the need for bank facilities in suburbs of metropolitan areas. There is, however, another aspect to the growth in the number of state banks that deserves analysis. Since 1954 thirty national banks have surrendered their charters and converted to the state banking system. Eleven of these occurred in 1969 alone.

One reason for this recent increase in national bank conversions to state charters was the desire to take advantage of the larger loan limit enjoyed by state banks. For a national bank, the legal lending limit on an unsecured extension of credit to one borrower is 10 percent of its capital accounts, whereas for a Texas state bank the corresponding limit to any one borrower is 25 percent of the bank's capital and surplus. For a small bank this difference is particularly significant.

However, according to Robert E. Stewart, the present banking commissioner, the overriding reason for the large number of conversions to state banks in recent years has been a desire on the part of management to free reserves.[8] National banks and all state bank members of the Federal Reserve System are required by law to keep a certain percentage of their demand and time deposits as reserves in the form of vault cash or on deposit with the Federal Reserve facilities in their district. In addition to legal reserves, all banks have by tradition maintained deposits with other banks in order to compensate those banks for various services rendered, as a partial source of liquidity, or in some instances merely as a complementary account. Member banks, thus, in effect carry two reserve accounts: one to satisfy legal reserve requirements and the other to serve as correspondent bank balances.

State nonmember banks are also required to maintain legal reserves, although the percentage required has normally been less than that required by the Federal Reserve for member banks. In addition, Texas law permits the reserve for state nonmember banks to be kept in the form of vault cash or on deposit with any state or national bank as long as the bank has capital in excess of $50,000 and has been approved as a reserve depository by the banking commissioner and no more than 20 percent of the state nonmember bank's capital, surplus, and deposits is held as an account in any one reserve depository. Therefore, the same funds the state nonmember banks keep on deposit with other banks as traditional correspondent bank balances normally qualify as legal reserves by state law.

The use of correspondent bank balances as legal reserves by Texas state banks that are not members of the Federal Reserve System allows those banks to operate with a lower cash position. This is reflected in the percentage of total assets carried as "cash and due from banks" for all Texas state banks, including fifty-six member banks, which is lower than that for all member banks in the Eleventh Federal Reserve District—15.6 percent compared with 20.8 percent as of December 31, 1969.

Closely associated with the recent trend of bank conversions from the national to the state system has been the large number of withdrawals from the Federal Reserve System by Texas state banks. On December 31, 1956, 129 state banks in Texas were members of the Federal Reserve System, whereas by December 31, 1969, there were only 56 state banks in the system. It is believed that the vast majority of these banks left the system in order to free reserves.

The desire to free reserves has probably been motivated by two factors. One has been the sharp increase in operating expenses and in the cost of loanable funds over the last fifteen years, and particularly since the early 1960s. In order to offset these costs and to maintain profit margins, bank managers have been forced to work their funds harder to increase revenues. Naturally, one of the first steps has been the investment of idle funds in loans and securities, which has resulted in a reduction in correspondent bank balances and reserves.

The desire to free reserves has also been prompted by a change in the controlling interest in some banks. Frequently the purchase of controlling interest in a bank by an individual or a group of individuals is financed with a loan from a second bank. The stock of the bank being purchased is pledged as security for the loan, and as compensation—in addition to the interest on the loan—the borrower usually keeps either all or a portion of his bank's reserve balances on deposit with the lending bank. Naturally, if the bank that is being purchased is a member of the Federal Reserve System, its ability to maintain a substantial balance on deposit with the lending bank is severely inhibited. Although the exact number is not known, Banking Department officials have indicated that a considerable number of banks have either converted to the state system or have withdrawn from the Federal Reserve System for the reasons mentioned above.

Of the forty-three state banks that liquidated voluntarily from January 1, 1946, to December 31, 1969, two dissolved their business, nineteen became national banks, fourteen were either sold to or assumed by other banks, six were merged into other banks, and two received charters but never opened for business (see table 4).

The two banks that dissolved their activities did so because there was insufficient business to enable the banks to operate successfully. The motivation for the nineteen conversions from state to national charters is unknown, but the reason is likely to have been an attempt to increase the stature and prestige of the institution. The last conversion to the national system occurred in 1964. With respect to the fourteen banks that were either sold or assumed by other banks, only three of the exchanges have taken place since 1949. Presumably most of the banks were merely unable to continue successful operation. Some of the reasons were insufficient business to warrant continued operation, lack of successor management, mismanagement, and internal financial difficulties. The same factors may have prompted some of the mergers that have been consummated since 1945. In one of the six, however, the motivation behind the merger was quite different from that in any of the others.

On September 30, 1969, the Bank of Texas, in Houston, merged with the Esperson State Bank of Houston. The unusual feature of this merger was that there was no such bank as the Esperson State Bank—it was chartered as a "phantom bank," a vehicle used to convert the ownership of the Bank of Texas to a one-bank holding company. The mechanics of this procedure were essentially as follows. First a holding company was formed. Then the holding company, together with at least five individuals—in this case directors of the holding company—applied for a bank charter in the name of Esperson State Bank, with the holding company owning all the bank's stock except for directors' qualifying shares. Upon obtaining the charter, they effected a merger between the Bank of Texas and the Esperson State Bank through an exchange of stock, with the individual shareholders of the Bank of Texas receiving shares in the holding company proportionate to their interest in the Bank of Texas. After the merger was consummated, the name of the Esperson State Bank was changed to the Bank of Texas. As a result, the original shareholders of the Bank of Texas became the owners of the holding company, which in turn owned the Bank of Texas. On the books of the Banking Department the charter of the original Bank of Texas was cancelled and the name of the Esperson State Bank was changed to the Bank of Texas.[9]

The "phantom bank" procedure for restructuring a bank's ownership to a one-bank holding company is also used to effect a merger between an independent bank and a multibank holding company. The procedure is essentially the same as that outlined in the Esperson State Bank-Bank of Texas merger.

Only 18 state banks failed in Texas during the postwar era that ended December 31, 1969, a small number indeed considering the 413 failures in the previous forty years.

After the closing of the Guaranty Bond State Bank in North Zulch on January 1, 1940, there was only one failure, the Valley State Bank of San Juan on June 25, 1949, until October 15, 1956, when the River Oaks State Bank of Fort Worth closed. Since the closing of the Fort Worth bank sixteen additional banks have failed.

Of the eighteen banks that have failed since World War II, the vast majority were very small institutions located in essentially rural communities. The largest bank that failed had total resources of $12,184,818; the smallest had resources of only $73,995; and of the total, twelve, or 66.7 percent, had total resources of less than $2,000,000. The largest of the towns in which the eighteen banks were located was Aransas Pass, with a population of 7,285, and the smallest was Sacul, with 170 inhabitants. Sixteen of the eighteen failures, or 88.9 percent, were banks domiciled in towns with a population of less than 3,500.

The concentration of the postwar bank failures among very small agricultural banks is attributable to a lack of sufficient business in their communities to support profitable operation of a bank. In some of the communities sufficient business has never existed and the banks should never have been chartered. Other communities have suffered from the general deterioration of rural Texas since 1940, when the population began to migrate to metropolitan areas. This deterioration has naturally had a negative impact on banks serving these areas. Their income has generally been insufficient to allow them to hire and maintain highly competent personnel, to modernize their operations and facilities, and to institute adequate safeguards and internal controls. In addition, their capital has normally been relatively small and their access to new capital limited, a deficiency that is of paramount importance to the rural banks because of the predominance and high risk of farm loans in their portfolios.

Although the rural location and small size of the banks that have failed in the postwar era increased their vulnerability, examination of official records has indicated that in most instances failure was actually precipitated by other factors. The primary causes included embezzlement, occurring in eight of the eighteen failures; bad loans, occurring in four cases; and overextension of loans to officers and their closely related interests, occurring in three of the banks. Other primary causes were customer overdrafts, a kite by a customer, and overextension of loans to directors, each of which accounted for one failure. The most common secondary causes were overextension of loans to close friends of management, which existed in six instances, and irregularities, which were detected in four of the banks. The most common irregularities were gross violations of the bank's legal loan limit and acceptance of loan fees by management.

Although changes in the structure of the state banking system in the postwar era were principally a by-product of a growing Texas, the structure was also affected by the regulatory and economic climate and by prevailing banking practices. For example, the previously noted conversions of banks from national to state charters and withdrawals of state banks from the Federal Reserve System appear to have been directly associated with perception of regulatory advantages for state nonmember banks. It is also likely that these trends were further stimulated to some extent by bank financing of changes in controlling interests in other banks. From 1945 through 1969, 103 banks left the Federal Reserve System, while 19 joined the system by converting to national charters. Other banks merged and at least one of these represented a restructuring to holding-company status. Of the 18 failures that did occur, none was caused by deficiencies in the banking system or by economic crises. As for the impact upon the structure of the state banking system, the postwar period could be characterized as one of growth and relative tranquility.[10]

Role of the System in Financing the Postwar Boom

Throughout its history the state banking system has played a major role in financing the Texas economy. This is perhaps most evident in the post-World War II era, when aggregate loans grew from a modest $180.1 million on December 31, 1945, to a staggering $4.3 billion by December 31, 1969—or by *2,288 percent*. During the same period the loan-to-deposit ratio of the system increased from a war-depressed 18.9 percent to a relatively high 61.5 percent.

The large increases in the volume of loans and the relative importance of loans in the employment of bank funds are reflections of the rising prosperity of Texas, the pent-up demand for credit following World War II, and the easy monetary and credit policies of the Federal Reserve that prevailed during much of the first decade following the war. Likewise, the ever-increasing desire for a higher standard of living has given rise to sharp increases in the legitimate demand for credit by the consumer, demand that in turn has stimulated the need for investment spending and short-term and intermediate-term financing by businesses. The banks of Texas, by meeting these legitimate demands for credit, have contributed to the continuing development of Texas and the well-being of its citizens.

The development of the state banking system in Texas has been associated in large measure with the rural areas of the state. In fact, most charters granted in the formative years of the system were issued for banks in small rural cities where the establishment of national banks had been precluded by minimum capital requirements of $50,000 before 1900 and $25,000 in the years immediately thereafter. Under these circumstances the ability to establish banks under state law with a minimum capital of $10,000 in cities having less than 2,500 inhabitants led to a proliferation of state banks in small rural communities. As a consequence, the loan portfolios of the system's banks were concentrated in agricultural credits and the fortunes of the state banks were affected accordingly. Since 1940, however, significant changes have occurred. The rural population has declined from 3.5 million, or 54.7 percent of the population, to 2.3 million, or 20.5 percent of the population in 1970, and the state's economy has become industrialized. Likewise, the state banks are no longer predominantly rural in location or in character. From 1945 through 1969 approximately one third of all new state charters were granted for suburban banks in Dallas, Houston, Fort Worth, San Antonio, and El Paso, and 74 percent of all charters granted were in metropolitan rather than rural areas.

The economic and demographic changes in Texas since 1940 have also significantly altered activities and policies of state banks. This is vividly reflected in the composition of their loan portfolios, which have changed as the state banks have met the needs and demands of their customers. Precise information about the composition of state bank loans is not available for years before 1955, when the Banking Department started compiling a detailed consolidated statement of the system's banks. However, it appears that most of the trends evidenced during the 1955-1969 period also appeared in the previous decade.

As might be expected, from 1955 through 1969 the relative importance of agricultural loans in state banks declined markedly. While on December 31, 1955, agricultural loans, excluding loans on farm real estate, accounted for 20.2 percent of total loans; by December 31, 1969, they accounted for only 7.0 percent. They had declined from their place as the third most important of the four major loan components—commercial and industrial, consumer, real estate, and agriculture—to the least important position.

In spite of the decline in the relative significance of agricultural loans, the volume of these loans in state banks approximately doubled, from $162.9 million in 1955 to $304.4 million in 1969, and the state banking system continued to play a major role in financing agriculture in Texas.

From 1955 through 1969 commercial and industrial loans and consumer loans increased in importance and real estate loans changed little in relative significance in state banks. Over the period, commercial and industrial loans replaced consumer loans as the largest single segment of state bank portfolios, accounting for 36.4 percent of total loans on December 31, 1969. These changes in state bank loan portfolios clearly reflect the changing role of the state banking system in Texas. The location of new state banks largely in suburban metropolitan areas, the deterioration of rural communities, and the greater industrialization of urban centers make it highly probable that most of the increase in commercial and industrial loans from $246.0 million to $1.6 billion occurred in the metropolitan banks. Because of the suburban location of many of these banks, it is likely that much of the increase was used to finance small to medium-sized businesses in the rapidly growing suburbs. The same can be assumed for the increase in real estate loans, which grew from $103.8 million, including farm loans, on December 31, 1955, to $545.9 million, excluding farm loans, on December 31, 1969. The state banking system has been extremely important in the transition of the population and the economy of Texas from rural-agrarian to urban-industrial.

As of December 31, 1969, loans to consumers were the second most important segment of the state bank portfolios, totaling $1.5 billion and accounting for 33.8 percent of total loans, compared with $257.1 million and 32.0 percent at year-end 1955. One of the most significant developments in banking in the postwar era has been in the field of consumer lending and services. Banks have played a major role in facilitating higher standards of living through the reasonable extension of credit. Today durable goods ranging from television sets to automobiles and airplanes can be financed with down payments of as low as 10 to 20 percent, with principal payments amortized monthly for terms extending to sixty months at reasonable rates of interest. Though no distribution by type of consumer loan is available for the composite of state banks in Texas for 1955, in 1969 loans to purchase private passenger automobiles were by far the largest component of consumer loans, comprising over one half of total consumer loans. Next in importance were single-payment loans for household, family, and other personal expenditures, followed by installment loans for personal expenditures, installment loans to purchase other retail consumer goods, and loans to repair and modernize residences.

Consumer installment loans are certainly not unique to state banks; however, because of their ability to serve consumers through suburban locations, state banks have been leaders and innovators in consumer finance. For example, two state banks in Dallas pioneered the use of bank credit cards in Texas.

On February 8, 1953, Weldon U. Howell, president of Highland Park State Bank of Dallas, and James C. Dycus, president of Oak Cliff Bank and Trust Company of Dallas, made a joint announcement introducing a new "Charge-Plan" credit card for the benefit of shoppers in their suburban areas. This announcement was momentous, not because of the impact that it had upon the banking and payments system at that time but because it was the first bank credit card introduced in the state—the precursor of the bank-card trend that has recently assumed vast proportions and is perhaps the first step taken in Texas toward a "checkless society."

Under the Highland Park State Bank-Oak Cliff Bank and Trust Company plan any shopper could apply for a "Charge-Plan" credit card. With the card the shopper could charge purchases at stores displaying an emblem denoting membership in the plan and be billed once each month for purchases made at all stores. Unlike present credit card plans, no arrangement was made for deferred payments. It was not necessary for the shopper to have an account at either bank, and no charge was made to the shopper for the service. Each bank set up a credit department for handling the "Charge-Plan" service.

Two years later, in February 1955, the Highland Park State Bank relocated and changed its name to the Preston State Bank. Under Howell's direction the Preston State Bank inaugurated "Presto Charge," a highly successful credit-card plan that later affiliated with "Master Charge," one of the two predominant bank-credit-card programs in the United States.

Texas state banks have indeed been very significant factors in financing the postwar boom in Texas. While continuing to be major suppliers of credit to the agricultural sector of the economy, they have also helped to finance the rapid commercial and residential development of our major metropolitan areas. They have been major suppliers of credit for working capital and for permanent capital investments in business and industry—for both large firms and small. They have provided construction loans as well as permanent financing on single-family and multifamily residences and on commercial buildings. The state banks have also helped Texans to enjoy higher standards of living by allowing the purchase through consumer loans of goods and commodities that would otherwise have been unattainable.

A by-product of the postwar economic changes in Texas and in the nation and of the changes in the state banking system has been increased competition in banking markets and financial markets generally. Banks have had to change their image and philosophy. In recent years bankers have actively solicited deposits and loans. Moreover, they have entered avenues of financing that before World War II were not considered to be in banking's traditional domain, such as leasing and factoring of accounts receivable. In these areas and in the more traditional fields of lending the competition from savings and loan associations, credit unions, insurance companies, and other lenders has been intense. Banks have also been forced to bid for funds in the open market in order to meet the competition from U.S. government securities, commercial paper, and other money-market instruments, as well as that from nonbank financial institutions. The result has been a sharp rise over the last fifteen years in the percentage of loans to deposits and in savings and other time accounts as a percentage of total bank deposits, accompanied by a commensurate increase in the cost of loanable funds.

In spite of the challenges posed to management by these changing conditions and circumstances, the state banking system has continued to grow and prosper while maintaining the soundness of assets and the safety of deposits.

Other Postwar Developments

Besides the extraordinary growth experienced by the system and its role in financing the economic expansion of Texas, the trend of conversions from the national to the state system, and withdrawals from the Federal Reserve System, other significant postwar developments in the state banking system in Texas include the bill passed in 1951 that provided for the self-support and independent administration of the Banking Department, the re-emergence of the branch-banking controversy, and the organization of the Association of State Chartered Banks.

The Self-Support Bill

The most significant legislative achievement concerning the state banks since the passage of the Banking Code of 1943 was the enactment in 1951 of a bill that provided for the self-support of the Banking Department. The law provides that all revenue generated by the department from examination fees and other sources be paid into a "special fund" from which sufficient monies can be appropriated by the Finance Commission to run the department. A sum of $4,000 is to be transferred each year to the General Revenue Fund of the state to cover the cost of services rendered by other departments of the government. Among the costs covered are those incurred by the state auditor, who is required to audit the Banking Department from time to time.

The most important benefit arising from the change in procedure is that it enables the department to pay equitable and competitive salaries to its personnel. Under the law the salaries of the commissioner, deputy commissioner, departmental bank examiner, examiners, and assistant examiners are set by the Finance Commission; that of the commissioner is not to exceed the governor's salary.

Before the revision of the law all of the revenue generated by the department was paid into the state treasury. It was necessary for the banking commissioner to submit a budget for each succeeding biennial period to the legislature for approval. As a result the department was forced to keep its salaries and expenses in line with other state agencies and commissions. The approved budget was so low that the department was able to pay its examining force only about one third the salaries allowed by the comptroller of the currency, the Federal Deposit Insurance Corporation, and the Federal Reserve System. Under these conditions it was extremely difficult to attract and hold competent personnel.

The Branch-Banking Controversy

The branch-banking question has been before the bankers of Texas for decades. In 1929 the Dallas banker Fred Florence strongly advocated that Texas bankers seek legislation providing for branch banking in the larger cities of the state.[11] The question came up again in 1933 before a committee of the Texas Bankers Association but was tabled because the prohibition could only be removed by submitting the question to the voters and that could not be done before 1935.[12] The issue subsequently was dropped.

As far as can be determined, the first legislation designed to permit branch banking in Texas was introduced in the regular session of the Fifty-first Legislature in 1949. That bill would have provided for statewide branching. It was reported favorably out of committee but was apparently tabled thereafter.[13] However, the issue did not die. In the regular session of the Fifty-second Legislature a branch-banking bill was again introduced, this time with the provision that branching be limited to the city in which a bank was domiciled. The bill passed the house without opposition. The proposed statute was then sent to the senate, where it was referred to the Senate Committee on Banks and Banking, from which it received a favorable report. In the meantime the bankers of Texas were informed of these developments and urged to voice their opposition. On May 5, 1951, C. E. McCutchen, president of the Texas Bankers Association, sent a copy of the bill to every bank in Texas, together with a letter asking the bankers to communicate to their respective senators their opposition to House Bill 713. As a result senators were "showered with telegrams, telephone messages, and letters from all sections of the state," and the bill was defeated.[14]

The most recent efforts to remove the prohibition against branch banking in Texas occurred in the fifty-ninth and sixtieth sessions of the legislature. In 1965, during the regular session of the Fifty-ninth Legislature, a bill was introduced to permit a bank to engage in business in more than one place in counties having a population of more than 200,000 according to the most recent census. If passed, the bill would have affected eight Texas counties: Bexar, Dallas, El Paso, Harris, Jefferson, Nueces, Tarrant, and Travis.[15] The branch-banking proposal encountered strong opposition from the state's bankers, however. At the annual convention of the Texas Bankers Association in Fort Worth the convention went on record as "opposed to branch banking in any form . . . " The following resolution was introduced by Berl E. Godfrey of Fort Worth, chairman of the State Bank Division of the Texas Bankers Association; seconded by Tom C. Frost, Jr., of San Antonio, chairman of the National Bank Division; and unanimously passed by the convention on May 4, 1965:[16]

RESOLUTION ON BRANCH BANKING

Whereas, Texas Constitutional and statutory provisions now prohibit branch banking in this State, and

Whereas, it is the uniform and undivided consensus of opinion of both state and national banks in Texas that the laws of the respective states should be controlling with regard to branch banking, and Texas banks are opposed to any Act of Congress which would permit branch banking without regard for state law, and

Whereas, a proposed Constitutional amendment, Senate Joint Resolution 42, to permit limited branch banking has been introduced and is presently pending in the Texas Legislature

Now, *therefore*, be it resolved by the Texas Bankers Association, assembled in general convention this 4th day of May, 1965, that this Convention opposes the proposal embodied in Senate Joint Resolution 42 to authorize submission of a Constitutional amendment to the electorate of Texas to permit branch banking in certain counties, and further, that this Convention is opposed to branch banking in any form at this time and supports and maintains the presently existing Constitutional prohibition against branch banking contained in Article XVI, Section 16 of the Constitution of Texas, and

Be it further resolved, that the Executive Vice President and the Administrative Council of this Association are instructed to advise the sponsor of Senate Joint Resolution 42, the appropriate Committee chairman and members of each house, and the Speaker of the House and Lieutenant Governor of this State that this Association is unequivocally opposed to Senate Joint Resolution 42 or any other proposal to submit to the voters of our State the question of amending the Texas Constitution to permit any form of branch banking.

Be it further resolved, that the Executive Vice President and the Administrative Council of this Association vigorously oppose any proposal in Congress to authorize branch banking without regard for the laws of the respective states.

The strong sentiment reflected by the foregoing resolution dissuaded further legislative consideration of the branch-banking bill.
Legislation introduced in 1967 during the regular session of the Sixtieth Legislature would have permitted branch banking in the four most populous counties of Texas: Bexar, Dallas, Harris, and Tarrant. However, the bankers of Texas had begun working against the measure in November and December 1966, before the opening of the new legislative session in January 1967. The opposition to the bill was made unquestionably clear to every legislator in "banker-legislator meetings" throughout the state. In view of the preponderance of opposition the bill was allowed to die quietly in the house without hearings or undue fanfare. A subsequent request for a legislative study inquiring into the desirability of branch banking in Texas was defeated by a vote of 114 to 5.[17]

The Association of State Chartered Banks

On September 7, 1962, the Association of State Chartered Banks in Texas was formed. Its purpose, according to its founders, was to seek equity in the laws between state and national banks, to disseminate among its members information and data of peculiar interest to the state banking fraternity, to prevent federal encroachment on state controls, and to preserve the dual banking system.[18]

The association was organized with approximately 96 percent of the state banks subscribing to membership. The first president was P. B. (Jack) Garrett, vice-chairman of the board of the Texas Bank and Trust Company of Dallas. The association also elected a vice-president, secretary, and treasurer. One state banker from each of the thirty-one senatorial districts of Texas served on the Board of Governors and seven of its members, along with the association president, formed the executive committee. The first year's dues were set at $.03 per $1,000 of total resources of each bank, from which $96,000 was initially raised. Headquarters were established in Austin and Sam O. Kimberlin, Jr., who had served as counsel to the Banking Department since 1956, was hired as executive director.

From the state headquarters association members were kept apprised of changes in rules and regulations of the comptroller of the currency, the Federal Deposit Insurance Corporation, the state Banking Department, and other agencies affecting banking, as well as case decisions of the courts that pertained to banking.

The most important work of the association, however, was in seeking legislation pertinent to the state banks. The most notable achievement in this respect was the passage of legislation by the Fifty-eighth Legislature, in 1963, that has saved the state banks over one million dollars each year in sales taxes and corporate franchise taxes, from which the national banks were exempt but the state banks had not been.

Shortly after the passage of the foregoing legislation the Association of State Chartered Banks became inactive, primarily because the Texas Bankers Association underwent a complete reorganization and assumed most of the functions of the Association of State Chartered Banks. In the fall of 1964 the Administrative Council of the Texas Bankers Association met with the Board of Governors of the Association of State Chartered Banks to urge the latter to join in a consolidated and coordinated effort to make the Texas Bankers Association the most effective banking association in the country. One of the first steps taken by the Texas Bankers Association toward this goal was to hire Sam O. Kimberlin, Jr., from the Association of State Chartered Banks as its executive vice-president. Another step taken was to move the Texas Bankers Association offices to Austin, the state capital, in order to facilitate the association's legislative activities. In view of the loss of its executive director, the accomplishment of its primary legislative aim, and the expanded activities of the Texas Bankers Association, the membership of the Association of State Chartered Banks voted to place the organization in an inactive state.[19]

As an inactive organization, the Association of State Chartered Banks has not been completely dormant. It has continued to recommend amendments to the State Banking Code and it contributes scholarship funds to various Texas universities for senior banking majors who are in need of financial aid. Finally, the association provided the financial support necessary for this history of state-chartered banking in Texas to become a reality.

Notes

1. "The Log of a Typical Texas Bank," *Texas Bankers Record* 33 (December 1942): 28-29.
2. "Ration Banking Costing Country Banks Plenty," *Texas Bankers Record* 32 (May 1943): 44 and 46.
3. "Task Force in Banks Are Women," *Texas Bankers Record* 33 (October 1942): 32.
4. "Banks at Last Awake to Menace of Socialized Credit," *Texas Bankers Record* 32 (March 1943): 18.
5. "Texas Banking Code before Lawmakers in 1943," *Texas Bankers Record* 32 (December 1942): 16.
6. "The Texas Banking Code Becomes Law," *Texas Bankers Record* 32 (April 1943): 6-9.
7. "The Texas Banking Code Becomes Law," p. 6.
8. Robert E. Stewart, banking commissioner, private interview held at the Banking Department of Texas on March 20, 1970.
9. Ibid.
10. Material pertaining to postwar bank failures was obtained from the last examination report on file in the Banking Department of Texas for each bank and from an interview with Commissioner Robert E. Stewart on March 20, 1970.
11. Fred F. Florence, "All Signs Point to a Prosperous 1929 in Texas," address before a meeting of the Fourth District Bankers, Waco, February 19, 1929, reprinted in *Texas Bankers Record* 18 (March 1929): 22-23.
12. *Texas Bankers Record* 22 (August 1933): 19.
13. *House Journal, Texas Fifty-first Legislature, Regular Session, 1949* (n.p., n.d.), pp. 177 and 1805.

14. *Texas Bankers Record* 40 (May 1951): 112.
15. Sam O. Kimberlin, Jr., "Legislative Roundup," *Texas Bankers Record* 55 (March 1965): 19.
16. *Texas Bankers Record* 54 (May 1965): 3.
17. Walter Johnson, "President's Address," address before the Texas Bankers Association, *Texas Bankers Record* 56 (June 1967): 8.
18. P. B. (Jack) Garrett, "Why an Association of State Chartered Banks in Texas?" *Texas Bankers Record* 51 (September 1962): 24-25.
19. Sam O. Kimberlin, Jr., interview on March 26, 1970.

Appendix

Banking Commissioners for the State of Texas 1905–1970

W.J. Clay, January 9, 1905-

R.J. Milner, January 17, 1907-
August 31, 1907 (no photo available)

Thos. B. Love, August 31, 1907-
January 31, 1910

William E. Hawkins, January 31,
1910-August 3, 1910

Frederick Von Rosenberg, August 4, 1910-January 6, 1911

B.L. Gill, January 17, 1911-July 10, 1913

W.W. Collier, July 28, 1913-January 23, 1915

Jno. S. Patterson, January 23, 1915-August 28, 1916

Chas. O. Austin, September 1, 1916-January 31, 1919

Geo. Waverly Briggs, February 1, 1919-April 1, 1920

J.C. Chidsey, April 1, 1920- August 1, 1920

J.T. McMillin, August 4, 1920- January 19, 1921

Ed Hall, January 20, 1921-
August 31, 1922

J.L. Chapman, September 1, 1922-
January 20, 1925

Chas. O. Austin,
January 26, 1925-
August 31, 1927

James Shaw, September 1, 1927-
July 12, 1933

E.C. Brand, July 12, 1933-
August 31, 1935

Irvin McCreary, August 31, 1935-
December 26, 1935

Zeta Gossett, December 26, 1935-
August 31, 1939

Fred Branson, September 1, 1939-
January 31, 1940

Lee Brady, February 14, 1940-
September 11, 1941

John Q. McAdams, September 15,
1941-April 15, 1944

H.A. Jamison, April 15, 1944-
December 1, 1945

L.S. Johnson, December 1, 1945-
July 1, 1947

J.M. Falkner, September 13, 1947-
June 30, 1970

Robert E. Stewart, July 1, 1970-
(no photo available)

LIBRARY OF DAVIDSON COLLEGE